CHILDREN OF
JIHAD

ALSO BY JARED COHEN

ONE HUNDRED DAYS OF SILENCE: AMERICA
AND THE RWANDA GENOCIDE

CHILDREN OF
JIHAD

A Young American's Travels Among
the Youth of the Middle East

JARED COHEN

GOTHAM
BOOKS

Though the author works for the U.S. Department of State, the views expressed in this book do not necessarily reflect those of the Department of State or the U.S. government.

GOTHAM BOOKS
Published by Penguin Group (USA) Inc.
375 Hudson Street, New York, New York 10014, U.S.A.
Penguin Group (Canada), 90 Eglinton Avenue East, Suite 700, Toronto, Ontario M4P 2Y3,
Canada (a division of Pearson Penguin Canada Inc.); Penguin Books Ltd, 80 Strand,
London WC2R 0RL, England; Penguin Ireland, 25 St Stephen's Green, Dublin 2,
Ireland (a division of Penguin Books Ltd); Penguin Group (Australia), 250 Camberwell Road,
Camberwell, Victoria 3124, Australia (a division of Pearson Australia Group Pty Ltd);
Penguin Books India Pvt Ltd, 11 Community Centre, Panchsheel Park, New Delhi – 110 017,
India; Penguin Group (NZ), 67 Apollo Drive, Rosedale, North Shore 0632, New Zealand
(a division of Pearson New Zealand Ltd); Penguin Books (South Africa) (Pty) Ltd,
24 Sturdee Avenue, Rosebank, Johannesburg 2196, South Africa

Penguin Books Ltd, Registered Offices: 80 Strand, London WC2R 0RL, England

Published by Gotham Books, a member of Penguin Group (USA) Inc.

ISBN-13: 978-0-7394-9367-0

Printed in the United States of America
Set in Galliard
Designed by Ginger Legato

While the author has made every effort to provide accurate telephone numbers and Internet addresses at the time of publication, neither the publisher nor the author assumes any responsibility for errors, or for changes that occur after publication. Further, the publisher does not have any control over and does not assume any responsibility for author or third-party Web sites or their content.

TO MOM, DAD, AND MY SISTER, EMILY:

THANK YOU FOR YOUR LOVE, SUPPORT, AND PATIENCE

CONTENTS

CHILDREN OF
JIHAD

PROLOGUE

LEBANON, 2005

For a third Wednesday in a row, I had lunch at a Western fast-food chain in Beirut, Lebanon. This time it was McDonald's. I was alone and American, but it wasn't the comfortingly bland Western décor or the universally recognizable taste of a Big Mac that drew me to one of Beirut's most popular fast-food restaurants. It wasn't homesickness at all that brought me to McDonald's; it was Hezbollah, one of the world's most notorious terrorist organizations.

The members of Hezbollah who invited me to McDonald's week after week did not fit the Western profile of Middle Eastern terrorists. Instead of tattered green military fatigues, they wore Armani jeans and Versace sweaters; their hair was not covered by checkered scarves or head wraps, but meticulously sculpted and styled; and rather than slinging Kalashnikov rifles over their shoulders, they lugged around bulky, heavy backpacks, more likely to be filled with books than bombs. When girls walked by, they didn't avert their eyes in an act of chastity; they whistled and gave catcalls that would have been equally at home at an American mall. The few shy boys contented themselves with juvenile comments to the group. The girls, independent-minded and cosmopolitan, would shout back, flirtatiously condemning the boys for their churlish behavior.

They always paid for my lunch, and each week there were new dining companions; most were other members of Hezbollah, but all were supporters of the group. Their political views—when expressed—were ultraextremist and they unabashedly shared them with me. But more often than not, we talked girls or sports. When we didn't discuss politics, it was easy to forget that these young men were considered by most of the Western world to be terrorists, especially in a cosmopolitan city like Beirut.

Beirut is one big paradox. The notorious green line that divided the city between Christians and Muslims during the country's fifteen-year civil war is visually unrecognizable, as it has been replaced by trendy outdoor cafés and clothing stores. The bombed-out buildings that haunted the Lebanese population with violence now take on an aesthetic appeal as they stand sandwiched between modern structures. On the surface, it seems that the city's historical divides have all but disappeared. But this is hardly the reality.

Socioeconomic disparity and religious tensions have become the modern green line. At the top of the socioeconomic chain are the entertainment districts of Monot and Gemayze, each of which boasts a vibrant nightlife and ostentatious display of wealth. When I walked the streets of these districts I felt more like I was observing a fashion show than a social scene. But just fifteen minutes from the outdoor coffee shops and valet parking at Starbucks and McDonald's is the impoverished and predominantly Shi'a south Beirut suburb of Dahiye, where residents are far more conservative and economically deprived than their more affluent neighbors. The conservative brand of Shi'a Islam and the dire economic situation in Dahiye have propelled Hezbollah into the role of community caretaker. With its headquarters based in these suburbs, Hezbollah wins popular support by providing housing, electricity, clean water, hospitals, and educational opportunities to local Shi'a. To the east of the Shi'a slums is the predominantly Christian section of Beirut known as Achrafieh; however, the only thing east and south Beirut have in common is that they are both located fifteen minutes from downtown. Like the Shi'a and the Christians, the Sunni also have their neighborhoods in Zarif and Verdun, where there is a mixture of wealth and poverty. The close proximity of each of these groups, combined with political, entertainment, and educational realms that bring them together for better or worse, make this diverse city a recipe for sectarian and political conflict.

Hezbollah, or "Party of God," has had a dark history as a terrorist organization. It began in 1982 as an Iranian-backed extremist Shi'a movement that sought to expel Israel from Lebanon, to attack American establishments, and to aid in the Palestinian quest for statehood. Historically, Hezbollah has dealt America some of its most devastating terrorist attacks: the bombing of the American Embassy in Beirut in April 1983, the bombing of the Marine barracks in October 1983, an attack that took the lives of 241 Americans, and a slew of kidnappings of Americans between 1983 and 1986. That doesn't include Hezbollah's history of violence against Israel, which, after a six-year hiatus, precipitated a major conflict in 2006. Well-organized, heavily armed, and closely tied with Iran, the military wing of Hezbollah continues to threaten Israel and has the potential to carry out many more terrorist attacks against America. Despite how well we all seemed to get along, my familiarity with the history of Hezbollah made me constantly suspicious of the young members I met in and around Beirut.

I was nervous around these young men. It didn't matter how Western they looked or how much we engaged in superficial small talk; I knew their history. For three weeks of fast-food lunches, I avoided telling them my last name or discussing my religion. Now, after just three weeks, they were ready to take me to Hezbollah strongholds. I didn't want any surprises; I churlishly thought if I revealed my Judaism at McDonald's, I would somehow be protected by the friendly American forces of crispy chicken sandwiches and supersized French fries.

I assumed my companions hated Jews and Americans. Hezbollah

is guided by a commitment to the destruction of Israel. They had kidnapped dozens of Israelis and Americans and prior to 9/11 they were responsible for more American blood than any other terrorist organization in the world. And why would I think otherwise? I knew that Hezbollah didn't believe in Israel's right to exist; I knew that Hezbollah had been labeled a terrorist group by the United States; and I knew that Hezbollah had conducted numerous suicide attacks around the world. So these young men weren't exactly the kind of people I would want to see my American passport with my Jewish last name. While they were always courteous, friendly, and even kind to me, I always took it for granted that these young Hezbollah had ulterior motives.

We developed a routine: They asked me what I wanted for lunch and after telling them, I waited patiently for Hezbollah to wait on me. Middle Eastern youth are drawn to fast food. Eating it is an expression of hipness, style, and cosmopolitanism. I once met a young mechanic in northwestern Syria who would actually travel seven hours to Beirut just to get Kentucky Fried Chicken. Every time I arranged for meetings with young people, they always picked a Western fast-food chain, like Dunkin' Donuts or Pizza Hut. At first I thought they were trying to accommodate me, but I soon realized it was their own affinity for American culture that was determining our meeting places.

I was a little more anxious than usual on this particular Wednesday. How the hell do you tell Hezbollah—days before you're set to travel to their stronghold—that you are Jewish? I imagined every scenario possible. Few of these had a positive outcome. Images of violent confrontation horrified me. The last thing I wanted was to come back to my apartment to a frightening surprise.

Before they even had a chance to put the trays of food on the table, I blurted out, "There is something I need to tell all of you before we go to Dahiye," which was the location of the Hezbollah stronghold.

"No problem, what is it?" answered Fouad, who had paid for my lunch three weeks in a row. He was the leader of the group and usually dressed in dark blue jeans and a green collared shirt. We had actually met at a café in West Beirut three days after I arrived in Lebanon when I interrupted him and his friends teasing a group of their female friends. His hair was dark and curly and smothered with hair gel. He was scruffy and he always had a smile on his face.

I decided to just say it. After taking a deep breath, I exclaimed: "My last name is Cohen."

They stared at me blankly.

Were they confused? Shocked? Angry? These awkward silences were always so uncomfortable and being the chatterbox that I am, I usually felt compelled to fill the silence. This time I did so with a collection of stuttering points, "I am Jewish, my family is Jewish, and while I am not extremely religious, I do practice Judaism."

Still nothing.

"I know that—" I started.

"This is not a problem," Asharaf interrupted, placing his hand on my shoulder. He was Fouad's friend, short and stocky, and hardly the picture of a terrorist. This was not lost on his friends, who always seemed to pick on him a bit. "We have no problems with Jewish people. We have no problems with American people. We hate the United States government and we hate Israel, but the Jewish and the American people have done nothing to us."

Sharif, another of the young men, chimed in as well. He seemed to be the most slick of the group. Like Fouad's, his hair was drenched in gel, but it wasn't an explosion of curls as much as a stiff slicked-back style. He wore a sleeveless shirt, perhaps to prove that he ventured to the gym every now and then. What he said surprised me the most: "You know, we have never known any Jews before, but we have Christian friends. We even have three Christian deputies in Parliament elected from the south as members of the Hezbollah Party. If there were Jews in Lebanon we would probably be friends with them. We know the difference between religion, people, and their governments. In fact, we love American movies and music and we really like Americans. But we want to see the United States government destroyed."

Had Hezbollah just told me that they didn't care that I was American and Jewish? Had they also said that if there were Jews in Lebanon they would probably be friends with them? I had thought membership in Hezbollah mandated a strict adherence to the Shi'a interpretation of Islamic law, which would seem to preclude all of the above possibilities. I was shocked.

I was constantly surprised by my encounters with Middle Eastern youth, as much in Lebanon as in Iran, Iraq, and Syria. My impressions of the Middle East were largely shaped and colored by the mutually antagonistic relationship between the older generations of America and of Middle Eastern countries. I learned from my travels throughout the Middle East, however, that the youth can only be understood as their own phenomenon. They are far more tolerant than older generations and seemingly more sophisticated in their ability to distinguish between people, governments, and cultures.

Technology and unprecedented access to the outside world have given these young people sources of entertainment and means for communication that their parents never enjoyed. They embrace connectivity that transcends politics, religion, and extremism. The young men of Hezbollah were a perfect example. One minute they uttered extremist rhetoric about the American and Israeli governments, the next they went to nightclubs and danced to American music, watched American movies, and talked favorably about the concept of "America," a land as positively mythic for them as for generations of chasers of the American dream.

Technology widened the generational gap, affording these youth the opportunity to communicate in new and liberating ways. I found youth of every political persuasion in the Middle East living multiple lives, separating their social and recreational activities from their ideological enterprises.

I wanted to see this multiplicity in every sphere possible. I wanted to feel and experience it all. I knew this meant going to dangerous places and putting myself on the line. But I wasn't new to this.

During my four years as an undergraduate at Stanford, I traveled all throughout Africa. These journeys began with an anthropological interest in studying other cultures and while my primary motivation did not change, the environments I actively sought out became increasingly dangerous.

I traveled to war zones where I encountered rebels, child soldiers, perpetrators of genocide, victims of various sorts, and ordinary citizens who learned to coexist with horror that is virtually impossible to imagine for most Westerners. And it was all relatively easy. If there was no entry permitted to a country or a region, I simply snuck in. When I was not permitted to do something, I simply did it anyway. In most of these areas, the law had completely broken down.

While in Africa, I developed an interest in human rights and conflict resolution. Whether it was sneaking into the Congo under a pile of bananas, running across the Burundian border, or taking the very dangerous risk of crossing the Congo River from Kinshasa to the war-torn city of Brazzaville, I realized that one day in these regions yielded more knowledge than six months in a classroom. The adventures were addictive, not simply for the exciting stories I'd later be able to tell, but because I walked away from these experiences with a perspective I couldn't have gained in any other way. I wanted to hear those voices that weren't heard and wanted to be a megaphone for them.

While in college, I filled my room with eight-by-ten photographs of children I had met, families that had taken me in, and individuals I had encountered. I didn't want to forget any of it. There was a slide show of images and experiences that constantly played in my head. The memories were equal parts jubilant, tragic, and terrifying. The mental slide show was not always easy to endure, but I appreciated the continuous reminder of what I had seen and experienced.

After 9/11, my interests began to shift. In my final excursion to Africa, I was shocked by the wave of extremist Islamism that seemed to be sweeping the continent. I had expected this in the coastal cities, where there was a historical Arab and Islamic influence, but it seemed to be gaining traction in central Africa as well. Poverty-stricken communities in desperate need of basic goods and social services have become ripe for infiltration by extremists who can garner support for a radical ideology simply by building a hospital or school. My fascination with this phenomenon led me to the Middle East.

Once I decided to go to the Middle East, I wanted my first trip to be big. I wanted to go to Iran.

CHAPTER 1

DESTINATION IRAN

IRAN, 2004

I t still baffles me that I was ever let into Iran. I was a graduate student at Oxford University, and while I was an innocent student of international relations, I hardly had a background that was conducive to the type of visitors the government of Iran hoped to attract. The flexibility of the Oxford academic schedule, along with the stipend I had from my Rhodes scholarship, made me more interested in using Oxford as a base for travel than a place to study. Iran became my first destination in two years of sporadic travel throughout the Islamic world. Getting there, however, was not without its headaches.

The traditional position of the government of Iran, a rigorous police state, is based largely on the regime's desire to undermine an American government viewed as too friendly to the State of Israel, which Iran hopes to see, in the words of its current president, Mahmoud Ahmadinejad, "wiped off the face of the map." So it didn't seem likely that the Iranian government would grant a young American Jew a visa. Historically, relations between the United States and Iran have not always been so poor. For much of the Cold War, Iran was one of America's principal allies.

For the regime in Iran, those years—the period during which the monarchical shah ruled Iran—represent something entirely different. Having ascended to the throne in 1941 at the young age of twenty-two, the shah had neither the experience nor the discipline to manage a country of such vast wealth. Most Iranians believed that the shah was essentially handing Iran's wealth to foreign companies, which benefited the royal family and the upper class but had detrimental effects on the majority of the population. Discontent brewed and manifested itself in leftist movements that ultimately resulted in the popular election of the socialist Muhammad Mossadeq as prime minister. Mossadeq's socialist platform called for nationalization of Iranian oil and expulsion of foreign influence from Iran.

Fearful of the potential loss of political influence in the Middle East, the American government looked for ways to reverse the socialist tide in Iran. In August 1953, the CIA, in a joint effort with British intelligence, staged a coup to oust Mossadeq. While the coup led to the return of the shah to power and a negotiated settlement on Iranian oil that was favorable to Britain and the United States, in the long-term the coup had planted the seeds for the 1979 Islamic Revolution. Twenty-six years of corruption and poor leadership by the shah led Iranians to scapegoat the United States for their troubles and label the coup as the precipitating factor for the calamitous socioeconomic and political situation in Iran. The allocation of blame on the United States accumulated almost exponentially during the 1960s and 1970s and ultimately manifested itself as a crucial aspect of the revolutionary platform, which led to the establishment of an Islamic republic in 1979 and the seizure of the American Embassy, with revolutionaries holding fifty-two Americans hostage for 444 days.

The hostage crisis, which came after the United States admitted the exiled and ailing shah for medical treatment rather than return him to Iran for trial, led the American government to sever diplomatic ties with Iran. Since then, the relationship between the United

States and the Iranian government has only grown worse and the Iranian government only less willing to grant visas to Americans.

Even though almost everyone I knew—experts and otherwise—told me I was wasting my time applying for a visa, I was determined. I applied four months earlier than I needed to, but after sixteen trips to the Iranian Embassy in London, it seemed that the net result of my diligent efforts would be little more than the further depletion of my rapidly dwindling scholarship stipend and unhealthy consumption of venti caramel macchiatos from Starbucks that I relied on as fuel to repeatedly make the two-hour trip.

As it turned out, however, the repeated obstinacy of the Iranian government—and my willingness to be repeatedly rejected—ultimately worked to my advantage. Over the course of my many visits to the embassy, I had the opportunity to befriend one overworked official. After a few months of wooing him in broken Farsi, I was able to make him sympathetic to my situation. In December 2004, twelve hours before my flight to Iran, I was granted a visa to travel to the country that President Bush had less than two years earlier labeled as one of the three members of the "axis of evil."

When the plane took off for Tehran, the men on the plane were drinking alcohol and only one or two women were covered. I asked the man next to me if alcohol was legal in Iran. He looked at me, gave a small chuckle, and drank his Heineken. I slept through the rest of the flight, and when I woke up on the runway in Tehran, I felt like I was on a completely different plane. The alcohol was totally gone and every woman on the plane had covered her head with a hejab, as is the law in Iran. What struck me most was the total change in mood. The vibrant and jubilant crowd who had taken off in London now seemed subdued and regimented.

As I walked off the plane and through customs, I was nervous. This was not the first time I had had border anxiety. But, unlike when I'd crossed the Congolese or Burundian borders, I wasn't afraid of bodily harm. What terrified me was the uncertainty. The media had shaped my impression of Iran as a deeply religious, anti-American, and extremist society, and now I was prepared for the worst, and I had heard that foreign nationals with valid visas were sometimes turned away at immigration for no apparent reason.

Tonight, however, there would be no such surprises. The woman behind the immigration counter was dressed in full chador and hejab and, in a stoic but friendly voice, welcomed me to Iran and stamped my passport. My first five minutes at Tehran Airport would turn out to be the only truly simple experience I had in Iran.

I breezed through customs and collected my bags and exited the airport to get a taxi, but was greeted by a short and stocky elderly man holding a sign with my name on it. It wasn't likely that there were many other Cohens passing through Tehran Airport at three in the morning, so I knew that the man was there for me. I was naturally a little bit suspicious, but at three A.M. and after a long flight from London, I was happy for a ride to my hotel and my escort seemed pleasant enough. I hopped in his car and we headed on our way. I would soon learn the "escort" was actually my minder.

As we drove from the airport to the hotel, I could see the expected images of notorious ayatollahs glaring from prominent billboards. The roundabouts that organized the intersections in Iran's busy streets were ornate with bizarre sculptures that looked like a cross between metallic folk art and something you would buy in a party store. As we got closer to the city center, I could see the chador-wearing women wandering the streets as we passed the Iran Freedom Tower, a large tripod structure strangely placed in the middle of traffic and resembling something one would expect to see in *Star Wars*. The initial glimpse at all of these images triggered few, if any, emotions beyond the usual excitement of being in a new place. There was, however, one exception to this: images of Ayatollah Khomeini and billboards reading "Down with USA" sent chills down my spine and reminded me that I was in a truly terrifying place. I had seen this kind of graffiti in other countries, but this was my first time in a country where such phrases were actually the party line.

In what would turn out to be a very poor decision on my part—one that would make my time in Iran extremely trying—I shared my plans for my time in Iran with my "escort."

I didn't know it then, but all Americans in Iran are required to travel with a government-assigned escort, or, as they euphemistically call it, "tour guide." These escorts, however, are tour guides in name only. The regime in Iran assumes that any American entering the country is a potential spy and therefore links him or her with these guides. These friendly tourism officers work overtime to make sure that American tourists have virtually no personal interactions with Iranian people.

I wasn't a tourist, but I wasn't savvy enough to know to keep that information to myself. As we drove, I explained to my escort that I hoped to conduct several interviews with top government officials while in the country. I had planned to do some of these interviews for my dissertation at Oxford on the history of U.S.-Iran relations, but more than anything, I wanted to give myself an excuse to research something in this closed society. This information made him visibly uncomfortable, but his uneasiness didn't fully register with me. Instead, I just went on. I told him that I had a list of Iranian leaders whom I would try to interview. The list included a number of notorious opponents of the regime, many of whom were either under house arrest or in prison.

My enthusiasm and excitement trumped my reason and I spilled virtually everything to my minder. My naïve candor about my intentions had set off alarm bells with my escort, who was responsible for keeping me and visitors like me from doing precisely what I had told him I was in Iran to do. Though I was eventually able to remove at least the overt shackles the intelligence apparatus would soon place on me—largely due to my comments that night—my trip was never comfortable. I was constantly followed by intelligence agents, some of whom identified themselves to me as such and others who operated covertly. My room and possessions were randomly searched and I was personally intimidated on countless occasions.

On my first morning in Iran, I woke up, eager to get out, meet people, and wander around Tehran. Academic contacts in the United States had arranged for a translator who would also serve as a guide and interview scheduler. Her name was Marwa and I had come to know her only through e-mail correspondences, but she seemed optimistic about helping me.

I walked over to the hotel reception and gave Marwa a call. I was anxious to meet her and excited to begin my research. No sooner had I hung up the hotel reception phone after telling Marwa to come to the hotel than I saw the same escort who had picked me up from the airport walk through the door.

Still not knowing exactly what his role was, I told him I didn't need anything and that my guide was on her way.

"Who is your guide? I am here, I am responsible for you," he told me.

I told him that was not necessary.

He grew stern and he insisted on waiting to talk to my translator. We waited for about twenty minutes before she walked in the front door of the hotel. She wore a red hejab, was slightly heavyset, and must have been in her late thirties. She had a big smile and spoke with a soft but high-pitched voice.

Marwa and the escort had an intense conversation in Farsi. I don't know what they talked about, but the outcome was Marwa telling me that she would make some phone calls and get back in touch with me. I didn't understand what had happened.

My nameless escort acted as if nothing dramatic had taken place. I once again explained to him that sightseeing in Iran was of secondary importance and that I had come to interview officials, but I soon found myself in the back of a taxi with this complete stranger, who had just had some kind of an ominous interaction with the person who was supposed to be guiding me. It was still far from clear to me what was going on, but I had figured out one thing: This guy had no interest in helping me.

The drive wasn't long and we soon arrived at the offices of a state-sponsored tour company. The room was relatively clean, with counters along the walls. There were three fully covered women who worked at the counter closest to the entrance, and after having spent almost all of my waking time in Iran with a cranky old man, I was delighted to be greeted by several very nice ladies. I enthusiastically practiced my Farsi with them, which seemed to at least spark some smiles. But I think this was mostly because my opening line was *"Doktar hayay Irani kheyli khoshghelan, vali kheyli hasudan,"* which in Farsi means "Iranian girls are very beautiful, but they get very jealous." They asked me how I found Iran so far and I joked that all I had seen was the airport and my hotel. One of the women reassured me, "Don't worry, you will see many nice things in Iran."

But each man who worked at the company was ruder than the next. They were bossy, demanding, and abrasive. This wasn't like my travels in Africa, where a smile, attempt at the language, and friendliness went a long way. Every friendly gesture on my part was rebuffed and met with icy looks and sharp words. My frustration rapidly grew into irritation.

They rushed me into the office of Mr. Sorush, the manager. Imposing at six feet four and sporting a large mustache, Mr. Sorush was not what I would describe as an approachable character. He wore his pants unusually high up and despite the belt being above his belly, he still looked overweight. I told him that I appreciated the offer, but that I didn't need a tour company while I was in Iran.

I explained that I was a student at Oxford and here to do research, but Mr. Sorush didn't even wait for me to finish and abruptly stormed out of his own office and left me there explaining myself to nobody but the photo he had of Ayatollah Khomeini on the wall. I waited for a while and the door finally creaked back open and Mr. Sorush came back in with my unnamed escort. He scolded me as if I had done something grossly illegal and promised he could make my stay in Iran very uncomfortable.

The escort had sold me out. I knew it. Or rather, I should have known it. He kept chiming in with tidbits of detail about what I had told him. Each time he did this, I turned with a look of disgust. I had been in the country for less than twenty-four hours and already I was being threatened with prison and a report to the Ministry of Intelligence. I had expected things to be difficult in Iran, but I'd thought trouble would at least wait for me to get over my jet lag. I quietly acquiesced and I think he felt as though his final point had struck a nerve. It was at that moment that he stood up, extended his hand, and said, "Well, Mr. Cohen, we are very happy to have you in Iran and I really hope you enjoy your stay. Please let me know if you need anything." I politely shook his hand and thought up every curse word imaginable in my head at the same time.

It was at this moment that I really began to feel that I was in a police state. The sense of adventure that I used to feel in Africa when I would put myself in dangerous situations was absent. This wasn't fun; it was frustrating and emotionally draining. It was as if Mr. Sorush, with his two-faced offer, was rubbing the discomfort I felt. Cursing under my breath, saying it would all be OK, naïvely trying to assume nothing would happen—none of this worked. My lack of familiarity with a police-state society made my imagination run wild—not with pleasant and blissful thoughts, but instead with visions of ominous possible outcomes.

That second night in Iran was difficult. I felt alone and uncertain about the direction of my trip. I had not yet seen the friendly face of Iran, my time up until this point clouded by the set of unsavory characters I had encountered. Not a single person had made me feel welcome. I spoke to my mother that evening, but because I guessed that my phone was tapped, I couldn't explain that I had been threatened with arrest. So when she asked me how I found the country, I responded sunnily.

"The people are so friendly, the sights are beautiful, and I am being well taken care of," I lied.

I woke up the next morning to the sound of the phone. It was Marwa, explaining to me that I just needed to sit tight for a few days. She didn't want to interfere with Mr. Sorush's company, but she would try to arrange interviews for me and meet with me in the afternoon. I wasn't surprised to find an escort waiting for me in the lobby and as he approached me, he extended his hand and said, "Mr. Cohen, don't worry, we will take care of all your needs while you are here. I am Mr. Shapour and I am at your service."

It was total bullshit, but I was trying to think positively and was willing to play along.

Shapour said he had a plan to take me to see what he described as "one of Tehran's most beautiful and exciting spots." We flagged down a taxi together and within thirty minutes we had arrived at our first destination, a subway station. We took the Tehran subway a few stops and we were there. It was the shrine to Ayatollah Khomeini, the late supreme spiritual leader of Iran and founder of the Islamic Republic. The shrine looked like a palace, with a large gold dome in the center and four towering gold minarets surrounding it. Like so many other monuments in Iran, this one was under construction. Everything always seemed to be under construction, yet I rarely saw anyone working. The weekend is Thursday and Friday in Iran, and because Wednesday is right before the weekend and Saturday is the beginning of the new week, the work ethic tends to be a bit lackadaisical on those days. When you combine this with the fact that in the summer it is dreadfully hot, in the winter it is terribly cold, and people take time to pray three times a day, it becomes obvious that very little time is left for work. The Khomeini shrine had separate entrances for men and women and a whole pile of shoes outside the entrance. Inside the shrine, there were not only visitors, but also at least half a dozen or so Iranians who had fallen asleep on the elaborate Persian carpets, while wrapping themselves in these intricately woven treasures as if they were blankets. I wasn't sure if they were homeless, tired, or trying to feel close to the late ayatollah. Located to one side of the shrine, the late Ayatollah Khomeini's body rested inside a coffin. It was protected by a room-size box, elaborately decorated with verses from the Quran and elaborately designed gold metal. Hordes of people flocked to his tomb to pay homage and embrace their dead spiritual leader, but recalling this man's history with my country, I had no interest in joining them.

Most of the hundreds of daily visitors are people who are either deeply religious, or still revere Ayatollah Khomeini and the principles of the Islamic Revolution. Others treat this as a minihadj, or spiritual journey. The women that I saw at the shrine were all covered, the children that I saw were all with very conservatively dressed parents, and the youth hanging around the shrine seemed to show great affection toward the site. This seemed like the norm in Iran, that this was a place where youth often came to pay their respects to their former leader.

From the Khomeini shrine, my escort took me to the Behesht-e Zahra martyrs' cemetery, which was just a ten-minute walk from the shrine. Along the way, young teenage boys offered me tea and biscuits. They refused to accept my money, which I later learned was a customary charade not to be taken literally, so when I learned this after the fact, I felt really guilty. Behesht-e Zahra cemetery is a powerful sight. The cemetery is gigantic, filled with tombs commemorating the martyrs. Cement tablets with the names of the martyrs fill thousands of rows throughout the cemetery. The cement tablets are protected by raised metal sheeting that form a canopy over the deceased. Each martyr is granted a shadow box that is decorated by the family. I could have spent days walking from shadow box to shadow box looking at what was inside. There were pictures of children, pictures of religious clerics, pictures of houses, and pictures of wives. I had never seen death as celebrated as it was at Behesht-e Zahra.

The mood of the cemetery was somber. This was not surprising, given where I was, but in Behesht-e Zahra death is both advertised and celebrated. It was not a quiet setting, either, as this seemed to be a gathering place in addition to a graveyard. There were plenty of women hunched over tombs in tears, but there were also groups of men just hanging out and laughing with one another. When I asked my guide if it was normal for so many people to hang around the cemetery, he explained that this is what they do on a Friday. After Friday prayer, hundreds of Iranians come to engage in celebrations to commemorate the martyrs as well as funerals to honor the fallen victims of war. Some come for the grief, others come because it is a fun afternoon activity and it is something to do.

Americans often refer to Operation Desert Storm, the 1991 war with Iraq, as the first Persian Gulf War. Behesht-e Zahra is a powerful reminder of what was truly the first Persian Gulf War, the Iran-Iraq

War that raged throughout the 1980s. In September 1980, Iraqi president Saddam Hussein invaded Iran and began a conflict that would last eight years and achieve nothing on either side.

The war was bloody. Use of chemical weapons, torture, and brutal violations of human rights were frequent methods employed by both sides. The eight years of fighting claimed an "estimated four hundred thousand deaths and one million wounded on the Iranian side and three hundred thousand deaths and nine hundred thousand wounded on the Iraqi side," although some estimates actually suggest an even higher death toll. As a comparison, the number of Iranian casualties actually exceeded the number of American casualties in the Second World War. In addition to the bloody consequences of the war, it was also financially draining. According to reliable sources, "by 1986 the economic costs of the conflict were already as high as $600 billion," including loss of oil sales.*

For Iranians, this was the first Persian Gulf War. I never would have understood this had I not seen the kilometers and kilometers of tombstones and the weeping women in chador falling onto tombs. In later conversations I had with young people in Iran, the Iran-Iraq War would always come up. They spoke of the magnitude of the horror, the death toll, the impact, and the humiliation Iran experienced during this period. While I can never truly understand what it was like to have lived through that war, just Behesht-e Zahra alone made me appreciate that it was no mere footnote in history, as the Western world tends to view it.

Shapour saw I was moved by Behesht-e Zahra, by its emotionally stirring shadow boxes and the haunting rows of tombs. He was careful to show me the tombs of the unknown soldiers, which consisted of small, unmarked cement squares. Shapour wanted me to see the death

---

*James Bill, *The Eagle and the Lion: The Tragedy of American-Iranian Relations* (New Haven: Yale University Press, 1988), 305.

toll and the anonymity of those who died in the war. Intertwined with the rows of unmarked tombs were carefully planted shrubbery and poles adorned with flags for the Islamic Republic. Shapour placed his own Islamic Republic flag on one of those poles. I found the cemetery moving; this war I had only read about in books became a visual reality. I saw the pain of those who had lost; I saw the magnitude of the casualties in the sheer number of tombs; I saw the importance of this to Iranian society by bearing witness to the mourning rituals of Iranians who had come to pay their respects. But Shapour may have pushed his luck when he took me to a nearby museum where I could see posters declaring, "USA Is the Biggest Terrorist."

Both the Khomeini shrine and Behesht-e Zahra affected me, and the fact that the government wanted me to see these sites did not reduce the impact. They were not, however, the "beautiful sights" Shapour had promised. That was still to come.

Shapour told me that our next stop would show off Iran's beauty. He failed to mention that it would take almost two hours to get there and that most of that time would be spent in traffic. When we finally arrived, I found myself in an environment that I would hardly call beautiful. We were in the mountains, but all I could really see was the huge cloud of black smoke that seemed to form a fluffy tent over the city of Tehran.

On some days, the pollution is so bad that people start coughing up black smoke.

We left the "viewing" area and headed to what Shapour claimed was a really good restaurant somewhat nearby. His motive, of course, was to keep me out of downtown Tehran and distract from the prospects of interviewing officials. We soon arrived at an isolated small pizza café. Without realizing it, however, Shapour had made a crucial mistake that gave me a glimmer of hope for my time in Iran: He had brought me to Iran's youth.

It was at this mountaintop café that I got my first view of an Iranian experience unfiltered by my government escorts. And I have the charged hormones of a few pairs of Iranian teenagers to thank.

As I first saw at that café, Iran has a lot more than religious shrines, martyrs' cemeteries, and the regime. It also has a bunch of kids, who constitute nearly 70 percent of society, having the same kind of fun that we enjoy in America. All that other stuff—the regime and its trappings—just makes it a little bit harder for them.

The youth bulge in Iran is not random. The massive human-wave attacks that took place during that war wiped out a substantial portion of an entire generation. The memories of the Iran-Iraq War are deeply embedded in the minds of Iranian youth, not just because they grew up with this violence, but because it is the very reason for the size of their demographic.

In Iran, boys and girls are not permitted to show affection in public, and there is a morals police that strictly enforces the rule. When the Islamic Republic was established in 1979, the intent was to exploit nationalist sentiments and remold society in accordance with the Shi'ite interpretation of Islamic law. Drinking, public relationships, and dancing were all viewed as blasphemy. But, as I learned during my time at that dismal café, even the most repressive measures are no match for teenagers on a mission to get some.

I ate my lunch and I watched couple after couple after couple sneak off into the nearby bushes for some "privacy." Every five minutes or so, the morals police would go into the bushes and roust the canoodling teens from their love nests. The teens would then wait a few minutes before heading right back into the bushes, where they'd stay until chased out again. It was a total charade. Still, I loved it. I was entertained, but I was also sympathetic. I remembered the anxiety of middle-school birthday parties, seventh-grade couples trying to sneak kisses every time an adult's back was turned. We may not have had the Revolutionary Guards or the morals police watching over us, but we had our parents. At the time, it seemed just as bad.

While Shapour finished his pizza at the café I got up to walk around. I had a difficult time approaching people, but I did catch up with one couple immediately after the morals police had caught them. Happy for the chance to talk to somebody other than my escort, I struck up a conversation with them. I tried to talk to them about politics and Iran, but they seemed eager to end the conversation and sneak off again right in front of the morals police. When I was younger and kids would sneak off at parties, they would just get grounded; in Iran, there were potential consequences. I was amazed by this. I felt I had seen another Iran; a more liberated and vibrant Iran.

On the ride back to the hotel, my guide, Shapour, was not quite so jubilant. He remained silent on the entire drive back, clearly unhappy about something. Back at the hotel, Shapour and I sat down in two green cloth chairs in the lobby. During the conversation, I leaned back and he leaned forward; it was clear who was in control. He looked at me with his big piercing eyes and a stern look that I would become all too familiar with.

"You know, you have to mind what you ask people. This is not America, we do things differently here."

"And why is that?" I managed, after a few minutes of stony silence. I knew it was the wrong thing to say, but I was frustrated.

"I think I will call up Mr. Sorush and have him tell the ministry that you are breaking the law."

I felt myself losing it. This was ridiculous. I had done nothing wrong and I had acquiesced to every demand made of me. Was threatening me really that entertaining?

"What law?" I snapped.

Shapour took out his cell phone and dialed Mr. Sorush. For about two minutes, they exchanged words in Farsi, but I caught none of it. He didn't tell me what was said in their short conversation, but he led me to believe that I might get arrested. I didn't know what to do. My phone was almost certainly tapped and people were likely reading or filtering my e-mails.

I had been in plenty of life-threatening situations before and had always found a way to stay strong. At that moment, however, it wasn't Shapour's threat of arrest or any fear of imminent danger that scared me so much. It was something different, a completely new feeling that I had never experienced before. For the first time in my life, I felt captive to psychological intimidation. My travels in Africa had put me in physical danger, but I'd never experienced anything quite so terrifying as my dwindling sense of personal freedom. All my phone calls, e-mails, conversations, and actions were closely monitored. People watched over my shoulder. Even when I thought I was alone, someone was always following me. I began to feel as if I could not think my own thoughts. Having always had the luxury of being able to express myself, I was devastated to have it all stripped away from me. I just lost it. It was that feeling I remembered all too well from when I was younger; eyes tearing, every ounce of energy focused on holding those tears back. In another context I might have started yelling at him, or I would have just stormed off; but, in Iran I just sank my head into my lap. I didn't want him to see how hard this was for me, but no matter how hard I tried, it was almost impossible to hold back.

I just got a glimpse of it. Iranians deal with Big Brother watching them on a daily basis. I truly sympathized with their situation. I tried to reflect on this as much as possible. In some ways it made things easier for me. As hard as things got, I could always find some kind of comfort in my departure date, the much awaited moment when things would return to normal. Most Iranians don't have this luxury. Without an escape, they simply find ways to coexist.

It was my weakest moment. I was alone in one of the most repressive countries in the entire world, and I had just broken down in front of a hostile intelligence agent. There was no sympathy from his end. Up until that point, I had considered myself strong. After all, I had snuck into the Congolese civil war under a pile of bananas, had stood face-to-face with perpetrators of the Rwanda genocide, and had met child soldiers in Africa hopped up on so many drugs that they easily could have viewed their guns as toys, not weapons, and ended my life right then and there. While these experiences were reckless, they did not even compare to the fear and helplessness I felt when I had been stripped of my freedom in Iran. It nearly broke me.

As if things couldn't have gotten worse, I realized then that I was out of money. Nobody had told me that I wouldn't be able to access my bank from Iran; I was told that Iran had ATMs and that even if my debit card didn't work, I would be able to take withdrawals off of a credit card or have money transferred to an Iranian bank. None of this was possible. Iran did have ATMs, but they only accepted Iranian credit cards (and most of them didn't even work for that). Because of economic sanctions, no American bank could transfer money into Iran. For the same reason, Iranian banks could also only give cash advances on Iranian credit cards.

I owed my guides and the appointed intelligence service money. I owed my hotel money. I had entered Iran with a combination of dollars, euros, and British pounds that amounted to no more than seven hundred dollars. Tehran is not a place to be broke and in debt, especially when I had already been threatened several times with imprisonment for nonexistent crimes.

The unfriendly faces grew less friendly still. My escort and the hotel manager both wanted me to pay them for the privilege of being intimidated and harassed, and I wasn't holding up my end of the bargain.

I tried calling my family, but my phone would cut out every few minutes or random voices would come onto the phone and make it impossible to speak. My family and I had decided that if I got myself in some trouble and was in physical danger, I would ask her if my sister had heard from one of her ex-boyfriends. This was our code.

My financial situation did not place me in physical harm and didn't warrant my drawing on the code, but the situation was nonetheless immediate. I connected with my mother down in Florida, where they were for Hanukkah. It took five days for me to get the money my parents sent. The transfers were complex and involved banks in London and random Iranian businessmen. Later I learned if you go to the central city of Esfahan and purchase a Persian carpet, you can route a credit card transaction through Dubai and get a cash advance off your credit card. For some reason, this transaction can only be made when buying carpets and only when they are purchased in Esfahan.

On the third day, Shapour once again greeted me in the lobby of my hotel and informed me that we were taking yet another trip to see Mr. Sorush. Mr. Sorush again threatened me and informed me that he had spoken to the ministry about me. He then advised me to spend the rest of the day at the hotel.

Would I be returning to the hotel to await arrest? If I were jailed in Iran, I could be held indefinitely, tortured, or worse. But that wasn't what scared me the most. If I were arrested in Tehran, there'd be no American Embassy to call and no diplomatic relationship to cite. I was totally alone.

Shapour put me in a taxi and told me not to leave my hotel. What a disaster this trip had been: I had run out of money, my research—which would rely on my ability to interview as many as fifty Iranian government officials—had failed within the first week of my trip, and now it appeared that I was about to be arrested for unauthorized journalism. After another emotional outburst, I was put in a taxi and told to return to my hotel. I would no longer be able to leave for any reason.

The taxi ride back to my hotel was the turning point of my time in Iran.

In the backseat, certain that I was being delivered to a fate whose terror I could hardly begin to imagine, I listened to the driver trying to make small talk. I wasn't exactly in the mood to chat, and I certainly wasn't in the mood for the elaborate game of charades that would break our language barrier. This young man, probably no older than twenty-seven or twenty-eight, was persistent and very interested in talking to me.

As we drove, I looked out my window and saw a gigantic picture of Ayatollah Khomeini on the side of one of the buildings. Willing to humor the driver's talkativeness, if not necessarily indulge his desire for conversation, I pointed to it and said simply, "Khomeini."

"Khomeini is very bad," he said.

"Well, what do you think about Rafsanjani?"

"He is very, very bad."

"Jannati?" I asked. Ayatollah Jannati is the cleric who notoriously declares "Down with USA, God willing," during his Friday prayer sermons.

"Very, very, very bad."

"What about President Khatami?"

"Medium bad."

It went on like this as I ticked through at least ten members of the Iranian leadership. Finally, I asked him what he thought of Ayatollah Ali Khamanei, the country's spiritual leader and the most powerful man in theocratic Iran.

He turned around to look at me. "He is like animal," he said.

I couldn't believe what I'd just heard. Had the harsh censorship and threats of the regime bypassed this candid, honest young man?

Out of curiosity, I asked him about the American leadership. I wasn't expecting anything positive

"What do you think of Condoleezza Rice?"

He smiled, "She helps us, very good."

"What do you think of George Bush?" I asked.

He looked at me with an air of pride and said, "He is like real man."

His hatred for Khamanei and admiration for George Bush slightly stunned me, but also excited me. I'd only heard the government line since arriving in Iran, but this young taxi driver gave me confidence that there was more to hear. When we arrived back at my hotel, I wanted to embrace the driver.

"How much do I owe you for the taxi?"

"Where are you from?"

It didn't appear that he had understood my question, but I answered his anyway.

I extended my arm to give him four ten-thousand rial bills (roughly four dollars) but he pushed my hand back ever so gently. I thought this was my second experience with what Iranians call *taroof*, a concept I had first learned of after I graciously accepted the free biscuits from the children in Behesht-e Zahra. *Taroof* involves offering something as a gift to demonstrate courtesy, when in actuality money is expected. There is usually a charade that follows, whereby three or four offers and refusals take place. *Taroof* is sometimes looked at as a cultural characteristic of saying one thing and meaning another. While some will argue this is the essence of this cultural tradition, most Iranians suggest that it is a politeness and a courtesy that they extend to one another.

After six or seven offers it became clear that either I was missing the signals, or this wasn't *taroof*, the Iranian custom of polite refusal. I finally asked him, "Is this *taroof*?" He assured me that it wasn't and that he simply loved Americans.

I took another twenty thousand rials out of my wallet and tried to give him more money. He again pushed my hand away. "You are American. I will never charge an American."

Despite my run-ins with Shapour and Mr. Sorush and the walls they placed before me, the taxi driver made me realize that all the real information was right in front of me. The vast majority of the Iranian population is under the age of thirty and these young people proved not only eager to talk to me, but also to be forthright in their displeasure for the Iranian regime. To this day, the Iranian people are some of the most pro-American people I have met in the entire world. The vast majority of Iranians—especially the youth—have a strong affinity for American culture, products, and entertainment and a substantial portion has at least an element of appreciation for the American government's unwillingness to pander to the Iranian regime.

I was not arrested that night, so I completely changed my objectives. Instead of seeking officials, I would learn about Iran by seeking out my peers throughout the country. The taxi ride without Shapour was evidence that the intelligence services in Iran were so preoccupied with preventing me from meeting with officials that they might not concern themselves with my new interest in the youth.

With a newfound sense of purpose, my confidence returned and with it came the ability to see the threats of Sorush and Shapour for the cheap intimidation tactics that they were.

Like so much else in Iran, my relationship with my guides became a charade: I asked to meet with officials, expressed frustration over the stagnation of my research, and complained almost incessantly about the problems the escorts were causing me. We would typically then have some kind of a disagreement or verbal argument, after which I would return to the hotel, playing the part of the defeated student. Certain that I was sufficiently terrified, my escort would head home.

It was at this point that I would begin my work for the day.

CHAPTER 2

REMOVING THE SHACKLES

IRAN, 2004

Making friends in Iran was surprisingly easy. When the vast majority of the country despises the regime, there is no shortage of opinionated youth. The leadership has deprived Iran's young population of a stable economy, civil liberties, and full access to an increasingly modernized and globally interdependent world. Students in Iran openly lash out at the regime and often preemptively vent to whoever will listen. I had seen subtle hints of this anger in my first four days in Iran, but it was not until the fifth day that I began to really take note of the anger and resentment among the youth.

That morning, I spoke to two Iranian academics I had become close with in the States. A paranoid e-mail I had sent them led to two phone calls very early in the morning. Hearing their voices and assurances was a relief. One of my contacts gave me the names and phone numbers of several individuals who, he assured me, would be able to help. He had been in touch with an influential official in the Ministry of Foreign Affairs, who, because of a past history together, was willing to call Mr. Sorush and arrange for me to have some autonomy from the escorts.

After Mr. Sorush and Shapour received that phone call from the ministry, I felt that my fortunes had been reversed. Up until that point, I'd only seen what the Iranian government wanted me to see, but now, Shapour asked me where *I* wanted to go for the day. It was a truly liberating moment for me when I told him I wouldn't be requiring his "assistance."

"I'm going to the university," I told him. "I don't need you to come with me."

The tables had really turned. It had taken five days for me to break free from Shapour, Sorush, and the rest, and though I knew that covert agents would still be following me around, my newfound independence was significant—psychologically and otherwise.

I turned my eye toward the universities. Historically, universities in Iran have served as notorious venues for student resistance. In 1999, students at the University of Tehran rioted in large numbers after conservative hard-liners closed a respected reformist newspaper. In response, the government—predominantly comprised of conservatives who want a more nonsecular and autocratic society—unleashed two of its militant forces—the Islamic Revolutionary Guards Corps and Ansar-e Hezbollah—on the student dormitories. The brutality of this notorious crackdown continues to haunt Iranians each time they consider taking to the streets. During the crackdown, some students disappeared, others were injured, and some were killed. Ever since 1999, the regime in Iran has kept a close eye on the university; the intelligence services have even recruited a network of spies within the student body to report on their classmates.

The gates at the University of Tehran were heavily guarded by armed soldiers and Islamic Revolutionary Guards Corps. The Revolutionary Guards, intimidating in appearance, wore dark green uniforms and held their guns firmly. Alongside the conservative clerics, the Islamic Revolutionary Guards Corps is one of the most representative features of the Islamic Revolution. Trained in the old American embassy, now called the "Den of Spies," these soldiers are the very embodiment of the regime's ruthlessness. They are a fearsome sight; to get past them, I used a trick I'd learned as a freshman in college. In those days before I turned twenty-one, I had learned to maximize the effectiveness of my fake ID by pretending to talk on a cell phone while trying to enter a bar or club. After I was denied entry at the main gate of the University of Tehran, I simply walked to another entrance, started an imaginary conversation on my cell phone, and walked right in.

The campus didn't look much different from an American university, with the notable exception of a Friday-prayer venue, several small mosques, and numerous pictures of Ayatollah Khomeini hanging on the sides of buildings. Students sat in scattered circular formations throughout the grass courtyards of the university. Other students crowded onto the stairs of buildings, perfectly situated for optimal people watching. Tired of sightseeing and eager to speak with students, I turned to enter the first building I saw. It was a three-story cement structure decorated with elaborate columns in front and preceded by a large staircase. On the front face of the building hung imposing portraits of both Iran's spiritual leader, Ali Khamanei, and the hero of the Islamic Revolution, Ayatollah Khomeini. Above all of this waved the flag of the Islamic Republic.

Inside, students were running wild, dashing in different directions, and forming pockets of loud, chattering social groups in every square inch of the lobby. Others ran to the cafeteria to get a sandwich or muffin before their next class. There were even some who I saw taking a nap on the floor. It reminded me of the period in between classes in an American high school, where students make use of those few minutes of liberation from the classroom.

As I weaved through the crowd of university students, I looked for one who might seem willing to help me. I had never found it difficult to meet people in another country. Having traveled to Africa about a dozen times, I had become accustomed to traveling alone. It didn't feel strange to approach random people or even go out in the evenings to a club by myself. It didn't bother me. Traveling extensively on my own has actually created a sense of curiosity about other people that has filtered into my everyday life. Wherever I am—whether it is New York, Oxford, or Kenya—I am always striking up conversations with strangers. Sometimes they think it is weird and suspicious, but to me it feels normal. Iran was no different. In fact, my initial reasons for going to the University of Tehran were selfish. I wanted to meet people I could talk to and some who could help me stay sane while in Iran. I needed people to explain to me the dynamics of what was happening and how to keep myself out of trouble. Given the misery of the first four days, much of which was due to my indiscretion in that first night's ride from the airport, I clearly had no idea how to fly under the radar screen in a police state.

Out of the corner of my eye I saw a female student standing in the middle of the room. She wore a long black chador, void of any individual characteristics; she looked like a silhouette. Her arms and legs were completely covered, as was her head. But when she turned around, I noticed her eyes right away. They were elaborately painted with blue mascara, eyeliner, and as it seemed, any other makeup product that one could possibly fathom using. Her cheeks were red and her lips covered in a noticeable light pink lipstick. Wearing elaborate makeup is just another way for women to reject the harsh dress codes imposed upon them.

Everyone else seemed as if they were in a rush, oblivious to what was going on around them and determined to get to their next class. She stood there looking in my direction and when it became clear that she was not going to approach me, I walked over to her. "Excuse me, do you know where Dr. Rezai's office is?" I felt slightly awkward asking this question because Dr. Rezai was a name I had created in a shameless effort to make friends.

She looked at me puzzled. "I am not sure of Dr. Rezai, are you sure he teaches here at the law school?"

I told her, "Oh, maybe I have the name wrong. You see, I have just arrived from the United States and I am hoping to talk to somebody about Iran and—"

She didn't let me finish; instead, she took me by the arm and guided me out to the courtyard. As I'd learn, Iranian women are not shy and are often extremely confident. Over a year later, she would tell me in an online instant-messaging conversation that she thinks I came up to her because she is more beautiful than the other girls. I couldn't deny this.

She smiled at me and said, "Wait right here. I have to meet with my law professor and then I shall answer all of your questions. You don't worry." Almost immediately after she returned, she extended her hand and introduced herself.

"I am Gita. What is your name?" She spoke with such a confidence and there was something incredibly engaging about this.

"I am Jared."

"Jrrrd?" she said as she tried to pronounce it.

"Ja-red," I said slowly in response.

"OK, Jrrrd, please don't go anywhere, I want to see if I can help."

I found a bench in the middle of the courtyard. Over the next forty-five minutes, I felt like an exotic creature on display in a foreign land. Random groups of students kept approaching me and asking where I was from. They all wanted to know the same thing: What do people in America think of Iran? There we were, citizens of two countries that are sworn enemies, all experiencing the same curiosity and eagerness to speak to one another. After about fifteen students had gathered around, one of the female students spoke up.

"We watched what happened on September eleventh. We saw it on the television." I hadn't even noticed her, but I began to notice a pattern. The female Iranians love to talk and take charge; hardly the image I had of women in a country ruled by Islamic law. She was kneeling behind the bench I was sitting on. She was a petite girl wrapped in her black chador as if it were a blanket keeping her warm. Her face was tiny and she had glasses that hung down on her nose. I was not sure what she was insinuating with her comment, so I responded with something benign.

"Yes, that was a tragic day for my country."

She nodded her head and adjusted her hejab slightly before tenderly offering her condolences. "You know on that day, all of Iran wept for America. We felt like our brothers and our sisters were suffering and we really wept."

I looked around the circle of students that had gathered around me and saw heads nodding up and down. And this touched me. The previous year there had been an earthquake in the ancient Iranian city of Bam, claiming the lives of more than twenty thousand Iranians. While Americans who watch the news likely registered this as a tragedy, I would imagine that few Americans wept on behalf of their Iranian brothers and sisters and I felt guilty that I had not previously offered my condolences for their losses.

Another female student spoke. She had very distinct features and glamorous eyes. Like so many other women in Iran, she had elaborately painted her eyes with dark mascara and artistically done her nails in dark pink polish. She had a completely different way of carrying herself than the other girl who had spoken. She sat comfortably and spoke with a confident and almost aggressive tone. "What do people think of Iran in America? Who do they think we are?" I thought about her question, as it seemed more rhetorical than anything else, as if she already knew the answer.

"I am not sure what you mean," I responded.

"Well, do they know we are not terrorists?" she demanded to know. "We are Muslim and we are proud of our religion, but that does not mean we are terrorists. Do people in your country know this?" She inched closer to me from her sitting position. "You must also know that just because we are Muslim and this is an Islamic republic, that does not mean that we like the mullahs or want this as our government. We hate them! They try to ruin our lives."

I wasn't sure how to contribute. I attempted to fill the silence. "I think part of the problem is that—"

She interrupted me before I could finish: "When you go back you must tell people that the Iranians have no problems with the Americans. Please tell them what you see here and tell them the truth. Tell them we love America and we really feel when America suffers. Make them know that we are not the same as our government and that we want to have America as friends." Her pleas rapidly evolved into a tirade on her disgust for the regime. She complained that the economy was growing worse by the day and instead of helping the people, the ruling elite simply pocketed the money from the country's oil. "They are all the same," she said, "they steal while we suffer. We are proud people and there is no opportunity for us. Sometimes we question what will be our future. We did not choose this government, but they still tell us how we must live and they give us nothing."

Gita returned with her sister. She seemed to think it was funny that I was surrounded by students, although I think I noticed a hint of jealousy. I thanked the students who were sitting with me and I turned my attention back to the sisters. Gita laughed and said, "I think you have made some friends." She laughed again. "You should get used to this. We don't see very many Americans. Everyone is going to want to tell you things." I laughed and invited the two sisters for lunch, but told them that because I didn't know Tehran, they would have to choose the place.

We broke the ice quickly when they saw how truly terrified I was to cross the street. They thought my trepidation was funny, but it was not without good reason. In Iran crossing the street is a challenge in and of itself. The traffic is atrocious, bumper-to-bumper at all moments of the day. Cars drive on whatever part of the road offers space, and it is therefore not uncommon to see vehicles of various shapes and sizes driving on the wrong side of the road. Iran is well-equipped with walkways that stretch over the road, but people seem to prefer throwing themselves in front of traffic to ensuring their safety. There are no emissions standards and as a result, clouds of black smoke hover over the traffic and filter into the street. The pollution is so bad that it occasionally even leads to the closure of schools. Women seem to cover more of their faces when walking near the road; using their hejab to keep smoke out of their mouths.

The sisters sensed my fear and Gita, who laughed as if this was the funniest thing she had ever seen, grabbed my arm and said, "Careful, my baby, come with us." She would jokingly repeat this every time we crossed the street for the next month. In Iran, it is often considered rude to use somebody's name, so direct addresses are often qualified with "my baby" or "my dear."

We arrived at a restaurant that the sisters assured me would be a typical Persian experience. A few paces inside, we descended a flight of stairs and I could smell the aroma of the cuisine. We walked along beautiful and intricately designed Persian carpets and were escorted to a corner table. The smell of saffron and cinnamon competed with a mixed aroma of mint and diced lime. My eyes searched the surrounding tables for the source of the delicious scent that filled the room. The tables were filled with lamb and chicken kebabs, rice dishes with vegetables, white yogurt, and beef dishes. I didn't know what they were called, so I would have to describe what I wanted to the sisters. Hopefully, I could try a little bit of everything during my stay in Iran.

Not long after sitting down, Gita and her sister, Leila, excused themselves to use the wash closet. They insisted that they would be right back and emphatically asked me if I would be fine while they were gone. Either they thought I was completely incapable of handling myself or they were anxious to demonstrate hospitality. I'd like to believe it was certainly the latter, as most Iranian youth I met were extraordinarily courteous.

Five minutes passed and the sisters returned. Only now, they were not the girls I remembered. In fact, I barely recognized them. The black hejabs were gone and the long black chadors had vanished. Gita returned wearing a red jacket and jeans. Her beautiful face was the same, but my eyes were immediately drawn to her hejab. I don't think I could even call it that: It was an ornate pink scarf with elaborate designs and blue flowers draped from her head. Her black hair poured out from the front of her scarf, which she had pushed to the back of her head. The scarf was so far back that I wondered how she kept it from falling off her head. She strutted back to the table, showcasing her transition from suppressed subject of the Iranian regime to liberated woman.

I hadn't thought much about the female attire at this point, but then again I had only met youth in the mountains and at the university. At the university, girls seemed to wear a black hejab, which is the head scarf, and a black chador, which is the long robelike attire that women were forced to wear after the Islamic Revolution. It never occurred to me that this might simply be their school uniform.

Even more remarkable than the transformation I witnessed with Gita and Leila in their physical appearance was the change in their personalities that seemed to accompany the new attire. When they sat down on both sides of me wearing their bright pink and blue head scarves, they seemed more comfortable, playful, and frivolous than before. They sensed I was intrigued by the metamorphosis I had just witnessed. Their sense was right.

Gita looked at me. "You know we don't like to wear these. The government makes us and we hate it so much. The black we have to wear for school uniform is so ugly and if I have to wear this I will at least have it be my own." It was remarkable; in just a few spoken words and a change in attire, the sisters showed me a powerfully yet subtle form of social resistance. While many Muslim women choose to wear the hejab, the Iranian women are not given any choice at all. In the absence of this choice, they feel as though wearing hejab or chador is forced endorsement of the regime, rather than adherence to Islam.

Many young Iranians feel similarly about attending prayer services. While many youth in Iran would like to attend Friday prayer out of a commitment to their religion, they choose not to. In Shi'a Islam, the dominant sect of Islam in Iran, a senior ranking cleric in every major city gives two sermons at the central mosque. The first is a religious sermon, while the second usually focuses on political or social issues. Most of the Friday prayer leaders in Iran are conservative clerics, and the sermons therefore tend to have a strict Shi'a interpretation of the Quran. While they vary in their style of speech, each holds one of the three highest ranks in Shi'a Islam: grand ayatollah, ayatollah, or hojatoleslam. The "Down with USA" and "Death to Israel" rhetoric that is often captured in the media usually comes from a Friday prayer.

These political sermons are hardly the representative phenomena they are often made out to be: Less than 3 percent of the population attends Friday prayers. This is a shocking statistic for a country that claims to be an Islamic republic and that just a decade ago required people to attend by law. Many of those who do attend Friday prayer do so because they fear absence will result in the loss of a job or, for students, the loss of favor with the university. It is not uncommon for a bystander to see the Friday prayer venue emptying out just before the political sermon. Most Iranians view Friday prayer as a forum that has been hijacked by the conservatives, and they have no interest in endorsing the regime with their attendance. Many people in Iran view the Friday prayer as having lost its religious essence. Instead, they see it as a mere forum for the regime to galvanize its few supporters and reaffirm its ideology.

Friday prayer in Iran is hardly the scene that it was in the initial years after the Islamic Revolution, when waves of Iranians washed into mosques throughout the country to hear the clerical icons who "liberated" Iran from the grip of the world's superpowers. The brand of

nationalism and religion that they advocated resonated in a revolutionary context. But it was not long before the prolonged Iran-Iraq War
and the reality of economic hardships made everyday life virtually unbearable for the Iranian people. The leadership fruitlessly tried to use
religion to keep a hold on their hearts and minds.

Despite a massive decline in attendance at Friday prayer, the government continues to force a visible presence. Every Friday, crowds
of people still walk as a mass through the streets, blocking traffic as
they stroll to the mosque. But the genuine fervor that surrounded
the Friday prayer in 1979 is long gone. Today, the politicization of
Friday prayer in Iran attracts mainly the most devout and the coerced.
The scene is almost a robotic display of indoctrination as crowds will
throw their fists in the air, repeating the words of fiery clerics such as
Ayatollah Jannati: *"Markbar Ameerika! Inshallah! Markbar Ameerika!
Inshallah!"* Not surprisingly, it is often these same people chanting
"Death to America, God willing," and those the government pays,
who participate in protests against the United States.

Given the imposed regulation of wearing hejab, the sisters demonstrated to me that while removing the head scarf was not possible
because of the legal consequences, the discomfort of compulsory dress
codes could be mitigated. They took ownership of the repression: If
the government forced them to wear hejab, they wore the hejab in a
style and manner that was farthest from what Iran's conservatives envisioned. They westernized the scarf and wore it on their own terms.

The hejab is a fascinating topic of conversation, especially among
youth. In every country in the Middle East, I encountered women
with various interpretations of the hejab. In Islam, the Quran states the
following with reference to concealing the body:

> And tell the believing women to subdue their eyes, and
> maintain their chastity. They shall not reveal any parts of
> their bodies, except that which is necessary. They shall cover

their chests, and shall not relax this code in the presence of other than their husbands, their fathers, the fathers of their husbands, their sons, the sons of their husbands, their brothers, the sons of their brothers, the sons of their sisters, other women, the male servants or employees whose sexual drive has been nullified, or the children who have not reached puberty. They shall not strike their feet when they walk in order to shake and reveal certain details of their bodies. All of you shall repent to GOD, O you believers, that you may succeed. (Sura al-Nur, 24:31)

It does not state in the Quran that a woman must cover her head, let alone her hair, face, and neck. The Quran explicitly states that women must conceal their genitals and their breasts. For Muslim women that I met, the hejab was a symbol of modesty; it depended on the individual if that modesty was represented from within—something women described to me as a "metaphorical hejab"—or by covering one's head or body.

The women in Iran, beginning with the sisters, made it very clear that the hejab had no meaning if they were forced to wear it. They emphasized how the Quran is meant to be interpreted in an evolutionary manner and therefore, it should be up to the women to decide what is meant by modesty.

In the absence of the freedom to choose, especially in Iran, the hejab has actually come to exemplify for many the exact opposite of modesty. In Iran, it is as if there is an unofficial competition among women to see who can have the best designer head scarf, who can have the brightest colors, and who can come up with the most fashionable way to wear the cloth. It always gave me a good laugh when I would walk behind someone and see the initials "CK," for Calvin Klein, or "DG," for Dolce & Gabbana. I spent more time with Gita than I did Leila and one thing that I noticed was that each time we met, she seemed to outdo herself with an even more intricate and elaborately decorated hejab.

While we waited to order our food, I shared with the girls a list of government leaders I hoped to interview while in Iran. I had typed a full two pages of leaders without much consideration for how such a list might be interpreted. Gita grabbed the list and muttered something in Farsi to her sister. I could see their faces turn from joy to disgust.

Both girls lifted up their menus so as to hide from potential eavesdroppers what they were about to tell me.

"Why do you want to meet with these people?" Gita asked me, simultaneously stern and dumbfounded.

"I want to learn about the politics of the Islamic Republic."

"If that is what you want, don't talk to these donkeys, they will only tell you lies, all lies! If you want to learn about Iran, they will only tell you bad things." Then she looked at me and said with a smile and a small laugh, "Luckily you have met me and I will not let you leave without knowing Iran. But you have to promise that when you go back you will tell people the truth about how we are; that we are just like you. We are not crazy people, we are not terrorists; we are not represented by the mullahs."

This hospitality from the Iranian youth was not only moving, but also indicated an itching curiosity and need to connect with the outside world. A number of students throughout Iran told me stories of how they have tried desperately to do so. Some write e-mails to the Associated Press, while others use MySpace, Orkut, and other online social networking sites that allow users to search for friends by country.

Young people have no means for political or social expression, and they are shielded from a world that is becoming more and more technologically advanced. They want to be modern, but the iron fist of an archaic regime prevents them from being so. As a result, they reach out to anything or anyone that can serve as a bridge to the outside world.

For the sisters and the numerous other youth I met while I was in Iran, I served as this bridge. From their perspective, they had one challenge while I was there: They wanted to demonstrate similarities between youth in Iran and youth in America and distinguish themselves from their government. They are proud of their country but embarrassed and even repulsed by their government. Gita and her hejab was an introduction to this paradox of pride and repulsion.

I learned more about this paradox on my trip to Shiraz and Esfahan. Unfortunately, I was accompanied in this trip by Shapour, who by that time I had given a variety of derogatory nicknames including "Ayatollah Assahola." I kept this to myself during the ride.

Esfahan is known to be one of Iran's greatest aesthetic treasures, with the Imam Square as its centerpiece. A truly spectacular site, the Imam Square consists of a plaza spanning two football fields, with a mosque on each side of the square. The two mosques are connected by a colonnade of stores and bazaars, selling everything from Persian chess sets to carpets and other artifacts. The centerpiece of the Imam Square is a tremendous fountain whose two streams cross about ten feet in the air.

The Imam Square was a center for activity. I saw children playing soccer, a man and a woman snuggling together on a bench, businessmen, families of tourists, religious clerics, and shopkeepers. The air in the Imam Square—trapped by the walls of four mosques—had a purity from the car pollution that I rarely experienced in other Iranian cities. I heard the sounds of people speaking, the air blowing, and water from the fountains spraying. As I walked around the bazaar that surrounds the Imam Square, I was in fact approached to buy one type of product. Iran has a serious drug problem, but I wasn't offered drugs at Imam Square. I wasn't offered alcohol either. Instead, I was approached repeatedly by various individuals asking me if I wanted to buy playing cards. Because of their association with gambling, the Iranian regime has banned playing cards from being either used or bought inside of

Iran. Not surprisingly, playing cards have become a hot commodity on the black market.

As I walked toward the central fountain in the Imam Square, I noticed that the cement benches that form a perimeter around the fountain were each carefully designed with large stenciled slogans of "Down with Israel" and "Down with USA." This was not graffiti; it was political messaging from the government of Iran.

These slogans do not represent the people of Iran, and in fact it is more common to see advertisements and products of Western culture than it is messages denouncing America and Israel. In Tehran, in front of the old American Embassy—the "Den of Spies"—one can find merchants selling pirated American DVDs on blankets. The selection was actually quite impressive: I found action movies like *The Rock,* patriotic allegories like *Independence Day,* and more than a few skin flicks.

Even for the many contradictions I'd already witnessed, this was pretty shocking, especially given the fact that the former embassy serves as the training ground for the Islamic Revolutionary Guards Corps. It is also symbolic of the tragedy of the relationship between the United States and Iran. When the shah fled Iran during the 1979 Islamic Revolution, he actively sought treatment for cancer in exile. After much debate and political disagreement, President Jimmy Carter agreed to admit him for medical treatment. Outraged that the shah would not be returned to Iran for trial and suspicious that this was part of an American plan to repeat the 1953 coup and restore him to power, protesters gathered almost immediately outside of the embassy.

On November 4, 1979, five hundred students, led by Abbas Abdi and spiritually guided by Ayatollah Khuiniha, climbed the embassy gates and seized sixty-one hostages, later freeing six. Some scholars and journalists suggest that Iran's current president, Mahmoud Ahmadinejad, was one of the students involved in the embassy takeover; however, the validity of this allegation remains uncertain. Immediately after the seizure, President Carter responded by banning the importation of Iranian oil and freezing all assets owned by the Iranian government and the Iranian Central Bank. A few months later, the United States banned exports to Iran and travel of American citizens to Iran, made it illegal to conduct transactions there, and severed all diplomatic ties between the two nations.

The hostage crisis lasted 444 days, and during this period Iran occupied the American airwaves and "took up much of the nightly network news." Immediately after the seizure of the embassy, "ABC scheduled a daily late-evening special, *America Held Hostage*, and PBS's *MacNeil/Lehrer Report* ran an unprecedented number of shows on the crisis."* In retaliatory mood fueled by the relentless demonstrations and anti-Americanism on display there, American politics and media contrived a picture of Iran as a country of religious fanatics, terrorists, and lawless Islamists. As was explained to me by Mohsen Sazegara, founder of the Islamic Revolutionary Guards Corps, "If you went to the embassy on every night for the first year of the hostage taking, on every street around the United States Embassy, every night you could see at least forty to fifty thousand people located over there until the morning." He recalls that "it was like a ceremony; there were even several vendor stations to sell popcorn, tea, and coffee."

Today, the front walls of the seized American Embassy are divided into panels, each painted with elaborate anti-American images. One panel is painted light blue with large red letters stating, "America Shall Face a Severe Defeat." On another panel, there are paintings of the American hostages, missiles with "USA" written on them, and American fighter jets. There are slogans all around the building saying, "Down with USA" and one panel that reads, "The United States of America, the great occupier regime, is the most hated state before our nation." The most imposing panel on the front gate depicts the

---

*Edward W. Said, *Covering Islam: How the Media and the Experts Determine How We See the Rest of the World* (New York: Pantheon Books, 1981), 82.

Statue of Liberty with a skull for a head. This same image is repeated in the form of a brass sculpture inside the compound of the old United States Embassy. Intertwined with the branches of trees along Taleqani Avenue, where the embassy is located, there are pieces of charred black fabric, the remains of burned American flags from the 444-day hostage crisis.

Had Shapour been in Esfahan with me, he probably would have stopped me, but he had grown tired and gone back to the hotel. I removed my camera from my bag and lifted it up to take a picture of the government-sanctioned graffiti. As I was peering through the lens, a body jumped in front of my camera. When I looked up, I did not see police or Revolutionary Guards Corps, as I had suspected. Instead, I saw a young man of about my own age. I thought he was making a childish joke at my expense, and I was annoyed.

He had long black hair, which he tucked behind his ears; the rest hung down to his shoulders. He wore a blue-and-white beanie that concealed the top of his head and he wore a pair of glasses with thick black frames. He was well-dressed, wearing finely pressed khaki pants with a white collared shirt and a blue sweater.

He spoke loudly and firmly to me, as if he was scolding my actions. "Why are you taking a picture of that?"

"Am I not allowed to?" I asked.

"You are allowed to, but please don't!" I lowered my camera and looked at him with great confusion. I still didn't understand why he cared.

"Where are you from?" he demanded to know.

"I'm from America," I told him.

He waited for a moment and walked closer to me. "You must not take pictures of these things. This does not represent the Iranian people! We don't want you to show these pictures to people in America so they will think this is us. We love the USA. If you look around and you talk to people, you will not see that we hate America. You will see the opposite. We listen to American music; we get our news from Radio Israel and Voice of America. The government puts these stupid signs here, this is not us. Ask anybody, they will tell you this."

His name was Omid and I asked him if he would be offended if I took a picture to remember this conversation. In Iran, I couldn't walk around with a computer and had to be careful even about taking notes because I was not authorized to be a journalist. The best way for me to remember things was by capturing particular scenes and memories on camera.

"You can take the picture, but please explain to people that this is the government and not the people," he reminded me.

I reassured him and extended my hand to formalize my promise, "I will."

Omid invited me to take a walk through the Esfahan bazaar with him. The bazaar reminded me of an intricate labyrinth. The smells in the bazaar changed with each corner I turned. One moment the aroma of Persian tea overwhelmed me, yet just a few paces in another direction the foul stench of hanging meat usurped that delicious spicy mint smell. As I strolled through this labyrinth of shops, I saw just about every type of Persian jewelry imaginable, stores that sold religious decorations ranging from framed verses of the Quran to pictures of the revered Shi'a Imam Hussein, and what became a repetition of the same types of Persian knickknacks: boxes, chess sets, pen holders, and other wooden objects, each with intricate gold, black, and white checkered designs. Some parts of the bazaar offered more universal goods, such as everyday kitchen supplies, shoes and clothing, and machinery such as Walkmans, tape recorders, and radios.

Omid walked me into a carpet shop that was inhabited by a group of his friends. They were all male and they sat in various positions throughout the carpet store. Some lounged on their sides, while others sat on stacks of carpets. The store was small, and while some carpets were displayed on the wall, most were piled on top of one another. I could smell the dust that had collected in this store; it was clear that business was not good. Three of us sat on small black stools and drank Persian tea, placed elegantly on a silver platter. He told them the story of how we had met and introduced me as the American who was taking pictures of the "Down with USA" slogans. The group of young guys gave me an unsparing critique of the regime: They told me they wanted the mullahs out of power and the freedom to choose their own leaders. They wanted access to the outside world and they wanted to be able to have the same social and political opportunities as Americans. It also became clear to me that this group of boys had no interest in international events. Whenever I would mention Israel, Iraq, or Afghanistan, the conversation always seemed to return to a discussion of their domestic troubles.

Omid and his friends were convincing and I heard similar opinions elsewhere in Iran. A few weeks later, I was in the southern city of Shiraz, at the Iranian version of McDonald's. Right alongside the fast-food menu, I saw pictures of Iran's president, Iran's supreme leader, and the Ayatollah Khomeini. As I was taking a picture of those photos, my friend Zahra playfully threw one of her French fries at me and inquired, "Why are you always taking pictures of these things?"

My new friends showed me that there were far more interesting images to capture and that Iran was more complex than the images the media uses to color our understanding of their country. Although it was only for a brief period of time, I was invited inside to witness their passive revolution.

CHAPTER 3

DEMOCRACY AFTER DARK

IRAN, 2004/2005

R*rrrrrrrrrrrrinnnnnggggg*.

The startling ring of the decades-old phone in my hotel room roused me from a deep sleep. I was just back in Tehran from my trip to Esfahan, Shiraz, Natanz, and Qom and thirteen hours of driving through a snowstorm with Shapour. Given how tired I was, it was surprising that I heard the phone ring at all, much less answered it.

"Jared?" responded a man with a Persian accent. I didn't recognize the voice, but it definitely didn't belong to either of my parents.

"Yes?" I muttered, slightly annoyed to have been awakened.

"Cirrus here. We met last week," the man's voice responded.

I vaguely remembered the name, but I had given the name and number of my hotel to just about every young person that I met in the hope that some would contact me. When Shapour was with me during the day, I would write my phone number down and give it to people while he was in the bathroom or while he disappeared for a few moments to run an errand. I couldn't quite remember where I had met this guy, but I guessed he was one of the kids that I met playing soccer in the Park Laleh.

"Hi, Cirrus," I exclaimed, trying to conceal the fact that I didn't know who he was.

He spoke with authority. "We would like you to come out with us tonight. We will pick you up in thirty minutes. Can you be ready outside?" he asked.

Without hesitation, I told Cirrus that I would be delighted to go out with them. As I got ready, I was exhilarated to have heard from Cirrus and in the back of my mind, I wondered if a young Iranian alone in New York would have been treated with the same hospitality that I was experiencing. I found the youth in the Middle East to be some of the most approachable people in the entire world and I admired them for it.

I have always found it revelatory that young people in the Middle East, which is the region where supposedly America is most hated, are friendlier, more open and welcoming, and more interested in engaging in conversation than their counterparts in Europe. This is particularly the case with Iran, where as an American, I felt more comfortable among the population than I did in my two years in England. Unfortunately, the strains and confrontations of the past twenty-six years have shaped the way many in the West, including the media, view the Iranian people. I knew when I returned from Iran people would ask me, "What is it like to be Jewish there?" or "What is it like to be American there?" I couldn't wait to let them know how warmly I was embraced by most Iranians I met.

I wondered what Cirrus could have possibly meant by "going out." This was an Islamic republic, after all. Alcohol was banned, nightclubs didn't exist, there were no bars, and the morals police had no other pastime than keeping young people from having fun. What could we possibly do?

It was New Year's Eve, and I was happy that I wouldn't be spending the night channel surfing between CNN and BBC and watching the ball drop in New York, where I'd otherwise be, drinking champagne at a bar or club with my friends and ringing in 2005 in style. I'd already spent one New Year's alone in a strange country: At the end of 2002,

I spent New Year's Eve in Burundi—which was in the midst of a civil war that had already claimed nine hundred thousand lives—and the following day in Rwanda, which was mired in its own bloody conflict with neighboring Congo. Needless to say, that wasn't quite my best New Year's memory, and I'd made a promise to myself never to relive that experience. And now here I was in the Islamic Republic of Iran, not a country known for its raucous celebrations.

My night out with these new Iranian acquaintances, however, was not to be about celebrating the New Year. The Iranian year is based on the old Zoroastrian calendar, which predates both the advent of Islam and the transformation of Iran to an Islamic state. In conjunction with this calendar, Iranians celebrate their new year in March so as to coincide with the spring equinox. Because the ancient symbol of Zoroastrianism was the burning flame, hoards of Iranians flood the streets annually and celebrate the new year by jumping over fires. These celebrations are an annual worry for the regime, as the number of Iranian people taking to the streets exceeds its capacity to maintain control.

Unclear about what the night had in store for me, I really had but one worry, that the hotel receptionist would tell my intelligence stalkers that I was going out in the evening. In Iran, this was a legitimate concern to have. The intelligence services are among the most sophisticated and far-reaching in the world. Iranian intelligence has agents in universities, hotels, and every other public venue one could imagine. For all I knew, the receptionist had been placed there just for the duration of my stay.

Tonight, I would be testing my tentative friendship with the evening receptionist, whom I'd gotten to know over the previous week. Small talk—"How do you find Iran?" and "I find it quite nice"—had evolved into substantive discussions about how badly he wanted to study abroad. It didn't matter to him where he studied, as long as it was not in Iran. He explained that he was applying to universities in Europe and asked if I would be willing to assist him in writing his essays and his application. This was a request that I gladly accepted.

He was a slender guy, with a peach-fuzz mustache and slicked-back hair drenched in gel. He was always in uniform: a white shirt, dress pants, and a black tie. Dangling from his shirt pocket was a name tag that read "Nezam." He smiled a lot and had a studious look about him. He was a very serious person, but every so often our conversations would turn into more playful discussions that usually involved him asking me what I thought of Iranian girls, and me responding with a diplomatic answer. I wanted to trust him, but I couldn't. I had to be suspicious of everybody. However, with time this trust would develop and Nezam would become one of the most important people I met in Iran.

While I never asked him to do so, Nezam and I had an implicit understanding that he would not reveal my secret evening escapades. We never discussed exactly what I was doing, but I think he knew. At later dates, friends of mine would come to the hotel for lunch or wait for me in the lobby and I only imagine he spoke to them while they waited for me to come down from my third-floor room. I could tell from his eyes, the subtle nods he gave me as I walked out the door, or the quiet laughter from his mouth when I would come home at four A.M. half in the bag that he knew I was having fun. He was glad I was skirting authority and seeing *his* Iran. We were brothers in defiance; Nezam was my ally. He could easily have gotten me arrested, tipped off intelligence services, or even threatened me for a bribe. But he never asked for anything except for me to listen to his story and work with him to achieve his dream of studying abroad. It was not unusual for me to speak to some of his friends on the phone when I passed through the lobby or to talk to others who had stopped by to seek my advice. I began to feel like a college counselor and discovered the reasons behind the massive "brain drain" phenomenon in the Islamic Republic.

Many young Iranians want to leave their homes and seek opportunities outside of the country. The lack of opportunity for upward mobility, the autocratic nature of the regime, and the dire economy have all contributed to the brain drain. If you ask Iranians what they want to do after their education, their first response is rarely "become a doctor," "become a lawyer," or "become a teacher." Instead, they are far more likely to say, "I want to get out of Iran." This collective wanderlust is not always a reflection of the feelings young Iranians have about Iran as such; rather, it is a statement that the country these young people love so much has nothing to offer them. Some youth will literally sit in front of Voice of America on their satellite televisions all day so as to learn or perfect their English. They spend countless hours on the Internet learning various skills—ranging from fashion to real estate—in the hope that one will yield a job opportunity.

I truly valued my relationship with Nezam and owe the comfort I experienced in the evenings to his unspoken trust. I would like to think that I reciprocated, but the value of what I did for him cannot be compared to the risks he took by protecting me and the loyalty he demonstrated by keeping my secret. When I was in Tehran, we sat down almost daily to talk about his hopes of getting an education outside of Iran. He had been studying engineering at the Polytechnic University in Tehran, yet he offered little indication that he would be rewarded for his hard work. I asked him once, "Why don't you want to stay here after you graduate from university?"

He looked at me and said, "I don't want to work for the mullahs." Unwilling to commit their futures to the clerical establishment, students find only grim opportunities for a real future in Iran. Some will join underground opposition, while others will go abroad; the vast majority, however, will end up in jobs that they are both overqualified for and uninterested in taking.

The Iranian economy is not conducive to job creation. It is structured as a state-run society and unemployment is rampant, with many experts estimating that close to 40 percent of the population is unemployed. While the government tries to argue that unemployment is a mere 13 percent, the young people who know the reality of the dearth of opportunities see through these attempts to mask the country's economic troubles with faulty statistics.

It is difficult to imagine how the country with the world's second-largest oil reserves, 10 percent of the world's oil, and the second biggest natural gas reserve can experience such economic troubles. The regime in Iran has a virtual monopoly on all forms of business and squanders most of the country's resources, enriching the kleptocrats in the ruling elite. Nezam, along with others I met, believed that to be successful in Iran meant that one had to basically sell out to the clerical establishment. Nezam also emphasized that "in Iran, this is not a real education. We learn the way the mullahs want us to learn. Why do we have to learn their way?" The history books are distorted and the curriculum is subjectively infiltrated with ideological prescriptions. Nezam, in common with many others, cares nothing about the ideology of the Islamic Revolution; he, and they, simply want to learn and don't feel as though they can do it in Iran. Nezam once asked me, "What happens one day if this regime is not here anymore? We will have learned the wrong things and we will not be prepared for opportunities in Iran after the mullahs have left."

In what would become my usual signal, I gave Nezam a smile and nod and walked outside to wait for Cirrus. In the passenger seat of Cirrus's Volkswagen was his friend Pedram. Pedram was in his early twenties, had a goatee, and wore glasses. His hair was straight and long, dangling over his ears. He was dressed very smartly, wearing a button-down blue shirt and a gray blazer. Sitting next to me in the backseat were two large white jugs, several bags of chips, two decks of playing cards, a couple of packs of cigarettes, and several jars of sour cream dip.

"Cirrus, what is all of this for?" I asked.

"No more sitting in your hotel at night," he said, laughing. He then repeated his quip in Farsi, and Pedram laughed.

"Do you drink?" Cirrus asked.

It suddenly became clear to me that the two giant white jugs sitting next to me were filled with illegal alcohol. I'm not generally a big drinker, but who could resist the opportunity to booze it up when the mullahs weren't looking?

The whole experience was beginning to remind me of my teenage years. Before we could buy alcohol legally, my friends and I would drink just about anything for the indulgence of a little bit of youthful insubordination. The foul taste of the alcohol in the white jugs would prove reminiscent of the concoctions we used to contrive from whatever we could smuggle from our parents' liquor cabinets. The only difference here—and it wasn't a small one—was the stakes. In high school, getting caught drinking will get most kids grounded. In Iran, getting caught with alcohol will almost certainly result in a lashing for the offender.

When I inquired about where he and his friends bought their alcohol, Cirrus told me that they used to call an illegal alcohol distributor, who would come over on a moped and deliver the goods. Cirrus and Pedram, however, had the fortunate connection of a friend in Tehran who prepared alcohol in his bathtub and sink, at least when his parents, with whom he lived, were away on vacation. Even though I drank the stuff, I would be lying if I didn't say I found it pretty rough and potent. Iranian moonshine.

All things considered, the setting seemed somehow familiar, and I found myself increasingly comfortable. As he drove, Cirrus talked about his romantic dilemma: He had been dating one girl for two years, but she was very conservative and pressuring him to get married, which Cirrus was not at all prepared to do, telling me he "still wanted to have my fun." He sounded like a typical American college student having a candid chat with a friend. They loved hearing stories about what American nightlife was like and I did my best to accommodate them with descriptions. While they thought the big clubs, fancy lounges, and lively bars that I spoke of sounded exciting, I was drawn to and excited about the prospect of underground secret parties in Iran. I guess we all want to experience what is unfamiliar to us.

Pedram also had a romantic dilemma. Unlike Cirrus, who had met his girlfriend in school, Pedram's love had developed over an Internet social network called Orkut. He described an Internet courtship that involved flirtatious messages, postings on each other's profiles, and eventually an arrangement to meet. "Jared, it was love at first sight," he told me. If the Internet has become a newly acceptable way for people to meet in America—JDate, Friendster, MySpace, and other sites—it did not surprise me that in a restricted and censored society, youth would look to digital connections as a replacement for clubs and bars.

What did surprise me was the digital freedom that Iranian youth experienced. The Internet is growing in Iran, and while owning a computer remains the luxury of the upper classes, the growing number of Internet cafés has made the Internet widely accessible to a broad swath of Iranians. The Internet is a place where Iranian youth can operate freely, express themselves, and obtain information on their own terms. As they communicate with one another, users of the Internet in Iran can be anyone and say anything they want as they operate free from the grips of the police-state apparatus. The Internet cafés allow young Iranians to interact over the World Wide Web without having to worry about the government tracing their IP address back to their homes. While many Iranians are still without Internet access, the number of those connected is rapidly increasing each day. Under the pretenses of an ambiguous or fake identity, young Iranians really do exercise a relative amount of autonomy in their thinking over the Internet. It is true that the government tries to monitor their online discussions and interactions, but this is a virtually impossible enterprise. The regime focuses most of its efforts on targeting the blogosphere and specific opposition Web sites for blocking. Resilient as they are, Iranian youth continue to find indirect ways to reach these sites that the regime blocks. The Internet is far too large and there are far too many sites for the government to effectively monitor what its youth say and do in this digital realm. The Iranian intelligence services have higher priorities, and simply put, they don't have the capacity to effectively deal with the explosion of the Internet. At times, the regime has attempted to slow the Internet, so as to make it so frustrating to use that Iranians will simply not bother. But this underestimates the commitment Iranian people have to their digital freedom.

The Internet is their democratic society. Even though the Internet is monitored, the youth have become extremely sophisticated in getting around the surveillance. They have become digital revolutionaries, creating, participating in, and popularizing chat rooms, blogs, and forums for discussion about everything from sports to politics. It has been stated that there are more than seventy-five thousand bloggers in Iran, with the majority under the age of thirty. The more high-profile blogs get shut down and replaced with an announcement stating, "According to the rules of the Islamic Republic of Iran, access to this site is forbidden," but the authorities cannot keep up with the volume.

Because the Internet is one of the newest sources of information and forums for expression, the government has tried to censor it. Despite the efforts of the Iranian regime, I actually found the authorities in Dubai—a city known for its relative social progressiveness, high technology, wealth, and entertainment—censored the Internet more successfully than those in neighboring Iran. One afternoon, while testing the limits of access in Iran, I was shocked to see that I could access the United States Department of Defense Web site, the CIA home page, and even the United States Department of State annual human rights report, where I read the following:

> The Government [of Iran's] human rights record remained poor, and deteriorated substantially during the year, despite continuing efforts within society to make the Government accountable for its human rights policies. The Government denied citizens the right to change their government. Systematic abuses included summary executions; disappearances; widespread use of torture and other degrading treatment, reportedly including rape; severe punishments such as stoning and flogging; harsh prison conditions; arbitrary arrest and detention; and prolonged and incommunicado detention.

As I surfed, I also found that a number of online networking sites were easily accessible, including the site where Pedram had met his girlfriend. I was also able to use online phone services, most notably Skype, which I actually found more useful than my wiretapped cell phone that my "guides" had given me. Many Iranians today are using Skype to practice English and make friends outside of the country. Using this program, users can search for other users from any country they want and actually call them.

In addition to telephone programs, most online messenger services were available, of which the two most popular were MSN Messenger and Yahoo Messenger. While these messenger services enabled youth to have hundreds of online contacts, I learned that these contacts rarely extend beyond the users' socioeconomic sphere.

Young Iranians take full advantage of these opportunities for expression and unfiltered information, and young people in Iran are spending a vast proportion of their free time on the Internet. I was shocked by the number of Internet cafés, and where there was no café, I was even more shocked by just how far some traveled to use one. Internet cafés have actually come to serve as new meeting places for young Iranians.

As we drove down the poorly lit streets of Tehran, Cirrus explained to me what he and his friends do in the evenings.

"It depends on the person," he explained. "But there is something for everyone." He told me that there are large parties for graduations, birthdays, and other special occasions, but there are also massive house parties. I heard hilarious stories about young people attending Halloween parties dressed as "clerics in the regime."

Pedram then chimed in, explaining that the behavior at the parties depends on the hosts, and that while some parties are tame, others feature belligerent drinking, rampant drug use, and promiscuity.

Cirrus laughed, removing one hand from the steering wheel to punch his friend in the arm, "I just told him that! Were you not listening?" Pedram's English wasn't that good and Cirrus liked to make fun of him for "missing things." Cirrus then told me that at these parties, it is not uncommon to see dancing, games of spin the bottle (called by a different name in Iran), and clothing that makes one instantly forget that one is in an Islamic republic. With these two as guides, I didn't feel bad about missing the New Years' parties back in the States.

But the nature of parties of Iranian youth also depends on the socioeconomic class of those participating. South Tehran is notoriously poorer than the northern part of the city and the youth from these regions tend to be stricter in how they dress, practice religion, and many of them also choose not to drink. But the youth in these largely poorer areas still know how to party. The parties are tamer, but nonetheless defiant of the regime, and take place behind the backs of the morals police. It is important to remember that the very existence of many of these parties violates the laws of the regime.

Youth in the slums of Iran are far more likely than their wealthier peers to use parties as opportunities to talk about politics and the status of their lives, and for many disadvantaged Iranian youth, parties are the only opportunity they have to express themselves freely and vent to me about their dire situations.

The underground parties in Iran are only one aspect of social recreation enjoyed by young people living under the harsh conditions. When they are not discussing politics, removing their traditional Muslim attire, or consuming alcohol at parties behind closed doors, Iranian youth gather in cinemas, restaurants, and hotel lobbies. They take day trips to the mountains, attend sports clubs, and meet for gatherings in public parks. Billiard halls are popular evening destinations and usually involve a stop at a local ice cream shop. Coffee shops and flavored-tobacco cafés have become the primary public meeting grounds for boys and girls looking to pass their phone numbers to one another from across the room.

The morals police do occasionally locate the underground parties and break them up. I heard stories about students getting lashes for either hosting or attending these parties. For young people in Iran, the parties are more than a source of entertainment. They are a forum for expression and a form of resistance. Every drop of alcohol they drink, every hejab that comes off, every beat of Western music they dance to, and every minute of entertainment they enjoy is representative of their rejection of the government in Iran. And it is a collective, if unspoken, effort.

While many Iranians have been practicing social resistance for years, their acts of defiance have taken on far greater importance than they did in the 1980s and 1990s. When the regime first came into power during the 1979 Islamic Revolution, it had overwhelming support from the Iranian people. The Islamic Revolution was first and foremost a nationalist revolution. Throughout the 1980s, the country fell into an eight-year war against Saddam Hussein's Iraq, keeping the country unified and supportive of the regime under the banner of nationalism. As the war dragged on—mostly at the behest of Iran's Ayatollah Khomeini—the realities of life under the Islamic Republic came to the surface. With the death of Ayatollah Khomeini in 1989, the regime lost its charismatic leader and architect of the Islamic Republic, and his original successor, Grand Ayatollah Ali Montazeri, was a dissenter against the continuation of the war. By this time, Iran's economy was in shambles, its infrastructure destroyed, and the regime's efforts to export its Islamic Revolution had been rebuffed at every attempt. What was left was a population that was traumatized by a war that had been raging for nearly decade, a nation suffering under a dire economy, and a population growing tired of waiting for the "better life" promised by the regime since 1979.

Because of the mass casualties of war and high birth rates, the next generation of Iranian youth emerged as the new majority. With the Iranian voting age set at fifteen, the mid-1990s saw an entirely new majority of young voters who began to express their frustrations with the regime. Unlike their parents, this generation had not lived through the shah's government. They did not remember the notorious secret police known as the SAVAK; they didn't remember all of the corruption. What they did know was that the regime they had been born under was failing to meet their needs and seemed unable to provide them with the life they deserved.

And in 1997 they voted for change and the reformist president Mohammad Khatami won an unexpected yet overwhelming victory. Since the creation of the Islamic Republic in 1979, the country had not seen any leader like Khatami actually win such a high elected office. Throughout the 1980s Iran's presidents had all been hard-line conservatives. In 1989, Iran saw the ascension of pragmatist president Hojjatoleslam Ali Akbar Hashemi Rafsanjani, but his promises for economic change and progress proved ineffective and instead revealed more about his corrupt tendencies than any patriotic commitment. Instead of presiding over a recovering economy, Rafsanjani, who was already extremely wealthy when he took office, moved onto the Forbes 400, the list of the wealthiest people in the world.

President Khatami, however, was of a different breed. He had come to the presidency promising reform, relaxation of restrictions on civil liberties, and economic change. He did not have his predecessor's history of corruption. He owed his surprise victory over the conservative candidates to the widespread participation of the Iranian youth in the 1997 presidential election. Young Iranians had taken his victory as a green light to embrace what the new president pledged to be new freedoms. In the first years of his presidency, students protested over everything from clothes to censorship. Initially, they gained small victories as Iran became more relaxed than it had been since the days of the shah. For the first few years of Khatami's presidency, it seemed that the voices of youth were louder than ever. This hope was short-lived.

In July 1999, more than twenty-five thousand students staged a riot at the University of Tehran after conservative hard-liners shut down a popular reformist newspaper. The response was harsh. Members of Tehran's police force stormed into the student dormitories and fired on crowds of Iranian students who were chanting, "Khamanei must quit," and "Ansar-e Hezbollah commits crimes and the leaders back them." In fact, the worst phase of the crackdown did not come from the police; it came from Ansar-e Hezbollah, the regime's quasi-official paramilitary organization tasked with punishing those who violate or disrespect the fundamental principles of Islam.

Within hours, the riots had spread to eight major cities outside of Tehran. In what is cited by Iranians as their version of the Tiananmen

Square massacre in China, Ansar-e Hezbollah entered the university, where they undertook a violent suppression of the riots. Numerous students were injured, hundreds were arrested, and one student was even killed. The most demoralizing aspect of this experience was not the crackdown itself, but the response of the reformists on behalf of whom the youth were protesting. President Khatami refused to denounce the violent suppression and instead stood by the regime's decision. Demonstrating even less support for the people who elected him, President Khatami did not attend that year's annual opening of the University of Tehran. It was at this point that youth came to see the reformists as just another branch of the conservatives, masquerading under a different name. Following the riots, many young Iranians came to believe that the reformists had simply used them to get elected but had little regard for their interests. These suspicions led many of the youth to see all government factions as one and the same. They viewed the supposed opposition as yet another extension of the theocratic establishment.

This disenchantment led some young Iranians to dislike the reformist movement more than the conservatives, arguing that at least the conservatives did not provide them with false hope. When I asked one Iranian student in Shiraz what she thought of the reformists, she replied with disgust that "all they have done is get the marriage age raised from nine to thirteen and allow women to wear nail polish. The women were already wearing nail polish, and nobody wants to get married that young anyway!"

With the reformists virtually eradicated from government and their lack of loyalty exposed, many youth do not believe that there are any officials in the government who can be influenced, nor do they feel that there are any politicians who will protect them if they speak out on their behalf. By the time hard-line conservative Mahmoud Ahmadinejad ascended to the presidency in June 2005, the conservatives could claim a monopoly over all major branches of the government.

This left little room for resistance and created a tremendous reach for the government to implement unopposed restrictions.

While these realities paint a grim future for the prospect of resistance in Iran, it would be inaccurate to suggest that Iranian youth have lost the desire to resist. While students and other young people are less inclined to engage in political protests, their willingness to participate in a passive resistance is paramount. This passive resistance is an underground and widespread social resistance that extends to every echelon of Iranian society. As the passive resistance in Iran presents an increasingly serious challenge to the regime, the leadership has become more and more adept at cracking down on offenders. The regime is under no illusion that it commands widespread support from the people and they recognize that this is unlikely to change in the future. Even so, they are committed to containing the social behavior of the youth. Their strategy is simple: The government of Iran keeps a certain arsenal of social concessions it has made that it will renege on if the population becomes too politically active. The government, for example, has generally looked the other way with regard to the stylish adaptations of the hejab, yet it has not been uncommon for them to tighten restrictions on attire after public protests or riots.

Cirrus, Pedram, and I arrived at their friend's house for the party. The house was located on a steep side street in one of the Tehran suburbs. It was a modest middle-class home, decorated with Persian carpets and a few decorations on the walls. The most prominent decoration in the house was the big-screen television, clearly the centerpiece of the house. Many Iranians do not get their news from the state-run television or radio but from CNN, BBC, Voice of America, Radio Israel, and a variety of other channels and radio stations. One of my Iranian friends joked with me that there is no reason to get a color television if you are going to watch Iranian state TV. When I asked why, he said, because "all you need to see is if the turban is black or white." The state-run television is mostly propaganda spewed by clerics, who wear either a black or white turban depending on whether or not they are descendents of the Prophet.

The satellite dish may be the biggest antipropaganda tool. The growing prevalence of satellite television is a phenomenon in Iran. Every time I stood on the roof of a building and looked down, there were clusters of dishes. Even in the slums of south Tehran, I saw satellite dishes that were larger than the metal or concrete shacks that people lived in. When I asked young people in the slums how people afforded satellite dishes, they would explain that communities pooled together resources to buy a few dishes for each cluster of houses. Even in the slums of Iran, young people can have access to the hit FOX drama *The OC* via Italian satellite! The program is undoubtedly risqué: Teens are shown using drugs, having sex, and abusing alcohol. An Iranian friend of mine told me over coffee that he was glad that they were able to get *The OC* by satellite because he thought it really showed the culture of youth in America. I met so many young people who told me that they watch Voice of America every day to learn English and hear what is going on in the news. They get movie channels, CNN, and BBC. Television watching is often a family affair, as dinner has moved from the dining-room table to tables in front of the big screen. The prevalence of satellite dishes in Iran led me to believe that this was the single most common technology that youth use for information; just about every young person in Iran has access to satellite TV.

Satellite dishes enter Iran illegally from Iraqi Kurdistan in the west and from the United Arab Emirates across the Persian Gulf and the Gulf of Oman. I actually saw smuggling, although not of satellites, when I was in eastern Iraq. Not far from the Iraq-Iran border, I watched mules make journeys up the switchbacks of mountains with cartons of cigarettes, bottles of alcohol, movies, and noncensored news. I didn't know it at the time, but apparently these mules also bring satellite dishes over the mountains of Iraq into Iran. In Iran, there are safe houses for the satellite dishes, which, if they can stay open long enough, serve as the distributor in different parts of the country. Black-market agents get dispatched throughout the cities, slums, and even rural communities to bring the satellite dishes and install them. An Iranian student I met in south Tehran told me, "You would never ask them where they got the dish and even if you did, they would never tell you."

Despite all of the cloak-and-dagger activity surrounding satellite-dish smuggling in Iran, the prevailing opinion among young people is that the regime itself is responsible for much of the black market business. While not officially taking part in it, mullah entrepreneurs privately run the black markets, or so the rumors go. An Iranian friend of mine in Kashan told me, "You should always know something about Iran: Any kind of illegal and forbidden things which are entered to this country surely have a strong protection by a powerful person. Otherwise they cannot move here."

Cirrus introduced me to about fifteen other young Iranians at the house party. Our evening consisted of card games and drinking. After about an hour, we heard a knock at the door. The girls had arrived. None of the girls wore a hejab and all but one of the girls was drinking. The large coats came off as well as the sweaters, revealing rather scantily clothed women. They were pretty good-looking. The hip-hop music followed and as at any party, the more people drank, the more they danced.

By four A.M., the party wasn't slowing down but I was beginning to fall asleep. Cirrus looked over his shoulder from a corner of the room and got everyone's attention. He raised his cup and said, "Jared, isn't it your New Year tonight?"

Startled, I raised my nodding head.

"Yes," I replied.

"We hope you are having a Happy New Year!" he exclaimed rather jubilantly. Others followed suit. I heard from one side of the room, "Welcome to Iran."

Not once did I witness any indication that these young Iranians were afraid of getting caught. These parties are important moments for them, giving them a feeling of freedom that they could not express during the day. For Iranians, this was their democracy after dark.

After-hours activity isn't limited to house parties. Two days after Cirrus's house party, I faked my minders and headed out for another evening adventure.

The streets of Tehran were virtually deserted. Instead of a luminous sky emanating from the lights of a vibrant downtown, the smog from a day of heavy traffic still lingered, and the cold of winter weather sent a chill through the air. In the evenings, there was an ominous calm that always reminded me that Iran is a police state. This atmosphere was not restricted to Tehran; I experienced the same eerie calm in Shiraz, Esfahan, Natanz, Kashan, and Qom. I was not surprised that some of the smaller cities had a quiet nightlife, but Tehran was supposedly the beating heart of Iran.

In what became an almost daily tradition, I found myself once again mistaking appearance for reality in Iran. There was so much happening behind the façade of this repressed society; without the right guide to show me the scene, however, I would never have experienced that reality. Tonight, my guide was a woman named Mariam, a twenty-five-year-old engineering student from Yazd, now studying at the Polytechnic University in Tehran. It was the students from this university that seized the United States Embassy in November 1979 and held fifty-three American diplomats hostage. Now, more than twenty-six years later, students from this same university were among some of the most hospitable people toward me, an American Jew.

Mariam and I had met the week before, during a chance encounter in southern Iran. She had come to Shiraz for the first time in several years to attend her cousin's wedding and we found ourselves in the same café. The coffee shop resembled a carefully built cave, adorned with Persian artifacts, elegant carpets, and booths for customers to enjoy a cup of tea or the taste of a flavored tobacco pipe. I sat alone in a booth and made eye contact with a group of kids in another booth. The girls huddled up and giggled before one of them stood up. Mariam soon approached me.

She had dark skin, long eyelashes, and rosy cheeks. Her attire was very stylish and while her head was adorned with a hejab, her dark hair—with blond highlights—concealed most of the green striped pattern. She wore a long blue coat with a white scarf that had frays at both ends.

"Where are you from?" she asked.

"I am from the United States."

She invited me to join her and her friends. They had an arsenal of questions for me. They wanted to know what life is like in America and they wanted to know what Americans think of Iranians. It was an entertaining exchange, but what really got me going was Mariam's insistence that I explain to her and her friends the whole phenomenon of using toilet paper, rather than water, when we use the bathroom. She seemed truly mortified by what she thought was just plain dirty. I didn't really have a good rebuttal because, frankly, it was a pretty good question. The best I could do in response was to explain that we do our best to shower from time to time.

"What are the three things that you want the world to know about you?" I asked, very curious to see how they viewed foreign perceptions of Iranians.

Mariam adjusted her hejab and looked right at me.

"One: We are not Arabs; we are Iranian. Two: We are not terrorists. Three: We like and we do everything like other youth around the world."

She reiterated this last point several times during the conversation and before I left she said, "You need to make sure you see Iran before you leave. Just wait until I get back to Tehran next week. I will show you."

Mariam wasted little time getting in touch with me after she got back to Tehran. In fact, she called me just as she was arriving back into the city limits, insisting that she wanted to take me out that night. Mariam picked me up on Taleqani Avenue in Tehran right in front of the mural at the old United States Embassy that depicted the Statue of Liberty with a skull. Mariam greeted me with the traditional three kisses on the cheek and insisted that I take the front seat, so I crawled into the front seat of her friend's Pontiac and introduced myself to her friend Nassim in the back.

Nassim was studying to be a teacher. She wore a long wool beige coat, a light hejab tied underneath her chin, and blue jeans underneath her jacket. From underneath the front of her hejab, I could see that her dark hair was lightened by blond highlights just like her friend Mariam's. This seemed to be the trend. Her skin was smooth and radiant from the makeup; her eyes were pronounced with blue mascara and her eyelashes were accentuated by thick black eyeliner. Nassim didn't care how the regime told her to dress; she did things her own way.

Wherever Nassim and Mariam were taking me, it was clear their purpose was to show me something special and different. If there was one thing I had learned in Iran, it was to expect nothing, and be surprised by everything.

I was itching with curiosity. "Nassim, where are we going?" I implored.

Mariam looked at me and answered on her behalf. "Don't worry, my baby, I think you will like this. You need to see all the sides of Iran."

We turned onto Fereshteh Street. Before my eyes caught a glimpse of the scene, I could hear the revving of motors, the beats of hip-hop music, and the repetitious sound of horns as if this evening was a cause for celebration. But as I would later learn, every night for the Iranian youth is a celebration. Fereshteh was more than a street; it was a phenomenon. The long street was packed bumper-to-bumper with cars and there was not an adult in sight. It reminded me of a high-school parking lot; each young person competing to see whose sound system is louder, whose windows are a darker tint, and whose window decals mark the hipper band. The rambunctious youth didn't constrain themselves to the confines of their souped-up vehicles. Confident boys, with their carefully sculpted hair, sat atop the roofs of their cars, doing what many adolescent males do in this situation: They ogled, pointed, and heckled. I saw three guys sitting on the hood of what looked like a blue sports car holding a large boom box that clearly had the volume pumped all the way up, as I could hear the distortion from the speakers' reaching more than their maximum sound capacity. Despite the time of night, these three boys sported dark sunglasses in an expression of coolness.

The girls were equally hip. Each face I saw was meticulously painted with mascara, blush, eyeliner, and lipstick. They all wore the hejab, but it was hardly noticeable. Each hejab was so elaborately decorated and pushed so far to the back of the girl's head that it looked more like a scarf than a head covering. Their fashion was the latest: designer blue jeans, stunning jackets, and shirts that were no different from what I might see in a night out on the town at home. In addition to the fashion and makeup, I kept noticing that some of the girls had white bandages over their noses, which was something I had also seen when I was in Shiraz. When I facetiously asked Mariam and Nassim whether nose jobs were the "in" thing in Iran, they explained that most of the girls who adorn themselves with the white bandages do so for status rather than healing. Mariam and Nassim were entertained by my disbelief that someone would actually pretend to have gotten plastic surgery.

Fereshteh Street was more than a forum for fashionable displays. It reminded me of a late-night traffic jam on Sunset Boulevard in Los Angeles. Within the traffic jam, of which we were now part, I found boys hanging out the windows of their cars, numerous girls not wearing their hejab, and even boys and girls dancing on the street and on the hoods of cars. It resembled a spontaneous block party.

Amid the horn honking and hip-hop music, young boys and girls engaged in paper exchanges across cars. Mariam and Nassim explained that the paper transfers I saw were the latest way for boys and girls to give their phone numbers. The girls insisted that I try my luck at this. Never shying away from a chance to live in the moment, I wrote my number on the back of a receipt, crumpled it up, and threw it at the car next to me. Much to my disappointment, the number hit the window and fell to the ground. It was a shame, too, because the girls in the car next to me were very attractive. Crumpled notes of paper are not the only method for number exchanges. In the same traffic jam, boys and girls used their mobile phones to send anonymous Bluetooth text messages to one another, electronically flirting and courting. I was amazed by how much young Iranians did on their mobile phones. Parties, meetings, gatherings, protests, are all organized anonymously by Bluetooth messaging. The cell phone is both a way out and a way in for Iranian youth as they seek to express themselves, while at the same time circumventing the state intelligence apparatus.

Fereshteh Street is not the only place in Tehran where younger Iranians, rambunctious in spirit, exercise their right to be youth. Jordan Street and Iran Zamin are two other youth hot spots. While each of these places has its own character—Jordan Street, for instance, is known for its drag racing—the general character and symbolic importance of these forums remains the same. This was the closest young Iranians could get to feeling normal, as if they were living in democratic societies where they didn't have to worry about the morals police or the intelligence services. They feel free on these streets and despite the fact that the morals police are just a few blocks away waiting to confiscate cars and arrest young socialites, they forget about the society they are living in so long as the music blasts, the fashion is displayed, and the interactions are flirtatious. The wild evening streets of Tehran offer a democratic lifestyle that Iranian youth can only enjoy after dark.

The parties, gatherings, and social indulgences that the Iranian youth showed me could themselves fill the pages of this book. They showed me a face of Iran that I hadn't known existed and the shared social activity that we experienced was an instant force that unified us. If one focuses on the parties and the social resistance it is easy to see the Iranian people as a tremendous asset for change in the Islamic Republic. But even if this passive resistance is the dominant characteristic of Iranian society, it does not tell the full story. There are those who chant "Death to America" and there are those who believe in the ideology of the Islamic Republic. While youth supportive of the regime are few and far between, there is one issue that seems to unify almost all Iranian people: the validity of Iran's nuclear aspirations.

CHAPTER 4

NUCLEAR PRIDE

IRAN, 2005

I was freezing. Using my sweatshirt as a blanket, I curled up in the back of the old, unheated Russian Skoda. When I'd made the hasty decision to drive from southern Iran back to Tehran, I hadn't anticipated a huge blizzard causing the trip to take at least three times as long as I'd thought it would. The blizzard led to massive congestion on the roads, and I struggled not to breathe in the thick black smoke from the line of cars and trucks in front of me.

After what had to have been at least thirteen hours in traffic, my driver and I emerged from the blizzard. The snow had disappeared and I now found myself in the barren desert of central Iran; it seemed we were now the only car on the road. Out the right side of the car, I could see an endless horizon of sand, and on the left, a snowcapped mountain range. I had thought that from Esfahan it would be a drive with no stops until we reached the holy Shi'ite city of Qom. Instead, we made an unexpected stop in Natanz.

I had nearly fallen asleep when my driver alerted me to an unusual attraction out the left window of the car. The car came to a brief stop as he pointed out his window: "Do you see this?" he asked me.

I saw what looked like a power plant or some kind of factory. There were clusters of large buildings, smoke coming out of cylindrical structures, and a serious fence encircling the compound. The fence was lined with machine gun towers, each separated from the next by only a few dozen yards. In what seemed to be yet another layer of defense, I could see small bunkers with antiaircraft weapons pointed upward.

The driver gave a small laugh.

"This is what causes all of these problems," he told me. To my left was the Natanz nuclear facility, the notorious site that had been exposed as a uranium enrichment plant capable of producing nuclear weapons.

Despite all of the current controversy surrounding Iran's nuclear aspirations, the actual nuclear program is relatively old. The Iranian nuclear program is often talked about as if it were a new phenomenon, but it began as an American-supported project in the late 1950s and early 1960s. At the time, Iran was America's principal ally in the region, aside from Israel. Throughout the early part of the Cold War, the United States had enjoyed a strong alliance with the Pahlavi monarchy in Iran and the Nuri al-Said monarchy in Iraq. When the Iraqi monarchy fell to a revolution in 1958, Iran was the last reliable ally among the predominantly Muslim countries in the Middle East.

When the United States worked with the shah to create the beginnings of the Iranian nuclear program, it was a task undertaken for a very different purpose from what is presumed to be the intention of today's very different regime. In 1959, the shah established the Tehran Nuclear Research Center at the University of Tehran. Run by the Atomic Energy Organization of Iran, the facility became the country's first and achieved operational capacity by 1967. The facility is built around its five-megawatt nuclear research reactor provided by the United States in 1967 as part of bilateral talks between the two countries.

The following year, Iran signed the Nuclear Non-Proliferation Treaty, in which Iran, along with other signatories, agreed to a wide range of issues ranging from disarmament and nonproliferation to the peaceful pursuit of nuclear energy. Under the auspices of the treaty, Iran has always been permitted to pursue nuclear energy for peaceful purposes, but the treaty forbids the pursuit of nuclear energy for military purposes.

With America as his ally, the shah initially had no reason to pursue a militarily oriented nuclear program. Additionally, during the 1970s, the United States and the Soviet Union also undertook policies based on détente, in which both parties at least appeared committed to nuclear arms reductions and some form of rapprochement. Despite détente, however, the shah still enjoyed the support of the United States for his nuclear aspirations. During the Nixon administration, Secretary of State Henry Kissinger envisioned an economically fruitful scheme that would use the allure of nuclear cooperation from private companies and the U.S. government to entice Iran to increase substantially its oil output. As a result, the shah began an ambitious plan to construct several nuclear facilities, using the current high oil prices and soliciting the help of willing American companies. In the late 1970s, President Carter called on the shah to relax his authoritarian grip on Iran and liberalize the economy, but this desire was viewed by many in the American government as separate from security interests in Iran.

Iran negotiated a number of contracts with private companies and American universities for supplies, personnel, and training for its nuclear program. It was during this period that Iran signed a cooperation treaty with newly nuclear India. Development moved quickly as the shah solicited French and Chinese support for the construction of nuclear facilities in Esfahan and Bushehr. In the years leading up to the Islamic Revolution, the United States and Iran had been involved in negotiations that would provide Iran with facilities for uranium enrichment and fuel reprocessing, two capacities that are needed to produce nuclear weapons.

Despite a change in the regime, a prolonged hostage crisis, and a war with Iraq, Iran continued development of its nuclear program under the auspices of the Islamic Republic of Iran. Not surprisingly, Iran under a new regime and led by Ayatollah Khomeini hardly had the sway with Western countries that the shah had enjoyed. In fact, Iran lost a number of its previous nuclear contracts with foreign governments and companies as a result of the Islamic Revolution.

During its eight-year war with Iraq, Iran experienced major setbacks to its nuclear program. Iraqi air strikes throughout the war caused substantial damage to Iran's nuclear facilities and made further progress impossible until they were repaired. While this was a setback, the government in Iran learned an important lesson about the distribution of its nuclear capabilities and drew on the Iran-Iraq War as its reason for constructing more clandestine and dispersed facilities.

The Iranian nuclear program resumed in the mid-1990s with an agreement between Russia and Iran for development of the Bushehr facility and an agreement with China for a conversion plant. Iran's specific nuclear activities were largely unknown throughout the latter part of the 1990s and it was not until a prominent Iranian dissident group blew the regime's cover in August 2002 that the issue returned to the forefront of the news. Led by Alireza Jafarzadeh, the dissident group announced that Iran had two clandestine nuclear facilities, including a heavy water reactor in the town of Arak and a uranium enrichment facility in Natanz.

In the time between the August 2002 announcement and my trip to Iran a few years later, the discussions and negotiations over Iran's nuclear program had degenerated into a game of cat and mouse. Germany, France, and the United Kingdom joined forces in what became known as the EU-3 to try and find a peaceful solution to the crisis. But as negotiations proceeded, new facilities were revealed in Iran and allegations of cheating and lying came from the United States.

I entered Iran in the midst of a worsening nuclear crisis. Just three months before my arrival in Iran, the International Atomic Energy

Agency—the principal international nuclear watchdog—had ordered Iran to halt preparations for large-scale uranium enrichment. Only months before I left for Iran, then–U.S. secretary of state Colin Powell had publicly declared Iran a growing danger and called for the United Nations to demonstrate resolve by sanctioning the Islamic Republic. Tensions were high.

Now, as I sat in the back of the car, engine still running, staring at one of the centerpieces of the conflict, I was surprised by how visible it was. The Natanz nuclear facility is enormous, resting at the base of a small mountain range in the middle of the desert. Its dozens of buildings are a short walk by foot from the main road, and its perimeter is demarcated by what I estimated as upwards of one hundred machine-gun and antiaircraft towers. They're not trying to hide it, that's for sure.

Back in Tehran, I couldn't get the Natanz facility out of my mind. Why hadn't I stayed longer to get a better look? Why hadn't I asked my driver to take me to the city center of Natanz to talk to some of the young people there about the nuclear program? Why hadn't I taken a picture to capture the memory? The answers to all these questions were stupidly obvious. I had no interest in starting off the New Year in an Iranian prison.

The concerns were real, but they seemed to be slowly overtaken by my disbelief that in just a matter of hours I could get from Tehran to Natanz. I didn't even know what I would do there, but I was certain that the small glimpse I had gotten on my way back from Esfahan would not suffice and I wondered if one of the many taxi drivers who had spurted out antiregime rhetoric to me would be willing to drive me back?

It had been an intense couple of weeks already. I had been hassled by the Iranian intelligence services for conducting interviews, meeting with members of the opposition, and violating the protocol that they had tried to lay out for me. I was on their radar screen, but that didn't stop me from pushing my luck. I had spent the early part of my trip to Iran running from intelligence officials, avoiding arrest, and attending wild underground parties. My attendance at these and in the festivities of the late-night street parties in Tehran was undoubtedly risky. After all, these young Iranians were breaking the law and I was right there with them. But the penalty for these escapades would be nothing compared to the potential consequences for the far greater risk that I was now entertaining.

I needed to be discreet because I was still stuck with my intelligence guide on most days, who certainly would have reported me should he become aware of any desire I had to return to the nuclear facility. This was different than talking to youth; if he had any idea where I was going and what I was doing, I would have been in serious trouble. One day, I contrived a story about how I was feeling ill and intended to spend the morning and afternoon strolling through the Park Laleh.

When the time came to depart, I felt kind of like I was back in high school, cutting class. All I could do was hope that the random taxi driver I'd selected hated the regime as much as the other couple dozen taxi drivers I had met. I was paranoid that everybody over the age of thirty worked with the intelligence services. I could just imagine what an intelligence report would look like that evening:

THE AMERICAN HAS STOPPED TO TAKE PICTURES OF THE NUCLEAR FACILITY AND IS ASKING THE PEOPLE IF THEY WANT NUCLEAR WEAPONS.

This was not a comforting feeling and when I got to Natanz, I was so paranoid that I barely spent any time there before turning around and heading back to Tehran.

*   *   *

The nuclear issue had been on my mind since the day I arrived in Iran. The first newspapers I read in Iran had headlines like "U.S. Produces Fake Nuclear Documents on Iran." Other headlines referred to "Iran's right to advance" and the "necessity of nuclear power." The regime was not shy about using government propaganda to promote their nuclear ambitions.

On the surface, the public perception of Iran's nuclear pursuits baffled me. I consistently saw Iranians adopting an intellectual posture of loving anything their government hated, and hating anything their government loved. I concluded that it was in this way that the majority of Iranian youth derived their political persuasions, but the nuclear issue didn't seem to fit my formula. The regime supported Iran's nuclear aspirations, and so did almost everyone else in Iran—including young people.

I wasn't shy about discussing various political topics, but I was always apprehensive about bringing up the nuclear issue. My hesitancy was bolstered by the first group of Iranian students that I had met at the University of Tehran, who assured me that at Iranian universities, there are students who are on the payroll of the intelligence services; I needed to be aware that these students might try to instigate the type of conversation that could really get me in trouble. Even people who I thought were helping me could very well be intelligence officials, and I was told to be mindful that I was being followed and only to talk about sensitive issues in a safe environment.

The nuclear issue first came up with a group of architecture students that I met in Shiraz. The group was spread out in an old historical mosque, doing what appeared to be a drawing exercise. They looked busy but not unapproachable. In what was the usual sequence of events, I approached two of the students and within seconds had a crowd of fifteen to twenty students surrounding me.

We began the conversation with small talk about my travels in Iran, but it did not take long for the conversation to turn to politics. The students and I spoke about the lack of freedom in Iran and concerns about the bad economy, and several of the students expressed worries that after they finished their architecture degrees, they would not be able to find jobs. Their concerns extended beyond job prospects as a number of others expressed their horror at a growing drug culture in Iran. I was reminded that the long border Iran shares with Afghanistan has led illicit entrepreneurs to capitalize on the turbulent environment that first prevailed under the Taliban and ceased to subside under President Hamid Karzai. Opium, heroin, and cocaine are tearing away at the social fabric of Iran by seeping into wealthy communities and trickling down into the most impoverished. Having seen their willingness to speak candidly with me, I asked the group of students what they thought of Iran's nuclear aspirations.

After only a few seconds of silence, I heard a high-pitched voice exclaim something from the back of the group. "What is the problem with this?" she asked me with a perplexed look on her face.

She was short, maybe five feet one or two, and wore a black hejab that she tucked in to her white, button-down jacket. She stood there with a stern look on her face and her hands tucked into her pockets. Underneath the jacket, I saw that she wore fashionable blue jeans and white sneakers, with the ends of her jeans slightly torn and resting almost perfectly on her shoelaces. She was clearly the most outspoken of the group, and on several occasions shushed some of the guys when they tried to speak.

This young woman didn't wait for me to answer. With the same stern look on her face, she made sure that I would not forget her words.

"You know, we have a right to advance too. The energy will be good for Iran and it will help us." She looked me right in the eyes with every word. She was abrasive but not unfriendly. Even with a large group present, she didn't give anybody else the chance to speak. She then yielded the floor to me. Her confident silence was as assertive as her words had been; her look said, "I dare you to respond to that." I told her that I understood the need for nuclear energy and that I, too, viewed such technology as advancement. But I asked her, "You say that nuclear energy will be good for Iran, but what if that energy is used to build nuclear weapons?"

Her hands went deeper into the pockets of her coat as she once again challenged me. "Well, so what? This doesn't harm anybody."

I told her that many were worried that the regime would either sell a nuclear weapon to terrorists or use it themselves, most likely on Israel. She dismissed this as hypocritical. "America used nuclear weapons against another state," she reminded me. I explained to her that the United States government dropped atomic bombs on Hiroshima and Nagasaki in the context of an armed global conflict and that many believed more lives would have been lost on both sides if the war was prolonged any further.

This didn't satisfy her.

"Well, if we want nuclear weapons, why should we not be allowed to have them? America has them, China has them, India and Pakistan have them, Israel has them; so many countries have them. Why can't we be the best too? Is it fair to say that we can't?"

I wasn't getting anywhere with her so I tried another approach. "Well, can I ask you something else?" I said.

She laughed and turned to the girl on her right and said something in Farsi. I think she seemed to like going head-to-head with me in front of her friends. More important, she clearly thought she was winning.

"*Bale*, ask your question," she said.

"What if I were to tell you that nuclear weapons will continue to keep the mullahs in power? Won't this worsen the economy and prevent you from getting democracy? Is it really more important than these things?"

I expected another crafty justification for Iran's desire for nuclear weapons, but she instead looked at her classmates and said a few sentences in Farsi. Everyone burst into laughter.

"What did you just say to all of them?" I asked, eager to know what was so funny.

She caught her breath as she tried to stop laughing herself.

"I said to them: Well, if it is between the nuclear program and the mullahs' staying in power, we don't need it that badly." So even though the youth believe it is their national right to have nuclear weapons, it is not worth the regime staying in power.

Although the regime wants nuclear weapons for its own self-preservation, Iran's nuclear aspirations have been propagandized into a symbol of Iranian pride. Newspapers and speeches by the Iranian government refer to a "right to master this technology" and a "need to advance the sciences." Given the sense of pride that is so deeply embedded in Iranian culture, it is not surprising that when nuclear weapons are presented through the lens of nationalist spirit, most of the youth are sold on the idea.

By galvanizing the Iranian people behind issues of national pride, and the sovereign rights of the country, the nuclear question has become the sole issue around which the regime has successfully mobilized mass support for itself. As a result, that issue has become too valuable an asset for the regime to forfeit on terms other than its own. One wonders if the youth can be made to differentiate between the abstract concept of nuclear energy and the dangerous reality of nuclear weapons. This is a challenge because they view both as part of a greater scheme for advancement. Each young person I spoke to seemed to individualize the idea of a nuclear Iran. For them, it was not about energy or weapons; it was about Iran moving forward and advancing. They become energized talking about this issue, in part because it is one of the rare political issues that they can actually talk about freely.

The architecture students I met in Shiraz represented a common trend among young people: They want the energy; they want the weapons; but they don't want them so badly that they would support keeping the regime in power in order to see Iran's nuclear aspirations achieved. In order to get to this final revelation, however, I would have to ask the right questions, and I noticed students rethinking their stance once I suggested that the weapons might keep the regime in power. All of a sudden they would want to know how and why that would happen and where I'd heard such an idea.

The typical security arguments for stopping a nuclear Iran do not resonate at all with the Iranian people. Iranians do not care as much about international issues as they do about their own immediate domestic concerns and their sense of Iranian nationalism. As a result, the suggestion that Iran might sell weapons to terrorists or use weapons on Israel does little to shift opinion away from dreams of a nuclear Iran.

I noticed that few young Iranians were aware of the domestic repercussions of pursuing weapons in addition to energy. They hadn't thought about the billions of dollars that were being allotted for the nuclear program, money that was desperately needed for other parts of the economy. Many hadn't given attention to the detrimental consequences this issue has had on Iran's standing in the world. Most important, few of the youth I met seemed to have entertained the idea that the government's desire for nuclear weapons was merely a scheme to stay in power. Whenever this last point was disputed, I would always tell my peers that a Kim Jong Il with nuclear weapons is much more likely to stay in power than a North Korean regime without nuclear weapons. Both because the analogy was simple and because Iranian youth are repulsed at the thought of their beloved Iran being compared to a rogue dictatorship like North Korea, I often made use of this comparison.

The economy is the most pressing issue in Iran and I always found it convincing to talk about how the money that was spent on the nuclear program could be used for economic programs. When it became clear that the nuclear program detracted attention—and funds—from rehabilitating the economy, young Iranians frequently shifted their priorities and cast aside their vision of a nuclear Iran.

Since my last trip to Iran, the danger of the nuclear program has been highlighted by the ominous statements of conservative president Mahmoud Ahmadinejad. His rhetoric surrounding Iran's nuclear program, coupled with calls for Israel to be wiped off the map, have led many to forecast the danger of a nuclear Iran. Even the United Nations imposed some degree of sanctions. While Iranians for the most part scoff at a president whom they find embarrassing at best, the international community is determining how to react to his antagonistic statements. Even though it is unpredictable what Iran might or might not do with nuclear weapons, one thing is certain: If Iran does acquire them, it is certainly not the president who will have the nuclear launch codes, as is commonly—and incorrectly—believed by many.

CHAPTER 5

"DEATH TO AMERICA"

IRAN, 2005

In June 2005, Iranians went to the polls to vote in the Islamic Republic's ninth presidential election. As in previous years, thousands of candidates were disqualified by the Guardian Council before the election. Seven men ran for president and not a single one gained enough votes to win outright; the top two vote-getters, former Tehran mayor Mahmoud Ahmadinejad and former president Hashemi Rafsanjani, would compete in a runoff election.

In the days leading up to the runoff, I received dozens of e-mails from my Iranian friends, all of whom were extremely concerned about the prospect of a victory by the hard-liner Ahmadinejad. One friend wrote, "Most of Iranians are worried and have hesitation about what is going to happen. It was unpredictable for us that he was the second and we have another round of election!!! He has told if he will be the president he wants to establish a real Islam like Taliban and he wants to force all the women to wear chador." This same friend went on to say, "My friends and I say he is similar to a monkey and if he is going to win, all Iranian should run away from Iran!!!"

Another friend of mine from Shiraz echoed this concern. She wrote, "All here are worry except the religious groups. We don't like to vote but this time we really have to because if Ahmadinejad wins, this country will be disappeared forever (of course it is now). The election is on Friday and we will see if we still have a country."

The day before the election my friend Sharzad wrote from Tehran, "Rafsanjani and Ahmadinejad are going for a second round of election, but how did that happen? When I asked most of the people, they told me they voted for Moeen or Rafsanjani. I don't know how Mr. Ahmadinejad, the most ugly man that I've seen, could come up????!!!!!" She explained that most people believed they should now vote for Rafsanjani because Ahmadinejad was too religious. Her forecast was that "if he be the president, all of us believe that none of the Iranian should stay in Iran." After Ahmadinejad was declared the winner, one friend wrote:

> You can't believe we are all shocked. I just got a chance that on Thursday my exams got finished and I graduated from university. I am lucky because surely Ahmadinejad will make women wear chador in universities. It is the biggest fraud in the Iran history. Today we couldn't even talk to each other because what should tell each other? A donkey has become our President. We are hopeless and I don't think that we can change anything because they react with a gun. Most decide to go out of Iran; so do I. As soon as possible I want to run out of here and I prefer to go to US. . . .

This e-mail expressed the sentiments of many Iranian youth I spoke to after the election. Especially upset were my Iranian Kurdish friends, who believed Ahmadinejad had played an active role in terrorism against the Kurds. They claim that in 1989 a young Ahmadinejad traveled to Vienna, where the Kurds and many others have suggested that he was was involved in the assassination of three Kurdish leaders who opposed the regime in Iran.

My young friends suggested that four factors led Ahmadinejad to win the presidential election in Iran. First, the conservatives mobilized

the Islamic Revolutionary Guards Corps, the Basij forces, Ansar-e Hezbollah forces, and all elements of the military apparatus to vote for
Ahmadinejad. Many members of the IRGC, Basij, and Ansar-e Hezbollah were bused from town to town, some of them voting as many as
twenty-five times. Getting Ahmadinejad in a runoff against Rafsanjani
was of the utmost importance for hard-liners. Many Iranians believed
the wealthy Rafsanjani was a crook; he was an easy target. In the runoff,
then, conservatives cast Rafsanjani as an out-of-touch kleptocrat and
painted Ahmadinejad as a populist candidate. Creating this dichotomy
was not difficult: Ahmadinejad was relatively unknown and could take
on whatever attributes his supporters desired, while Rafsanjani's lust
for wealth was legendary.

Second, while the hard-liners were getting out their base—by any
means necessary—many young people in Iran remained on the sidelines. Most believe the 2004 *Majles* (parliamentary) election had been
hijacked by conservatives; these young people saw no reason why
the presidential election would be any different, especially given how
many reformist candidates had been disqualified before voting had
even begun. Given the low turnout of reform-minded youth, the well-
organized military and proregime contingency were able to stage a
reasonable showing.

Third, the precedent of the 2004 Majles elections led the conservatives to believe that they could commit widespread election fraud with
virtually no consequences or backlash. In 2005, they were not worried
about widespread violence, riots, or action by the international community. It has also been suggested that the government scheduled the
most important university exams at the time of the election, reasoning
that students would be too preoccupied with their studies to go to the
streets for demonstrations or riots.

Finally, the conservatives needed to prevent a victory by Rafsanjani.
They didn't want him to get credit either for cutting a deal on Iran's
nuclear program or, conversely, for pushing forward with it in the face

of international opposition. Whatever the ultimate course he chose to take, Ayatollah Khamanei, the true leader of the Islamic Republic, needed a president he could control.

Despite the international concern and hand-wringing over Ahmadinejad, who has turned out to be just as conservative as the youth feared, the presidency in Iran is a relatively weak office. To ascertain which members of the government speak with the force of the regime, one must first understand the tremendous complexity of Iran's governance structure. At the top of this chain of command is Ayatollah Ali Khamanei, who is the supreme spiritual guide and has the power to make all final decisions and revoke those of others. Ayatollah Ahmad Jannati chairs the Guardian Council, the authority charged with interpreting the Iranian constitution. In this position, Jannati has the power to disqualify presidential and parliamentary candidates. The Guardian Council also has the authority to reject any law passed by the parliament, or *Majles,* as it is called in Persian. Another noteworthy branch of the government is the Expediency Council, tasked with the responsibility of resolving disputes between the Majles and the Guardian Council as well as serving as a consultative body to the supreme spiritual leader. Other notable branches include the Expediency Council, which will choose a new supreme leader upon Khamanei's death; the Judiciary; Parliament; and the National Security and Intelligence apparatuses.

These branches of government, as well as the advisors and clerics that comprise them, are the movers and shakers of the Islamic Republic. The president is absent from this list, as he is kept in check by each of them. Even the few powers that the president is given are easily checked by the supreme spiritual leader. There are 177 articles of the Iranian constitution, none of which grants the Iranian president any final power or decision-making capability in Iranian policy. The ultimate check on the Iranian president comes in Article 113 of the constitution:

After the office of Leadership, the President is the highest official in the country. His is the responsibility for implementing the Constitution and acting as the head of the executive, except in matters directly concerned with the office of the Leadership.

So if Ahmadinejad doesn't have the power in Iran, what is all the fuss about? There is the obvious point that he is part of the regime and therefore his statements reflect at least in part those of his colleagues who do actually exercise power. But Ahmadinejad doesn't need decision-making power to influence. Even if his message doesn't necessarily resonate with the majority of young Iranians, he speaks in such a way that it resonates with anti-American populations from Venezuela to Lebanon to Pakistan. His ability to fuel the anti-American fire with words across sects, ethnicities, and nationalities is part of what makes him so dangerous. But his words have also fueled an even larger fire. His rhetoric has taken the nuclear issue to an entirely different level and brought it to the forefront of international security concerns. While the world cautiously determines how to resolve the conflict peacefully, Iranian youth fear the worst. Ahmadinejad is being used by the regime as a scare tactic.

As the world responds to the government's rhetoric, young Iranians attentively watch the news on their satellite televisions and they read the news on the Internet. They hear rumors about what will happen to their country and they wonder what these rumors will mean for them. Do more Security Council sanctions mean war? Will the United States come into Iran and overthrow the regime?

Young Iranians dream of a change that will bring them opportunity, but they do not want this change to come through violence. As children, they lived through eight years of war with Iraq and don't want to experience that horror again. Still, they are obsessed with the idea of change. Young Iranians can tell you exactly what they want, but they make assumptions about the relative ease through which such change can be brought about, particularly when it comes to the use of force. In 2002, at the onset of the United States bombing campaign in Afghanistan, there were pockets of Iranian youth holding signs that read "Bomb Us First." Similarly, I met Iranian students throughout the country who joked that the United States is paying the price in Iraq for jumping the queue; these young people wanted the Iranian government overthrown before the Iraqi government. This is their way of saying that they want a new regime in Iran, although their words are not meant to be taken literally.

These same youths were always careful to remind me that they would never tolerate a foreign boot on their ground or a foreign tank rolling through their streets. They have a tremendous amount of pride and it was amazing how many times students would draw on the historical examples of Mossadeq in 1953 or even Alexander the Great's burning of Persepolis, as evidence for what happens when foreigners get involved in Iranian affairs.

The day after my trip to Natanz, I arranged to meet a group of students for lunch. I wanted to talk to them about possible responses to the nuclear crisis. The basic consensus among these students was that, if given the choice between violent change or allowing the regime to remain in place, they would rather try their luck with the regime. Most Iranians take a positive view of the United States, but any American involvement in a violent revolution, sure to bring back memories of the Iran-Iraq War, will quickly sour that association. Currently, the admiration young Iranians have for the United States is based more on America's symbolic position as the antithesis of the Iranian regime than on any specific policy. The wrong specific policy, however, would supersede the general affinity Iranians feel for the United States. As one of the students, a native of Natanz, said to me, "I love George Bush, but if he invades my country I will hate him."

*   *   *

In Esfahan, I had met a family in the Imam Square, with two daughters who were just a few years younger than I. While they were cordial to me, they showed great support and admiration for Iran's supreme spiritual guide, Ayatollah Ali Khamanei, and the Islamic Republic; they were also very religious. As soon as I told them that I was American, one of the girls went into a tirade about America's "criminal support for Israel" and the American "murder of Palestinian people." Her comments didn't offend me; if anything, I'd expected to hear such things far more often than I had. In Iran, state-designed history books and massive propaganda campaigns teach young people oversimplified bumper-sticker slogans; if their families reinforce these beliefs, they will likely hold them themselves. These girls were clearly influenced by a very conservative father, who was not shy about sharing with me his own viewpoint, which I would categorize as a more extremist version of what his daughters had expressed.

The conversation continued about the Arab-Israeli conflict for about fifteen minutes and I rarely got a word in. Indoctrination is easy to detect because those who have been most affected by it are the least willing to engage on relevant issues. When discussing contentious issues they want to preach, not discuss. Once she found out I was Jewish she inquired, "Why don't you want to be a Muslim? I think all people should be Muslim." And my rebuttals didn't seem to make much sense to her; I would repeat over and over again, "I think we are all children of God and how we choose to embrace that relationship is the choice of an individual," but made no headway. This was my standard response to questions about my religion; I had been trained to give it by a few concerned mentors back in the United States. As it turned out, it was usually unnecessary; in this case, it proved more perplexing than effective.

The conversation did not degenerate completely, as a shift from the topics of politics and religion brought us to similar curiosities. The same girl who had given me a state-sponsored history lesson in "America's oppression of Muslim people" now smiled at me and asked, "Are the buildings in New York really like we see on TV? I think it is not possible and if it is, then it must be with the hand of Allah." I proceeded to tell her about glass elevators, buildings that were over a hundred stories high, and what it feels like to walk down a city block in downtown New York. She loved hearing this and she grew more curious with each description. I had never thought about it this way before, but in the same way I had always traveled places to see ancient ruins and marvelous achievements of the world's oldest civilization, young people in the Middle East want to come to America to see modernity at its best.

When I asked to take a picture with them, they looked to their father for permission. He agreed, but only if he stood between me and his daughters dressed by choice in full chador.

At the University of Tehran, I met several girls who would not stand within several feet of me when we spoke. I stopped them outside of the on-campus mosque to see if I could ask them a few questions. Each was dressed in full black chador all the way down to her feet. Their faces were ovals surrounded by black head-scarves that covered every strand of hair, and they wore no makeup.

These girls were quick to remind me that they had no problem with the American people or the country, but they were very comfortable lashing out at the American government. They emphasized that it is America's "support of Israel" and "oppression of the Palestinian people" that is creating problems in the world. The girls were emphatic about reminding me that they are tired of America pushing its weight around.

"But who is to blame for Iran's domestic troubles, such as the economy?" I pushed.

The shortest of the three girls spoke up.

"America has the sanctions on Iran, America supports Israel, America attacks Islam; these are the things that make for our troubles in

Iran." The other girls nodded in agreement. She sounded as if she was muttering a propaganda headline.

"What do you think should be America's role in the Middle East?" I asked, trying to deduce what they thought of the war in Iraq and the prospect of American intervention in Iran.

One of the other girls spoke. She was tall and thin, and unlike the other girls, she spoke with a very angry tone. It was as if she saw me as a representative of the government. She asserted that even though Saddam Hussein is the enemy of Iran, "the Americans should not have come to Iraq and should not have invaded the Iraqi regime, because there were other means to control the country and that regime, there were other options put forward by European governments, and the invasion was not worth all this bloodshed and this violence in the name of democracy." She had a lot to say and there was little room for my words.

"It is doubtful whether American presence in the country, in the region, will actually enhance the chances of democracy," she continued. "People will always see this American democracy as imposed on the regime, so it will always have this stigma attached to it. They do not feel emotionally attached to this democratic experience and it will have a boomerang effect and will result in the opposite and make it antidemocratic."

This girl, at least four years younger than I am, had rendered me speechless. She was so articulate and so passionate in her words that I didn't know what to say. She then issued what sounded to me like a warning.

"America should know that its presence in the region is a threat to Iran, this is part of the same old story of how the Americans are a danger," she cautioned. "The Americans are no longer a danger; they are a *closer* danger residing in the east and in the west. Even if the economics change, the danger is still there with their presence."

This stank of indoctrination for me. Indoctrinated youth were everywhere. In southern Tehran, I went into some of the poorer areas, where I encountered similar, if more populist-tinged, rhetoric. Some youth I met there believed that the regime protected them and safeguarded their livelihood. I couldn't understand how they could have so much confidence in a government that squanders its country's resources and wastes funds needed for the economy on corrupt enterprises and a radical foreign policy.

Every chance I got, I would ask students to explain to me, as I put it, "Who are the youth who chant 'Death to America'?" What I learned is that there is not one answer to this question, as such "Islamic Republic fans" are pulled from various strata of society. One Iranian student explained that the youth who support the regime "come from the stomach of the Islamic Republic government." This was a cute analogy, but I didn't quite understand it.

"What do you mean?" I asked.

"Imagine you are thirteen or fourteen years old and you are confused about what happens around you because you don't know the reality. Then someone appears and wants to bring you up the way he wants, so he tries as well as he can to change your mind."

"But where do they find these youth?" I probed.

"Most of them come from poor families because they show them that rich people and the people who think modernly are taking their rights for life. So they wash their brain with the old model of Islam and they tell them that is justice."

"And what do they tell them?"

"They tell them that anybody except them is evil, it doesn't matter who they are. This can be America, Israel, or even other Iranians." She continued by explaining that agents of the regime support the poor families with money, but she reminded me that this is not for the well-being of these families; it is to buy them off. Rather than actually changing the policies to provide for better social services and opportunities, the regime takes advantage of the short-term needs of the impoverished by giving them immediate cash. They take advantage of the lack of education by scapegoating others and casting themselves as the protectors of the poor in the face of Western secular imperialism.

Many of those targeted for indoctrination are the families of martyrs from the Iran-Iraq War. Following eight years of bloody war, hundreds of thousands of families had been affected by it. Some had lost fathers, husbands, and sons, while others had lost houses and businesses. With hundreds of thousands of soldiers throwing themselves before the front lines of the war in massive human-wave attacks, a substantial portion of the previous youth generation was killed, incapacitated, or disappeared. Immediately after the war, the Iranian government began investing in the minds of these families, in particular the youth who had lost one of their kin. The war was blamed on America, Israel, and the West; the Islamic Republic government was cast as the great protector of the people's security and well-being. The Martyrs Foundation and government-sponsored schools, with their regime ideology, reached out to the impoverished communities and the slums. The ideology was believable to these youth simply because the only money they received was from the government and they didn't have any other information. Some of these youth actually do buy into the ideology, but more often than not, subscribing to it is a reflection of ambition rather than loyalty.

Ultimately, support for President Ahmadinejad, even among the lower class, is based on little more than his rhetoric. He has failed in his actions and already lost much of his support base. When Ahmadinejad ascended to the presidency, he promised economic change at the expense of secularization; not only has society become more nonsecular but the economy has also worsened. The difficult time he had in getting his ministers confirmed illustrated his ineffectiveness within the Iranian government circles; given these circumstances, many are questioning how he can execute an economic agenda.

It is important to note that the small minority who support the regime are not limited to the impoverished. There is a very real, if minuscule, segment of the population who can be classified as true believers. These true believers are the ones who subscribe fully to the ideology of the Islamic Republic and want a fully nonsecular government. They attend Friday prayers, they participate in demonstrations (although many of them receive money for this), and they hope to become the next generation of the ruling elite. Almost perversely, these true believers are often driven more by ambition than by true belief, as such. The true believers I met in the universities aspired to be head of the Guardian Council, president of Iran, or ministers in the government, and becoming a true believer is the only way for them to do this. They are deeply religious, but so are other members of the population who despise the regime. The key difference is that the true believers show a willingness to sell out to ambition.

Among the true believers, there are also those who are the kin of the inner circle of the ruling elite. These families have prospered under this regime and know that whatever follows will lead to a lower quality of life for them and their families. As a result, they hope to keep the generational support alive by following in their fathers' footsteps and by supporting the regime in all of its policies. Having been socialized in the homes of the inner circle, they have no reason to reject a status quo that has brought them wealth, opportunity, and personal prosperity.

While the impoverished and the true believers are key components of the regime's support base, the most important and stable support base they have is among the youth who participate in military and paramilitary activities.

In addition to the traditional military, some elements of Iranian youth are actively involved in the Basij forces, Ansar-e Hezbollah, and the Islamic Revolutionary Guards Corps. Each of these organizations serves a different purpose, but they all allow for youth participants to hold positions of social and political prominence. It is empowering for these youth; they are given uniforms and authority to command over the population. For those who have grown up either humiliated or impoverished, the military is a great way to get ahead and is a way to experience a level of power and comfort that is not enjoyed by the vast majority of Iranian young people. These youth do not live in fear like the rest of the population; instead, they take part in evoking fear. Because many of these youth lack a strong education, they actually enjoy a relative position in society that far exceeds what they would otherwise have.

These military organizations are integrated into Iranian society so as to maintain order and keep the regime in control. While the traditional military are responsible for protecting Iran from outside threats, these state-sponsored paramilitary organizations are designed to maintain domestic stability, i.e., to keep the population suppressed. The Basij forces can best be thought of as volunteers for military service. Not surprisingly, they are usually young and come from the poorer and less educated segments of society. The Basij forces first came to prominence during the Iran-Iraq War by providing bodies for the human-wave attacks against southern Iraq. At present, the Basij are supposed to be role models for their peers and are tasked with enforcing proper ethical conduct. This enforcement has often been violent and has caught the attention of groups such as Human Rights Watch and Amnesty International.

My first encounter with the Basij forces came outside of the old United States Embassy on Taleqani Avenue. Just as I was taking a photo of a mural that read "America Shall Face a Severe Defeat," I was grabbed on my arm by a Basij troop, who could not have been older than sixteen. He was a kid; his clothes were too big for him, his hair was disheveled, and he had but a little bit of scruff right above his upper lip.

He didn't speak English, but he grabbed my camera and was able to mutter, "What are you doing here?!" and "What is this?" in an aggressive tone.

I tried to stay calm. I had encountered numerous child soldiers in Africa, who were hyped up on gunpowder and drugs and armed with loaded AK-47s. Those child soldiers viewed violence and murder as a game and I truly feared them. There were no consequences for their actions and they saw me as a figure in a video game. I had come into contact with these child soldiers in the Democratic Republic of Congo, Burundi, and the Republic of Congo. They toyed with live grenades and fiddled with loaded guns the way I'd played with action figures when I was their age.

I didn't consider myself too tough for the Basij forces, but I had become accustomed to staying calm when confronted by military and paramilitary figures speaking to me in ominous tones. Besides, the Basij troop that confronted me was about as threatening as a kid demanding my lunch money. In the United States, he would not even be old enough to drive; and more notably, unlike the child soldiers in Africa, he had a wooden club instead of a semiautomatic weapon.

Regardless, I was in a new place and I didn't know in what ways this kid could cause trouble for me. So I played the game. Fortunately, I had just interviewed the former Iranian vice president and I had the picture on my digital camera. As soon as I showed this kid a photo of me shaking hands with Sayyid Muhammad Ali Abtahi's, he left me alone, first admonishing me not to take any more pictures.

I saw the Basij forces in other parts of Iran, but I rarely saw them commanding much respect. At the universities, they have their own rooms where they watch over the activities of the students. The students, however, mock them as a "bunch of children and want to be Hezbollah students who know nothing about life." One student explained that "they just sit there all day and wait for any motivation against their interests so that they can scream and yell and pretend they are important."

In Shiraz, I saw an eighteen-year-old Basij trooper approach a group of girls and tell them to cover up. The girls were wearing multicolored hejabs, but pushed so far back on their heads that it looked like they would fall off. Outside of the hejab, they wore completely Western clothing. I was several yards away, so I couldn't make out what was being said, but the reaction of the girls said it all: They just looked at him and laughed. As he persisted, they talked back to him and walked away. In theory, the Basij command respect and an important place in society, but in practice, they are scoffed at by the majority of the population for being uneducated parrots of regime ideology.

Ansar-e Hezbollah plays a similar role to the Basij forces, although it acts more independently. The organization is best thought of as the Iranian regime's vigilante group of personal thugs. Their official duty is to uphold Islamic codes in Iranian society, but they are also used to do the regime's dirty work. When riots or protests spiral out of control, Ansar-e Hezbollah usually takes the first crack at quelling the tides of dissent. They played a substantial role in suppressing the student riots in 1999, and as an elite paramilitary group, they continue to intimidate. Dressed all in black, they are seen by the population as the equivalent of a gang of government thugs, traveling from district to district looking for protests and assemblies to crack down on. They are essentially suppression-happy, often seen using primitive weapons like metal bars and chains and speeding around on their motorcycles. As one of the most conservative and fundamentally Islamist groups in the country, most youth fear this gang of thugs.

The final group of regime supporters in the military is the Islamic Revolutionary Guards Corps and the Special Qods Force wing of the organization. Trained in the old United States Embassy, the Revolutionary Guards can be considered an elite military parallel to the traditional Iranian military. The youth of these two organizations join for the same reasons as those who join Ansar-e Hezbollah and the Basij, except this group represents the elite of the impoverished, ambitious, and deeply ideological youth who support the regime but are not in the inner circle of the ruling elite families.

Contingents of each of these proregime factions can be found among the youth at the various universities, but the interactions these members of the ideological minority have with their fellow students illustrate their marginal place among the larger masses of young Iranians. In one of the many conversations I had with Gita, one of the sisters who had first shown me the youth's view of Iran, I asked of the proregime youth, "What were they like in school socially and in the classroom?"

She hated these types of questions. "Once I saw one of these boys and girls were talking together, but with a two-meter distance and they refused to look at each other," she said, describing proregime students. She laughed in the middle of her story. "Everybody laughed at them and thought they were crazy and that they would always stay crazy."

"What do you mean crazy?" I asked.

"These girls do not have clean faces, they don't have woman faces," she replied.

I really didn't follow so I asked her to explain further.

She tried again. "I mean they don't go to salons, they don't do their eyebrows, and they don't manicure their nails. They don't take care of themselves or care about looking nice. It is the same with the men; they just grow beards and wear the same clothes every day."

I shouldn't have laughed, but I did.

I asked her what the teachers and other students feel about their presence on campus.

Again, she became energized with disgust, explaining that "the only people who like them are those that are just the same as them."

"Do they do well in school?" I inquired with curiosity.

Unfortunately, these kids do well in school. Gita reminded me that the universities are government-run, so they tend to favor those who support the regime. This complaint of proregime favoritism is even shared by some faculty, one of whom explained to me that the standards of the universities have been lowered so that those who support the regime can graduate with better grades. He told me that critical thinking has been slowly squeezed out of the curriculum and professors who have been there for twenty years cannot get promotions, yet hard-line conservative professors can be promoted after just two years.

I pressed Gita further. "Do the students who support the regime ever try to impose their beliefs on others?"

"Oh!" She jumped at this question as if she had forgotten to touch on this. "Yes, a lot they do! They always try to criticize other students and make the universities more Islamic."

I asked how they do this.

"From time to time they have some announcements and have some gatherings."

"What kind of announcements?" I inquired.

"For example, when they see that some boys or girls wear the modern clothes or more Western clothes, they will try to humiliate them in public. But this is difficult, because most of us like wearing these clothes so we just ignore them."

"How many people at your university would you say support the regime?"

"I don't think it can be more than five percent. You know, they think everything against their will is corruption."

Fortunately, those who chant "Death to America" are only a fragment of the population. Despite the loyalty that they appeared to have for the regime, I saw this loyalty as relatively fragile. Despite the fact that the regime attracts most of its supporters by exchanging money for ideological enthusiasm, the regime cannot actually afford to subsidize a massive support base. Since much of the regime's loyalty is tied to what it financially provides for that support base, the loyalty is precarious at best.

Given the constraints of intelligence services, time, and traffic jams, I saw as much of Iran as I could have. When Shapour drove me to the airport on my last day, I still couldn't stand him but I had a big smile on my face, because he really had no idea what I had been doing while he wasn't around. When he left me at night, when he left for the afternoons, when he arrived to meet me after lunch, or when he let me be for the day, I had been learning about his country from the very people he didn't want me to meet.

I arrived at the airport five hours ahead of time for a flight that left in the middle of the night. I really didn't anticipate I would have any problems. My experience in Iran had been turbulent, but my new Iranian friends had helped me get through what would have otherwise been a difficult experience. They opened up a new world to me and showed me the important distinction between appearance and reality in Iran.

While I waited on line to get my boarding pass, I was approached by two members of the Islamic Revolutionary Guards Corps. They gestured me to come with them. What could they do now? I just wanted to get on the plane without any hassle. I assumed this was a routine check. It wasn't.

They asked me what I had in my bags. I told them there were books, clothes, and some artifacts that I had bought. It didn't matter what I said or what the content of my bags were; they wanted something. I stared blankly and was gestured to follow them into a room. They told me to leave my bags behind.

I spent the next four hours in the room, where I was given coffee and biscuits. Nobody spoke to me for the first thirty minutes as I sat there alone on a tattered yellow couch.

The door creaked open and a slender Revolutionary Guard, who looked to be around twenty-eight, sat down next to me. He informed me that if I wanted to leave Iran, I would need to pay a thousand dollars. Was he crazy?! I didn't have that kind of money and even if I did, I certainly didn't see why I should have to give it to him. I had done nothing wrong. But this was not how he saw it. Each time I asked what the fee was for, he would ask me to wait a minute and then disappear for another thirty minutes.

Several hours went by; I still sat in the same room on the same tattered couch. My mood began to change; I had become fed up with these antics. Another hour of this charade went by. It was now just one hour before my flight and I started to realize that there was a decent chance I would not be allowed to leave Iran. I didn't know what they wanted me to do; I didn't have the money they asked for.

Just thirty minutes before my flight, a member of the Islamic Revolutionary Guards Corps came into the room and once again demanded money. I pulled out my wallet, opened it up, and showed that I had five hundred dollars in there. He looked at it, pulled it out of my wallet, and counted it in front of me. After nodding his head in satisfaction, he then presented me with my boarding pass and allowed me to check my luggage.

As I boarded the plane and looked out the window while it took off, I felt a huge burden lifted off of me. It was as if I could think my own thoughts again and feel comfortable again. But I was also grateful for the hospitality and openness showed to me by some of the Iranian youth.

As the plane reached cruising altitude, I remembered an experience that will always remind me of just how many wonderful surprises Iran had held for me and of the encouraging reality that lurks beneath the surface of a repressive regime.

*   *   *

It was my first Saturday in the country, and though I rarely spent the Jewish Sabbath in any form of religious observance, I was looking for a synagogue. I had run into some trouble: I didn't know how to say either "Jewish" or "synagogue" in Farsi. I was also hesitant to ask anybody for help, assuming that most Iranians shared the anti-Semitic sentiments of the government and afraid of the reactions my questions might provoke.

Knowing that I would never find a synagogue without asking somebody, I tentatively approached three or four people. They were all cordial, but had absolutely no idea what I was looking for. Just when I was ready to quit, I spotted a young person, a student by his appearance. He looked to be about my age; he was clean-shaven, with his long hair tied into a ponytail. He wore a leather jacket and was listening to a Walkman when I approached him.

I introduced myself, and he told me that he was an engineering student at Polytechnic University in Tehran.

"Do you know if there is a synagogue in Tehran?" I asked him in English.

"Synagogue? Is it a hotel?" he answered, perplexed.

I tried to explain, still in English, "I am looking for the place of the Jewish people."

His face showed no sign of recognition, but he seemed committed to helping me find whatever it was that I was looking for.

I pulled out a piece of paper, and drew two hands pushed together in prayer. He didn't seem to understand. I then drew my best approximation of a map of Israel and he just shook his head.

"Mosque for Israel?" I finally ventured.

He seemed to understand immediately, exclaiming, *"Bale, Kaneeba Haim!"*

I didn't know what the "Kaneeba Haim" was, but I wondered if this young man still didn't understand what I was looking for. After all, I might have been looking for a synagogue that didn't exist. For the convenience of my search, I had decided to assume that there must be Jews in Iran, but I didn't yet know if they practiced publicly in synagogues or worshipped only in private, fearful of an unfriendly regime.

I thanked the young engineer and was on my way. I got into a taxi and told the driver my destination, Kaneeba Haim. I was curious what this "mosque for Israel" would turn out to be, though I doubted that it was in fact a synagogue.

But after a fifteen-minute ride to a section of Tehran I'd not yet visited, a synagogue is exactly what I saw—or at the very least, what appeared to have once been a synagogue. As we pulled up, I saw a four-paneled metal gate, with a turquoise sign. Written in Hebrew, Farsi, and English, a sign above the entrance read: "Synagogue Haim Iran." The synagogue looked closed—perhaps permanently—and the neighborhood seemed dead. But when I gave the metal door a nudge, it swung open, revealing the largest Jewish compound in Tehran.

These compounds—many with multiple synagogues—can be found in various parts of Tehran and other Iranian cities. I had assumed—logically, I thought—that whatever small Jewish community remained practiced in secrecy. After all, Iran is a country that gave the Israeli Embassy to the Palestinians; the roundabout circling the building is called Palestine Square. In the center of the square is a large metallic statue of "Palestine," with sculptures representing Palestinian guerrilla militants. All throughout Iran's cities, the government has erected signs and billboards that read "Down with Israel" and "Death to Israel." The government of Iran has for decades provided funds to Hamas, Hezbollah, and other Palestinian militant groups committed to the destruction of Israel. Officially, Iran is about as anti-Zionist and anti-Semitic a country as exists in the world today.

The capital city of Tehran, however, is home to eleven fully functional synagogues, each one catering to an active congregation. There are even two kosher restaurants. Further, in some parts of Tehran, one can find a Muslim mosque, a Zoroastrian temple, a Christian church, and a Jewish synagogue, all within blocks of each other. Having spent time in these neighborhoods, I still don't know what's more remarkable: the religious diversity or the total lack of tension one might imagine such diversity would create in a country like Iran.

As I wandered aimlessly through the courtyard of the compound, I was spotted by the curious eyes of children, all of whom bore the distinctively distracted expressions of young escapees from a tedious religious service. Surprised and excited by my appearance, one of the young boys grabbed me by the hand and brought me inside; the others covered their mouths and laughed. I suddenly found myself in the vestibule of a small but crowded synagogue. There was an altar, an ark holding a Torah, and two rows of benches. The men sat on one side and the women sat on the other. The synagogue itself was not large, but boasted a congregation of about fifty men and women, most of whom appeared to be in attendance for Shabbat services. The only indication that I was still in Iran was the fact that all the women still wore the hejab, the head scarves required by Islamic law. It was a bit strange seeing observant Jewish women in traditional Muslim attire.

It took only a moment for everyone to notice a stranger in their congregation. The service abruptly stopped and all eyes turned on me. I could only imagine what they were thinking. Fortunately, one of the teenagers there spoke English. I explained that I was Jewish and wanted to attend services. The blank stares were immediately transformed into welcoming smiles. Within a minute of revealing myself as a Jew looking for a place of worship, I was embraced by the rabbi, surrounded by young worshippers, adorned with a tallis and yarmulke, and led to a seat on one of the benches.

"*Shabbat shalom,*" the elderly Iranian rabbi said as he reached out to embrace me. His curly hair stuck out from underneath his yarmulke and his face was wrinkled and kind. I smiled back at him, thrilled to be attending Shabbat services in the Islamic Republic of Iran. After days of being tailed by menacing intelligence agents and struggling to keep my fear and anxiety in check, I was overcome with relief and joy to find myself in a situation that was even remotely familiar. The irony, of course, was that the worshippers at this particular synagogue were far more observant than I had ever been; I had difficulty simply following along with the service. The very existence of this synagogue and the vibrancy of the place was yet another indicator that things in Iran weren't always as they seemed.

Minutes later, I was brought up to the bima, the raised platform where the rabbi stood. I chanted along with the Iranian rabbi, gleefully fumbling through the words to songs I hadn't heard since my bar mitzvah.

CHAPTER 6

THE CALM BEFORE
THE STORM

LEBANON, 2005

Upon returning to the United States, I publicly shared my stories of partygoing youth in Iran who despise the regime and love American culture. I spoke on television and the radio and I participated in public forums where "professors" from the University of Tehran were present; I was so eager to discuss my experience that I overlooked the likelihood that these "professors" would report my comments back to the Iranian government.

At the time, I was unable to talk about anything but Iran, and I became obsessed with a desire to see every inch of the country. I had even made arrangements with a friend's father to live with the Qashquai nomads in southern Iran and to drive up the Iran/Afghanistan border. I also flirted with the idea of crossing from the southwestern province of Khuzestan into the southern Iraqi city of Basra.

I was sitting at a Starbucks on Cornmarket Street in Oxford when I received a phone call from the Iranian Embassy in London. My visa application had been denied; I would not be allowed to return to Iran, and I was devastated. Forcing myself to look beyond Iran, I decided to base myself in Lebanon, where I could get to Syria and Jordan by taxi and where I could easily fly almost anywhere in the Middle East. So, in June 2005, I left for Beirut and began a long journey that would take me into the heart of Middle Eastern youth culture.

The first thing I noticed about Beirut was how absolutely modern the city looked and how unbelievably gorgeous the people were. Beirut certainly reminded me of Paris, the city to which it is frequently compared. At night the city has its sophisticated trendsetters, its snobby self-important types, and its collection of families who just want a quiet night out. There are also, of course, the occasional drunken teenagers stumbling around the city streets, street peddlers, many of whom are Syrian children, old men selling roses, and even a now notorious guy who makes money by creeping up behind people and yelling, "Beirut!" only then to try selling them maps of the city. They may be different characters, but they are all there to be seen. Walking down one street, I could find distinct traditional Arabic music, yet I could turn a corner and hear 50 Cent or Beyonce. No matter what part of town I was in, there were always the easily recognizable sounds of revving engines. While on occasion these were the sounds of beat-up old cars, they usually emanated from a Ferrari or Lamborghini and were deliberately advertised by whatever spoiled kid was behind the wheel of the car his dad gave him. The more vibrant parts of town with bars, restaurants, and clubs were well-lit, but most of the city had an eerie darkness, which, while one might have expected it to be ominous, was made safe by the masses of young Lebanese on an exodus from their favorite bars to the hot late-night clubs.

The vibrancy of the Beirut nightlife is juxtaposed against the elaborate mosques that reminded me that Lebanon has its conservative sides and the war-torn buildings and bullet-holed statues that placed this all in historical context. The presence of tanks, armed guards, barricades, checkpoints, and jeeps packed with scruffy Lebanese Armed Forces were yet another chilling piece of evidence that beneath the fun lay brewing tensions of a fragile security environment. The occasional Mercedes or BMW with the yellow-and-green Hezbollah flag offered a stark reminder that this was not your typical party city. But despite all these reminders, Beirut just didn't seem to be the war-torn place that it was. The tension seemed deep below the surface and it was easy to assume that the plague of violence in this country was a thing of the past, or so it seemed.

On my first night in Lebanon, I headed to Monot, one of Beirut's most vibrant nightlife districts. Located just next to downtown Beirut, Monot has something for everyone: Western bars, Arab nightclubs, outdoor restaurants, and more. In the summer, every night is like spring break in an American city, as trendy youth from a wide variety of backgrounds wander the streets in search of the next party and Saudi men attempt to flaunt their money downtown in the hope of meeting a girl much younger and more attractive than themselves. These Saudi men would try their ostentatious courting rituals just next to down-town in Monot, except most nightclub owners know that if they let Saudi men in, they will never see another Lebanese girl come into their club. On that first night out in Beirut, I met two guys named Ziad and Walid. They were sitting at Monot's Ice Bar discussing the current political situation in Lebanon, which at the time I really couldn't even begin to grasp. Ziad had a long face and big eyes. His hair was a buzz cut and he was built like a football player. A towering six four, he was a physical presence, but when he opened his mouth he sounded more like a gentle giant. Walid had short hair, dark skin, and a very clean-cut look. His face was scruffy, but, it seemed, deliberately and fashionably so rather than through laziness and poorly maintenance. They looked like a couple of frat guys, drinking the night away on the stoop of the fraternity house. When I approached them, they were perched at an outdoor seating area, scouting for girls.

After some friendly conversation, Ziad and Walid invited me to a beach party on the following night. The next evening, Ziad picked me up and we drove thirty minutes south to Jiye. The party took place at an open bar near the beach, but the crowds of young Lebanese dancing flooded onto the street and onto the beach itself. The outfits were outrageously stylish, with some women in hejabs and others in bikinis, one even adorned with my country's flag. The young Lebanese were dancing to a mix of American hip-hop and Arabic dance music. The greatest burst of energy seemed to arise when a DJ combined the Western and Eastern music with techno beats that made one's heart pump; when certain songs would come on, everyone would start pumping their fists in unison. It was like an enormous *Soul Train* line.

That night, I met Muslims, Christians, and Druze; I met Palestinians, Syrians, and young people from all over the Middle East. The groups were mixing freely and nobody was talking politics. I would spend much of my time in Lebanon at social events just like this one. I visited nightclubs where the bouncer might have been a Shi'ite member of Hezbollah, the bartender a Sunni member of the Future Party, and the patrons Maronite Christian, Druze, and even Jewish. The dance floor might have been filled with members of rival political groups or religious sects, and there might have even been a few terrorists there; all sides of the Lebanese civil war would be represented, but with the lights low and the music loud, you'd never be able to tell who was who.

At first, I was shocked; this was certainly nothing like Tehran. In Iran, for example, one would never see a Basij troop at a party with underground youth; in fact one would never see Basij at a party of any kind. Lebanon was quite the opposite: Everybody—secular, religious, Christian, Muslim—partied, and everybody partied together. Maronite Christians who by day would profess their disdain for Shi'a Muslims and Shi'a Hezbollah operatives who spent their afternoons raging against Christians would come together at night and put aside their differences. I would later learn that most one-night stands crossed sectarian lines. In a culture in which premarital sex is considered taboo and the exposure of such behavior carries serious consequences, young Lebanese have discovered that members of rival religious groups make perfect anonymous partners. There are even stories of girls going to the doctor and paying eighty dollars for reconstructive surgery to make sure the physical results of that night are reversed. Outside of bars and clubs, religious rivals rarely mix: Sleeping with the enemy is the best way for Lebanese youth to guarantee that their nighttime indiscretions never see the light of day.

In my time there, I would find Lebanon to be the most divided country I'd ever visited, a nation ridden by political, ethnic, and religious differences. But those differences never made it past the velvet rope: When Lebanese young people are out at night, they don't talk politics or war and they don't acknowledge Christian, Muslim, or Druze; the youth simply party as Lebanese.

From the rooftop of one of my favorite bars in Beirut, there was a clear view of the site where former prime minister Rafik Hariri was assassinated in March 2005. The bombed-out cars, shattered windows, police tape, and exploded buildings were all still there; I could even see a gigantic crater in the ground where the actual car bomb had detonated.

Although I was in Lebanon in a time of relative peace, there were at least three or four car bombings when I lived in Beirut, including one in the heart of Monot. I heard each one, and one of the bombings sent vibrations through my apartment. There were a number of other occasions where I mistook the lighting of fireworks for the explosion of a car bomb. Lebanese youth are particularly fond of fireworks; it is somehow fitting that in Lebanon, the sounds of celebration are often indistinguishable from the sounds of war.

To be sure, Lebanese youth were not unaffected by the bombings. Every time there was an explosion—which, due to the prevalence of firecrackers and fireworks, was quite often—young people would get on their cell phones and make sure their friends were unharmed. But they wouldn't be stopped from living their lives. Car bombs didn't stop young people from setting off fireworks and they certainly didn't stop them from going out. The day after a bombing was usually quiet, but within a day or two, the clubbers would be back out in full force. After a car bombing killed the head of the Lebanese Communist Party, many youth decided to go to the downtown street where the bombing had occurred and cheer for Lebanon; it was an act of defiance and resolve. If anything, each bombing only solidified the commitment of young Lebanese to rise above the violence of their parents' generations.

Even the villages, while not boasting the urban infrastructure of Beirut, had a progressive feel to them. The façade of comfort and extravagance can easily cast a shadow over the economic hardship, the seemingly embedded sectarian divides, and the dearth of opportunities in Lebanon. But it is just a façade: Young Lebanese often hide their true economic class behind imitation designer clothing, knockoff handbags, and cars that required the family to take out a loan.

In the summer of 2005, optimism in Lebanon was at an all-time high and by the summer of 2006, Lebanon was a country that seemed to have it all. The Syrians had left the country, tourist revenue was flowing in, and political rivalries seemed less important than embracing a prosperous future. These were changes the Lebanese youth could take credit for. Despite the potential, the country remained fragile and within one year's time Lebanon once again found itself serving as a battleground, this time between Hezbollah and Israel in July 2006. For the Lebanese youth, these sounds of bombs, these sites of rubble, and these violent clashes were all too familiar, as war once again stripped them of everything. Born into a Lebanon that was occupied by both Israel and Syria, Lebanese youth have never—until very recently—experienced sovereignty and have suffered through a perpetual identity crisis. Are they Arab or Phoenician? Are they Shi'a or Sunni, or are they Muslim Lebanese? Are they Maronite, Greek Orthodox, Druze, or are they just Lebanese? And, what authority—Lebanese or Syrian—are they subject to? Some Lebanese youth have even gone as far as getting blood tests or swabs from their inner cheek to determine their true identity. For decades, the Syrian presence in Lebanon and the influence of the Hafez al-Assad government in Damascus made Lebanon a virtual extension of the Syrian police state. The terrorist attacks orchestrated by Hezbollah throughout the 1980s and 1990s gave the impression that Lebanon was a terrorist state, yet another source of isolation for the Lebanese youth. There was little concept of justice, freedom, or autonomy. The infighting within religious groups became as common as fighting between religions, causing many Lebanese youth to grow up without a sense of identity. The fighting between and among groups influenced social perceptions and embedded certain stigmas and stereotypes within the Lebanese mind-set. Lebanese based their loyalties not around ideology, belief, or education, but instead derived their identities from the groups, organizations, and coalitions that protected them.

It is impossible to talk about Lebanon without appreciating the significance and impact of its fifteen-year civil war. While Lebanon's history is long and complicated, the conflicts and tensions of today have their roots in the past. Although the war didn't begin until 1975, tensions in Lebanon had been brewing since 1943, when Lebanon gained its independence from France. The 1943 National Pact gave Christians a dominant role in the national government, with a majority of parliament and the office of president reserved for Christians. Other leadership positions were to be held by Muslims (including prime minister, reserved for a Sunni), but as the demographics of Lebanon shifted, the country's two major sects of Islam—Shi'a and Sunni—increasingly challenged what they saw as the disproportionate power of the Christian minority.

The conflict that precipitated the civil war was not simply between Christians and Muslims, however; differences among the various sects of Islam and Christianity in Lebanon also played a major role in the hostilities. Sharing only antipathy toward the Christians, Lebanese Shi'a, Sunni, and Druze did not quite form a united front. The historic divergences among the three groups, particularly within Lebanon, offer a bit of explanation.

The rift between Sunni and Shi'a Muslims dates back to 632 A.D., when the Prophet Muhammad died without any direct offspring. The Sunnis believed that Muhammad's successor could be chosen through consensus, but the Shi'a argued that the only path of succession was through the direct descendants of the Prophet. Today, the vast majority of the world's Muslims are Sunni, with Shi'a Muslims representing only about 20 percent of the world's total Islamic population.

In Lebanon, however, the Shi'a constitute the majority of the Muslim population. Lebanese Shi'a have been deeply influenced by the region's sole Shi'a power, the Islamic Republic of Iran. Further radicalized by the civil war and the Israeli invasion of Lebanon, the Lebanese Shi'a youth of today are, if anything, more religious and ideologically rigid than Shi'a living in Iran.

Yet it is the Sunni, though a minority of the Muslim population in Lebanon, who play the most influential role in politics. Many of the wealthiest and most influential families in Lebanon are Sunni; guaranteed the office of prime minister, the Sunni control the most powerful position in the Lebanese government. The Lebanese Sunni have always been wary of the more populous and more religious Lebanese Shi'a, who they believe are interested in taking control of the Lebanese government. Unique among their Sunni brethren across the world, Lebanese Sunni favor a secularist approach to government; most are bitter opponents of the religious Shi'a of Hezbollah.

Lebanon is also home to a small but important Druze population. Typically associated with Muslims, the Druze are actually practitioners of a distinct and secretive religion that originated in Egypt in the tenth century. Much of the Druze faith is based on the Hikma (Book of Wisdom), which is only provided to those who have proven themselves to be devout Druze. These informed initiates, known as the *uqqal*, shave their heads, grow long and curled mustaches, and wear neatly wrapped white turbans. A copy of the Hikma was stolen and published during the civil war, but much of the religion remains a mystery. Viewing themselves as the original inhabitants of Lebanon, the Druze are a very proud people and bristle when they are lumped with Lebanon's Muslim population.

Lebanon is also unique among its neighbors in that it has a substantial Christian population that once outnumbered the Muslim population. Most of Lebanon's large Christian population is Maronite, a sect that split from the Roman Catholic Church in the fifth century. While some have Assyrian and Semitic roots, most Maronites are Phoenicians who converted to Christianity during the early part of the first millennium when St. Maron and his disciples came from northern Syria to Mount Lebanon and converted the local inhabitants. Today, the Maronites are one of Lebanon's primary groups.

When Muslim invaders entered Lebanon in the seventh century, the Maronites managed to find sanctuary in the mountainous northern region. Like many Jews, Maronites remain purposefully aware that they were forced to practice their religion in isolation and hiding. It was important to my Maronite friends that I understood the historic perseverance of their people: They wanted me to see how Maronite churches were hidden in the cliffs of the Cedar Mountains and how their ancestors had carved crucifixes and symbols of Jesus on the backs of trees or into the rocks of the mountains. During a tour of churches in the Cedar Mountains, one friend told me, "You see these churches? You see these forests? You see these cliffs? This is our story of survival."

Following the Muslim invasion of Lebanon, the Byzantine Empire came to the aid of the Maronites, making it possible for the group to practice their religion under military protection. Through the assistance of the Byzantines, the Maronites actually became such a strong military force that they were eventually paid tribute by the Umayyad caliph in exchange for assurances that they would not challenge the Sunni caliphate.

When the Crusaders came to Lebanon in the twelfth century, the Maronites reunited politically with the Catholic Church by assisting in their military expenditures against the Muslims. While the alliance with the Crusaders proved beneficial for the Maronites in the short run, it led to great feelings of resentment among Muslim communities in the region. Further, the emergence of the Ottoman Empire in the sixteenth century saw a growing Muslim influence over the region. Throughout the duration of Ottoman rule, the French government, however, vowed to protect all Christians living in the Ottoman Empire, and the Maronites were able to flourish and continue solidifying their community. When the Ottoman Empire collapsed during the First World War, the Maronites began to make a push for self-rule, which was eventually granted by the French Mandate in 1920. While the Maronites enjoyed self-rule, Lebanon's Muslim and Druze populations became discontented, loathing perceived treatment as second-class citizens.

The 1943 National Pact, then, materialized in the context of dual fears harbored by both Christians and Muslims. On the one hand, Christians feared losing control to the demographic reality of a Muslim majority and a union with Syria; on the other hand, Muslims feared the close relationship between Maronite Christians and imperial governments, in particular France. After several rounds of negotiations between Maronites and Muslims—mostly Sunnis, as the Shi'a still had very little power—the National Pact stated that the government's top posts would be distributed along religious lines and the Lebanese parliament would be comprised of Christians and Muslims in a ratio of 6:5. This governmental design, also called a confessional system, was meant to be a short-term solution that would eventually evolve into something more democratic. Instead, the confessional system only exacerbated already heightened tensions and provided the structural factors that would lead to the Lebanese Civil War.

The growing discontent coincided with shifting demographics. The 1932 census stated that Christians outnumbered Muslims, but it had become obvious since then that the demographic makeup of Lebanon had been moving in the opposite direction. In the years following the establishment of the State of Israel, Lebanon also became home to hundreds of thousands of displaced Palestinians, who, while living as refugees, were mostly Muslim.

Tensions in Lebanon increased dramatically following a 1970 crisis in Jordan in which King Hussein nearly lost control of his country to a Palestinian insurrection. After successfully restoring order using the Jordanian Air Force and the threat of American intervention, King Hussein expelled thousands of Palestinians from Jordan. Many of these Palestinians were relocated to Lebanon, where they joined the growing community of Palestinian refugees from previous Arab-Israeli wars. Many of these newcomers had taken part in the fighting against King Hussein and found a logical union with the recently created Palestine Liberation Organization, which was then based in southern Lebanon.

Prior to 1975, tensions in Lebanon were high, but most of the violence consisted of isolated incidents between Palestinian militants and Israeli forces, and a handful of clashes between the Lebanese army and the Palestian Liberation Organization in 1969 and 1973. Everything changed on April 13, 1975, when a group of Palestinian gunmen, in an attempt to assassinate Christian leader Pierre Gemayel, killed four members of the right-wing Christian Phalangist Party, including the son of prominent Phalangi leader Joseph Saadi. Responding immediately, vengeful Phalangists attacked a bus in the Beirut suburb of Ain al-Rummaneh, killing twenty-seven Palestinian passengers. A cycle of reprisals and counterattacks began and lasted until 1976. In one such set of reprisal killings, known as Black Saturday, Christian Phalangists erected roadblocks around Beirut and slit the throats of anyone carrying a Muslim identity card. Muslim parties followed with their own set of attacks, and by the end of the day three hundred Christians and Muslims were dead. These incidents were no longer isolated; instead, they were the links in a chain of events that would lead to civil war.

One month later, Christian Phalangists seized the Palestinian camps of Qarantina and Tell al-Zaatar, massacring Palestinians inside. Palestinians from Syria now came to Lebanon to aid in the struggle. Joining together with the predominantly Druze Lebanese National Movement and its leader, Kamal Jumblat, they raided the town of Damour just south of Beirut and cleansed it of Christians. This Palestinian-Druze Union successfully pushed the Maronite Christians back to East Beirut and Mount Lebanon and led to the division of the city between the Christian East and the Muslim West along what became known as the green line.

In 1976, a concerned Syrian president Hafez al-Assad worried that the engagement of Syrian Palestinians in the Lebanese conflict might actually compromise his authority over his own population. Al-Assad, conscious of his status as one of the dominant leaders in the region, did not want to see Lebanon fall to Palestinian control. While he had supported the PLO activities since the late 1960s, the fast growth of the organization precipitated fears in Syria that the Palestinians could threaten the status quo. As a result, he sought to mediate an end to the conflict by proposing an adjustment to the National Pact that would shift the ratio of Christians to Muslims in parliament from 6:5 to 1:1. These efforts were fruitless, as Druze Kamal Jumblat and his influential Lebanese National Movement pushed for a complete eradication of the confessional system, from which the Druze were largely excluded.

With talks breaking down, the fighting persisted. By January 1976, the Lebanese army of nineteen thousand men had collapsed; its soldiers took their weapons and either went home or joined one of an array of belligerent groups. In the absence of a national army, the Palestinian militias became the dominant military force in Lebanon. It seemed that while the Lebanese Christians, Muslims, and Druze were plagued with factionalism and rivalry, the Palestinians might seize the moment and actually take control of Lebanon. Hafez al-Assad grew increasingly concerned and decided to intervene to aid the Maronite Christians and avoid a complete collapse of the Lebanese state and the spread of violence into Syria; the last thing al-Assad wanted was to face the same Palestinian military challenge that his rival King Hussein had experienced in 1970. In May 1977, Syria sent twenty-two thousand troops to Lebanon, and by November of that year, the Syrian army entered West Beirut and put a temporary end to the two years of fighting. While his initial objective was to stabilize the immediate region, al-Assad's ultimate goal—which was eventually achieved—was to establish a pro-Syrian government and transform Lebanon into a Syrian satellite state.

The warring parties, however, would not allow Syria to move into southern Lebanon, where Palestinian and Israeli fighting led Israel to undertake a push into Lebanon in 1978 that saw its forces reach the outskirts of Beirut. With the Israelis fighting the Palestinians in Beirut, Phalangists fighting Muslims in Beirut, and the Syrians fighting everybody, the city turned into a bloodbath. In just a matter of months, eighteen thousand people lay dead on the streets of Beirut, and in the two years of fighting from 1975 to 1976 it is estimated that more than seventy thousand Lebanese were killed. The Israeli raid was short-lived and Israel eventually withdrew on the condition that it would be replaced by a United Nations force. Syria, however, remained.

Everything changed once again in 1982 when the Israeli military, responding to continuing border conflict between Israel and the Palestinians, launched a full invasion into southern Lebanon with the objective of removing the Palestinian Liberation Organization from the country and standing up Maronite leader Bashir Gemayel as president of Lebanon. Not only did the Israelis fail to root out the Palestinian Liberation Organization (PLO), but in the midst of this invasion, Palestinian militants allegedly assassinated the new Christian president, Gemayel. In an act of revenge, Phalangist militias entered the Sabra and Shatila Palestinian refugee camps and undertook a horrific massacre that is to this day used against both Christians in Lebanon and the Israelis who condoned the action. The Israeli military again reached as far north as Beirut, eventually occupying all of southern Lebanon.

In August 1982, a multinational force led by the United States entered Lebanon. Their responsibility was to oversee the evacuation of all foreign troops and the PLO from Beirut, but the force did more harm than good. The American presence inflamed hostilities, and 1982 saw the birth of Hezbollah, the rise of its Shi'ite rival Amal, and several militant Palestinian groups. Terrorist attacks on the United States Embassy and the United States Marine barracks led to the collapse of the multinational force and the withdrawal of the United States from Lebanon.

Fighting persisted throughout the 1980s, with little movement toward mediation. The already unstable Lebanese government had failed to oversee the election of a successor to President Amine Gemayel—the brother of the slain Bashir—whose term expired in 1988. As a result, Lebanon had no government, with dozens of paramilitary and militia groups each vying for power.

In 1989, the Arab League oversaw the Taif Agreement, which officially ended the Lebanese Civil War. The Taif Agreement modified but did not abolish the confessional system. Under the terms of the agreement, Lebanon would have a Maronite president, a Sunni prime minister, and a Shi'a speaker of parliament. The parliament, which had previously represented Christians as the majority, was now to be divided 50/50 between Christian and Muslim deputies.

By the time the Taif Agreement had been reached, the war had lasted almost fifteen years. Initially a war between Muslims and Christians, it had spiraled into an orgy of violence that saw not only Christians and Muslims killing each other, but Christians killing Christians and Muslims killing Muslims. By the end of the civil war, as many as a hundred fifty thousand to two hundred thousand people had been killed, an additional three hundred thousand had been wounded, hundreds of thousands had been displaced, and millions had been traumatized, and the economic damage exceeded 20 billion dollars.

While the civil war that ravaged the country came to an end in 1990, the alienation and humiliation of the generation of Lebanese who had come of age during the conflict persisted under a prolonged Syrian occupation of Lebanon. As long as the Syrians remained in Lebanon, Lebanese youth had little reason to believe in the democratic process of their country. They were under the impression—quite correctly—that Syrian politicians were making laws and ruling under the banner of the Lebanese government. In this context, elections mattered very little, as they were not believed to hold any potential for change. Democracy seemed to be a distant concept so long as the Syrian occupation persisted.

Nearly two years after the Syrians left Lebanon and the one-month war between Hezbollah and Israel ended in August 2006, Lebanon faced yet another challenge to its nascent democracy as Hezbollah moved itself into downtown Beirut in an effort to collapse the internationally recognized government. Nine months later, the relatively unknown Al-Qaeda affiliated Fatah al-Islam added fuel to the fire by launching an insurgency from the Palestinian refugee camp Nahr al-Bared in northern Lebanon, reminding the world that Lebanon's conflicts are multidimensional. And so the perpetual cycle of tension and violence continues.

The scene was awesome. People danced on tables, hands were in the air, and the beats from the oversized speakers sent vibrations throughout my entire body. Every now and then the DJ would shut off the music and let the crowd drive the lyrics. The energy was magnificent. The place was packed and I had to weave my way through the crowds to find a small portion of the sand where I could find room to dance. The thought that I was in a Middle Eastern country didn't even cross my mind as I looked around and saw girls wearing hardly anything, guys in their bathing suits, and couples making out all around me. At the bar, people lined up to do shots, not just out of the glasses, but off of each other's necks and stomachs. There was nothing conservative about this place.

The beach party finally ended at six A.M. and Ziad, Walid, and their friend Naylah decided we should head to a club. We went to a place called B0-18; it had a retractable roof, Gothic décor, and thumping house music. As we walked in, I also noticed that there seemed to be a lot of men dancing with and kissing other men and a lot of women dancing with and kissing other women. Homosexuality has been banned by most Middle Eastern governments, but I would hear of gay youth in Syria, United Arab Emirates, Iraq, and even Iran who would ingeniously use their Bluetooth cell phones to organize underground parties and raves.

The club closed at seven A.M. and as it turned out, on that morning Lebanon was holding the last round of its first elections since the withdrawal of Syria the previous year. After the assassination of former Lebanese prime minister Rafik Hariri—widely believed to have been perpetrated by agents of the Syrian government—the Lebanese people largely put aside their sectarian differences and began calling for the end of the Syrian occupation, which had by then lasted more than twenty years. Even before Hariri's assassination, the United Nations had passed a resolution calling on all foreign troops to leave Lebanon; the international pressure brought by UN Resolution 1559 bolstered this new Lebanese nationalist movement. In March of 2005, hundreds of thousands of Lebanese came to Martyrs' Square in Beirut to make their demands heard. They held Lebanese flags, painted the colors of Lebanon on their bodies and faces, and celebrated unity between Christians and Muslims. The only times Lebanese came together like this were for soccer matches and at nightclubs; these demonstrations, later named the Cedar Revolution for the image on Lebanon's national flag, represented the first time Lebanese had come together to do something other than party. And the revolution was successful: Syria withdrew its troops and Lebanon was finally sovereign. The elections taking place that morning would be the first practical manifestation of that sovereignty.

I was at this point deliriously tired, but I was thrilled when Naylah insisted that we all drive together to northern Lebanon to witness the election in Tripoli.

Naylah was particularly vocal about the election, largely because she supported a different candidate than the rest of the group. Like Ziad and Walid, Naylah was a Maronite Christian, but reflective of Lebanese politics, she is part of a different Maronite political faction than the two of them. She insisted that she was the one to show me the elections. Naylah was one of the more energetic people I had met in Lebanon. She had curly black hair, lots of freckles on her nose, and her two favorite topics of conversation were house music and politics.

While we were driving, Naylah explained that voting in Lebanon was for coalitions and alliances. For instance, Michel Aoun's pre-dominantly Christian Free Patriotic Movement Party was aligned with Hezbollah, the largest Shi'a party and historic enemy of Aoun, against Future, the predominant Sunni party and ally to Aoun during the Cedar Revolution. None of this really made any sense to me. Naylah explained that the only thing I needed to understand was that just as groups had allied and fought with each other during the war, they were now aligning, realigning, and breaking alliances in the name of politics. Even with this in mind, I found Lebanese politics nearly impossible to understand. I had such a difficult time deciphering who was aligned with which party and what groups were affiliated with what platform or politician. Trying to appreciate the complex dynamics among the groups and the historical contradictions of many of the alliances was enough to give me a constant headache.

Naylah was a big supporter of Michel Aoun, who led one of the two dominant Christian parties in Lebanon. Aoun had been the interim president of Lebanon at the end of the civil war, but when he spoke out against the Syrian occupation, he was forced into exile. However, like everything in Lebanon, there are multiple sides to every story. Today, many Maronites believe that it was not his anti-Syrian rhetoric that forced him into exile. Instead, many suggest that Aoun's actions merely prolonged the violence in 1989 and 1990, leading not only to the final and most devastating blow to the Lebanese Christian community, but also to Aoun deserting his troops and fleeing to the French Embassy in October 1990. Back in Lebanon for the first time in fifteen years, Michel Aoun was a very controversial candidate. A Christian and a staunch enemy of Hezbollah, Aoun shocked the Maronite community by aligning himself with the terrorist party in June 2005. Illustrating the complexity of Lebanese politics, Aoun needed Hezbollah support to gain enough votes from Shi'a to win the election in the north. Likewise, Hezbollah needed some Christian support. Even with all the phony alliances and marriages of convenience between Lebanese political parties, many felt that Aoun had gone too far.

As we drove up the highway, almost every car was adorned with the flag of one of Lebanon's political parties. Some waved a white flag with a round circle and the Lebanese cedar tree in the middle: This was the flag of the Lebanese Forces Party, led by its incarcerated leader, Samir Geagea. I saw other cars waving the yellow flag with the green rifle in the middle, the signature symbol for Hezbollah. The Aoun supporters, or the Aounies, as they were called, adorned themselves in orange. As an Aounie, Naylah would honk her horn and raise her arm in the air every time we saw an orange flag coming out the window of a car. Fittingly for Lebanon, it was like a party all the way to Tripoli, as people rode on top of their cars and stood up through the sunroofs.

"Naylah, is it always like this during election time?" I asked.

"No, this is different," she replied sharply. "This is our first election as Lebanese. Since I have been born we have never had elections without Syria occupying our country. Now we can choose our own leaders instead of these corrupt politicians that Syria puts in place to destroy our country."

When we arrived in Tripoli, it was a spectacle. There were rallies and gatherings of all parties in parking lots, in front of stores, in clusters of cars, and in public parks. Naylah took me to a parking lot where hundreds of people stood with the orange flag of Michel Aoun. Most of these participants were young and seemed to be mere teenagers, so I assumed Lebanon had a low voting age. This didn't seem so strange to me: In Iran, young people can vote when they are fifteen years old.

"How old do you have to be to vote in Lebanon?" I asked Naylah.

"Twenty-one," she replied.

Most of the youth I saw out on election day were not even old enough to vote. For them, the election was about something more than voting and campaigning and taking part in the electoral charades; this election was about feeling truly Lebanese for the first time.

Naylah wasn't the only one who opened up to me. Lebanese youth were very friendly and they were quick to welcome me to Lebanon and ask me what I thought of their country. Lebanese girls would flirtatiously ask me if I found them *"heloue ketir"* and I had to concede that they are very beautiful, although I got fed up with boosting their massive egos. Lebanese youth carry themselves with confidence and their self-possession is amplified by their possessions: Image- and status-conscious young Lebanese wear nice things and drive nice cars. I was shier than usual about approaching people randomly; I felt like an underclassman in a high school cafeteria, trying to get a seat at the table with the cool seniors.

I needed an excuse to break into the scene, especially once I realized that my Arabic would be less useful than I had anticipated. I had studied classical Arabic but found that it was unrecognizable in Lebanon. Speaking classical Arabic in Beirut was like going to New York City and speaking Shakespearean English, so I got myself a colloquial Arabic teacher to help me adjust to Lebanese Arabic. The lessons proved to be very helpful and certainly made me more comfortable approaching people, but on a subsequent trip to Morocco almost a year later, I approached a shopkeeper and said in the Lebanese dialect of Arabic, *"Keefak?"* meaning "How are you?" To a speaker of the Moroccan dialect of Arabic, the word is unrecognizable; he thought I was saying fuck you. The interaction became hostile and awkward and I ended up buying an ugly necklace to shut the shopkeeper up and calm him down.

I spent my first few days in Lebanon developing and distributing surveys that covered a range of topics that included the Syrian withdrawal, democracy, religion and politics, Hezbollah, and American foreign policy. I was certainly interested in the results, but I was really hoping to use the surveys as a way to strike up conversations with Lebanese youth. I had deliberately devoted the last section of my five-page survey to United States foreign policy, knowing that this topic would evoke passionate debates. Two students whom I had approached randomly at the American University of Beirut had even been kind enough to sit with me for three hours and translate the entire survey into Arabic.

Over the next week, I meandered around the university campuses of Beirut, distributing my survey to every young person I encountered. This was not Iran: I didn't have to sneak into the universities and I didn't have to be mindful of intelligence services or Revolutionary Guards who wanted to arrest me. I operated with ease. In fact, I wasn't the only person handing out surveys: Lebanese youth take full advantage of their freedom of speech, and often mistaken for a student myself, I, too, filled out a number of surveys on issues like sex and religion.

Because I was handing out as many as fifty surveys a day, I was interacting with tons of young people. I exchanged phone numbers with many of them and it was not uncommon for students to ask if they could take me out at night or to their homes for dinner or to various parts of Lebanon. I received my first such invitation at the Lebanese American University, located in downtown Beirut and considered by many to be one of Lebanon's better universities. Like the American University of Beirut, the Lebanese American University was founded by American missionaries in the nineteenth century and originally established as a school for girls. It was not until after World War II that it became an integrated four-year university. The university has a student body of more than six thousand students from various backgrounds, although Shi'a Muslims are the most highly represented.

It was a relatively slow afternoon and most of the students either were in class or had gone home for the day. In the lower part of campus, I noticed a stunning girl sitting at one of the picnic tables. Her curly hair was highlighted with blond strands and she had accentuated her big eyes and long eyelashes with mascara.

I approached her and asked if she would mind filling out a survey. After assuring her that it would only take about ten minutes, I waited patiently at a nearby table. After a few moments, she signaled that she had finished and I walked over to her.

"I have so much to say about this. You know, it can't be explained so well in a survey," she told me.

I took this as an invitation to ask more questions. She introduced herself as Hibah and we decided to meet later.

*　　*　　*

Hibah and I sat at T.G.I. Friday's on Marrad Street in downtown Beirut. Marrad Street is one of the most popular spots for young people in Beirut; it is also one of the city's best places to people-watch. I found it hard to believe that just eight years earlier it had been virtually deserted; the gorgeous outdoor restaurants had been mere rubble and the busy streets had been filled with weeds and mortar shells. Today, T.G.I. Friday's is one of many Western fast-food chains in Lebanon; one has a better chance of finding a Starbucks (there are five in Beirut), Dunkin' Donuts, or Pizza Hut in downtown Beirut than in just about any European city and even some American cities.

It should be noted that despite the beauty and grandeur of areas like Marrad Street, Beirut isn't all modern and luxurious. The slums of Beirut, just a fifteen-minute taxi drive from downtown, are cramped, impoverished, and plagued by infrastructure problems. The poverty and degradation of these slums provide a fertile breeding ground for the extremism that well-organized groups like Hezbollah are spreading.

Hibah was a Sunni and a big supporter of the Future Party, led by the young politician Saad Hariri. The Lebanese Sunni, who follow prominent families rather than religious clerics, rally mostly around the Hariri family in Lebanon. The Hariri family became prominent through its business ventures in telecommunications, oil, banking, and television; Rafik Hariri served as prime minister of Lebanon on two occasions, first from 1992 to 1998 and then from 2000 to 2004. For his skill in guiding Lebanon during its period of reconstruction after the war, even critics of Hariri came to respect and admire him for refurbishing the country to something it hadn't been since before the war. It was his assassination on Valentine's Day of 2005 that sparked the Cedar Revolution, and for many Lebanese, the Hariri family continues to drive Lebanese politics. Through Rafik's son Saad, an influential deputy in parliament, the prominent Sunni family virtually dictated the results of the Lebanese elections whose last round of voting I'd witnessed on my first night in Lebanon.

Immediately after we sat down, Hibah told me that she would try to help me, but that she was not much of an activist and tended to avoid politics. A lot of young Lebanese say this, but it's rarely totally accurate. Young Lebanese live and breathe politics; born and raised in the crucible of war and occupation, even the most apathetic and apolitical Lebanese young person would look like an activist next to the average American youth.

It was then that I noticed that Hibah had dressed to impress. She wore a dress and makeup and actually looked rather fancy. I, on the other hand, was wearing Birkenstocks, jeans, and a T-shirt. Had I accidentally stumbled onto a date?

While we waited for our food to arrive, I asked Hibah about the magnificent changes that had taken place in Lebanon just a few months before my arrival.

"Jared, you must understand, we never knew who we were," she told me.

"What do you mean?" I asked.

"We grew up with bombs in the streets and Syria occupying our country. We were always controlled by Syria and afraid to discover who we are."

Like most Sunni youth, Hibah considered the Syrian occupation to be the defining struggle of pre–Cedar Revolution Lebanon; she hardly mentioned the Israeli occupation of southern Lebanon. To many Shi'a youth, the Sunnis had it backward: They saw the Syrian occupation as positive for Lebanon because Damascus supported Hezbollah against Israel. For Sunnis like Hibah, however, the end of the Syrian occupation was the beginning of Lebanon's future.

I asked Hibah what changed after the Syrians left.

"We became Lebanese," she replied.

"What do you mean you 'became Lebanese'?" I asked.

She blushed and looked down at her food. Then she looked up, smiled, and continued.

"On that day when we all went to Martyrs' Square, I didn't care so much what it was all about. My friends were all going and it seemed fun. But when I got there, something happened to me. I had never realized how Lebanese I was until that moment." She was referring to the unprecedented unity between Christians and Muslims as they stood together and called for one Lebanon, without a Syrian presence.

When we finished dinner, Hibah insisted on taking me to Martyrs' Square, the main plaza in downtown Beirut and the epicenter of the Cedar Revolution. I figured that this is what she had meant when she responded to my survey by saying, "It is easier to show you." The plaza was only a five-minute walk from the restaurant.

I was still confused about whether or not she considered this a date or a friendly meeting to chat about Lebanese politics. For simplicity's sake, I decided to assume the latter, which proved to be the right call. Hibah became a good friend and was actually extremely helpful in getting some of the Hezbollah guys she knew to speak with me. As it turned out, several of them had crushes on her and she felt perfectly comfortable asking them if they wouldn't mind meeting with me or letting me conduct some interviews.

Hibah led me to the center of Martyrs' Square. In one direction I could see the Mediterranean Sea, while in another I could see a gorgeous mosque and the old rubble of what was once a popular movie theater. We walked toward a statue of three people in the middle of a rotunda. The monument was marked with bullet holes, remnants of the war. All around the plaza, I saw tents and graffiti left over from the demonstrations against the Syrians. Hibah explained to me that young Lebanese had dropped out of school or taken leave to camp in tents, vowing not to leave until Syria left Lebanon. She showed me the graffiti on the walls, some of which had been written in marker and some in paint. One slogan read, "Christians + Muslims = Lebanese." Another etching said, "Together hand-in-hand for a better Lebanon." I saw, "Kill the Lion," a reference to Bashar al-Assad of Syria (*assad* is the Arabic word for lion). I even saw one piece of graffiti that read, "Lahoud pull out my ass hurts." Emile Lahoud is the pro-Syrian Maronite president of Lebanon; he has been widely derided by many Lebanese youth for his obsequious relationship with the Syrian government. These slogans reflected the deeply patriotic sentiments that Hibah wanted me to see, not just hear.

"We haven't always felt these things," she told me. "We were never able to. We always were controlled by Syria. When Syria left, it gave us a chance to look at who we are and what we want. The protests of March proved that we could do this."

While most active youth took part in the Cedar Revolution with the intention of getting Syria out of Lebanon (or just enjoying the biggest party of the year), there were some who counterprotested. At the time of the protests, Hezbollah performed counterdemonstrations with a pro-Syrian slant. This was not surprising, given that Syria's financial, political, and logistical support for Hezbollah had contributed to the organization's success in remaining a relevant player in Lebanese politics. I interviewed several young members of Hezbollah who took part in these demonstrations; they told me that despite their generally pro-Syrian perspective, their intention had not necessarily been to keep Syria in Lebanon. As one Hezbollah youth told me, "We appreciated the support Syria had given Hezbollah and felt obliged to say, 'Thank you for your help and have a peaceful departure from Lebanon.' "

Many Lebanese youth will agree that the day that Syria pulled out of Lebanon was the day they became Lebanese. In a country where the previous generation tried to settle sectarian differences with the violence and bloodshed of an extended civil war, today's youth have tried to put this dark chapter of Lebanon's history behind them. Through their voices, demonstrations, and commitment to change, Lebanese youth brought about the collapse of the pro-Syrian government and the end of a prolonged Syrian occupation.

They have taken a major step forward, but I wonder whether Lebanese youth will continue to break the patterns of the past. With Syria out of Lebanon, Lebanese youth can no longer blame all of their problems on occupation. True, in Shi'a areas there was a temporary Israeli occupation in its war against Hezbollah in the summer of 2006, but this was different from an eighteen-year occupation. More significantly, they must move past the traumas of their war-torn childhoods. The current generation of Lebanese youth were born into a society characterized by alienation, humiliation, and suppression; they were raised in a country where bombings and shootings were a daily occurrence. And so they distracted themselves from the bleakness of their lives with social and recreational indulgences. Their escapism was wholly excusable: During both the war and the Syrian occupation, there was little reason to believe that Lebanon would change; one can hardly blame Lebanese youth for trying to make the best of an awful situation.

Superficiality, a more substantive part of Lebanese youth culture than many people realize, has shielded young Lebanese from the realities of the difficult and traumatizing environment that they associate with their childhood. But it must not be mistaken for reality: While many young Lebanese drive expensive cars, wear extravagant clothes, and attend lavish clubs, they do not want you to know that they live with their parents and share a small room with their two brothers. They do not want you to know that their parents had to take out a loan so that they could drive a fancy car. They want to create the appearance that going out is an easy luxury, and they will not reveal that they didn't eat dinner so that they could afford to buy a single drink, which they nurse all night. They do not want you to know that every day they worry about their future and what will happen when they no longer have their parents as a source of income. Young Lebanese loved to talk about international issues with a foreigner like me, but in truth, it's the economy and the lack of opportunity that really frustrate them. It was only through building and nurturing friendships with Shi'a, Sunni, Druze, and Christians that I realized these sad truths.

Superficiality has become a crutch, and Lebanese youth have grown tired of the charade. One of my friends once said to me, "I love this country, and that is why I hate it so much." Lebanese youth are frustrated by the disconnect between Lebanon's potential and its reality.

They embraced the nightlife and are truly proud of Lebanon's cosmopolitanism, but behind closed doors, almost all young people will admit they want to leave. They love Lebanon but fear that it has nothing real to offer them. Students would always tell me that there are sixteen million Lebanese (nine million in Brazil) and only four million of them live in the country. Lebanon is experiencing a massive brain drain, and as in Iran, the emigration of so many young people is a direct result of the domestic troubles that the government has failed to address.

Though momentum from the Cedar Revolution is beginning to fade and hostilities between Hezbollah and Israel are destabilizing Lebanon, Lebanese youth remain poised to build upon their newfound sovereignty. Although still given to scapegoating and superficiality, Lebanese youth are breaking the patterns of the past by embracing democracy—even if they don't like to call it that.

My friend Ziad and I were walking down Marrad Street one afternoon when he stopped and pointed his finger to the crowds around us.

"Do you see all of these women with their makeup and fancy clothes?" he asked.

"Yes," I said.

"Do you know where they are from?"

I assumed they were from Lebanon, but Ziad corrected me.

Government propaganda in Tehran with the infamous revolutionary slogan
"Down with the U.S.A."

Poster in Behesht-e Zahra commemorating
the downing of an Iranian Airbus by an
American battleship in 1988.

Iranians going to Friday prayer in the holy Shiite city of Qom.

Iran's version of McDonald's in Tehran.

Built in the ninth century, the tomb of Fatima, sister of Imam Reza, is the centerpiece of the holy Shiite city of Qom.

Young Iranian girls adorn the full chador and blue jeans in Ruhollah Circle near the late Ayatollah Khomeini's home in Qom.

A rabbi chants at the Synagogue Haim in Iran, one of the twenty-seven synagogues scattered throughout the country.

On a hot summer day, children swim in the rivers and lakes of northern Iraq.

At Halabjah, the infamous city where Sadaam Hussein gassed thousands of Kurds in 1988.

Roundtable discussion with Kurdish Iraqis from the Kurdistan Iraq Student Union in Arbil.

Internet cafés in Iraq are a sanctuary
for young Iraqis.

Iraqi Assyrians playing video games at a youth
center in northern Iraq.

In the old Al-Ansar region of northeastern Iraq, young boys in Tawela listen to
the beats on their boom box.

Hezbollah and Amal go to the streets to celebrate the election results
in June 2006.

Children play in the rubble that surrounds a soccer field in the Ayn al-Hilwah
Palestinian camp of southern Lebanon.

A typical street scene with the canopy of wires and children on the streets in a Palestinian refugee camp.

A fight breaks out between two boys from rival Palestinian groups.

Terrorist training camp in Ayn al-Hilwah where militants practice shooting and guerilla warfare.

A display of a scandalous woman in Allepo, Syria.

Bedouin children

"They are mostly from Saudi Arabia and others are from the Gulf States. Do you know why they come to Lebanon?"

"Why?" I asked.

"Because here they are free to do as they please."

I thought about this for a moment, but I think Ziad could tell I was a bit confused.

"What do you mean?" I asked.

"They can behave as human beings naturally want to behave. They don't have to hide under the rules of their governments." Ziad put up his hand as if to demonstrate that a light bulb had just gone off in his head. "I can show you," he told me.

Just then, Ziad reached into his pocket and pulled out his small Motorola mobile phone. I watched him activate his Bluetooth mechanism so he could connect to other Bluetooth users. I could see him eyeing the half-dozen or so tables of women all sitting together. Within a few moments, he showed me the screen of his phone, which listed the nearby Bluetooth devices his phone had detected. The names were obviously fake. It reminded me of the Internet cafés in Iran, where all the young people's online identities contained sexual innuendos or references to Western rappers.

I then watched Ziad type a text message:

I AM WEARING A RED T-SHIRT AND STANDING AT THE TOP OF MARRAD STREET.

He pressed send, and off it went to all of the people whose names had come up on his Bluetooth network.

Within moments, I watched table after table of Saudi and Gulf women turn around and look at him.

"You see?" Ziad said to me as he laughed to himself.

One thing is certain: There was more political and social freedom, in Lebanon than in any other country in the Middle East. As Ziad showed me that day, Lebanon's progressive reputation made the country a destination for youth from Saudi Arabia, Iran, Jordan, Egypt, and across the Middle East.

While the social and political progressiveness of Lebanon provided temporary relief for Lebanese youth and Arab tourists who came to enjoy the country's freedoms, the young Lebanese now have a long road ahead of them. They have suffered tremendously on their path to freedom, and Lebanon still has its share of serious, structural problems: Its sectarian divides are still deeply embedded in the culture; religious allies are beset by political rivalries; and resentment from the war still brews under the surface.

Worse, Hezbollah is ushering in a new era of violence, instability, and occupation in Lebanon, giving young Lebanese a legitimate excuse to revert back to scapegoating and superficiality. A year before their war with Israel, I had the opportunity to spend some time with young members of Hezbollah.

CHAPTER 7

THE ALL-NIGHT "PARTY OF GOD"

LEBANON, 2005

Even the members of one of the world's most extreme groups were not immune to Lebanon's charms. I ate with Hezbollah at McDonald's, Pizza Hut, and various other fast-food joints. I sometimes saw the same Hezbollah guys at nightclubs, dancing, trying their luck with the ladies, and even sometimes drinking. These self-proclaimed pious Shi'a mixed with groups that were their sworn enemies by day, chatting with whomever they fancied. Their affiliation with the terrorist group Hezbollah was unrecognizable when they were out; instead, they blended in and constituted another handful of youth in the nightclub dancing to that summer's hottest music.

The Hezbollah I met in the summer of 2005 were what many believed was representative of Hezbollah after 2000. It seemed that they had abandoned all military objectives beyond controlling the disputed Shaba Farms territory in the Golan Heights; they seemed more committed to Lebanon than loyal to Iran; and they seemed to be moving in the direction of political integration rather than violence. But the Hezbollah that the world saw attack Israel in 2006 was a dark reminder that all the while Al-Qaeda had been projecting itself into the terrorist spotlight, the older, more established, and likely more sophisticated "Party of God" had only been hibernating. Shocking the world and perhaps even its own members, in 2006 Hezbollah burst back onto the scene with a blast of rocket fire.

Hezbollah was first conceived after the Israeli invasion of Lebanon in 1982. As Israel entered southern Lebanon, it was primarily the Shi'a villages that suffered the worst of the combat. At this same time, the clerics in Iran were spouting rhetoric of exporting their Shi'a Islamic Revolution. From the Iranian perspective, this was the perfect opportunity to make inroads into Lebanon, while at the same time winning favor in the Arab world by establishing Iran's credentials against Israel. Lebanon was a perfect target for Iranian intervention: The Shi'a were the largest group in the country and the population had become radicalized as a result of the Israeli invasion. As a result, the clerics in Iran seized the moment, dispatching two thousand of their elite Islamic Revolutionary Guards to eastern Lebanon's Bekaa Valley.

Hezbollah was created with three purposes. First, the paramilitary organization was to use guerrilla tactics to rebuff the Israeli invasion and push the Israeli Defense Forces out of Lebanon. Second, Hezbollah was to be an arm of Iran that would work toward exporting the Iranian Revolution. The most pious and capable Lebanese Shi'a were recruited as operatives committed to bringing about an Islamic Republic of Lebanon that would mirror Iran's theocracy. Third, Hezbollah committed itself to the destruction of the State of Israel and the return of Palestine to the Palestinian people.

Hezbollah has never been an organization that acts with autonomy. It has been developed and sustained by logistical, material, and financial support from both Iran and Syria. Hezbollah's allegiance with Iran began with the Shi'a loyalty commanded by Ayatollah Khomeini, but it has been estimated in the international media that Iran provides around $100 million in aid to Hezbollah annually. This aid comes in the form of weapons, training, cash, explosive devices, and funding

for the social and philanthropic activities that Hezbollah uses to garner support for the organization. The Bonyad-e Shahid, or Martyrs
Foundation, is largely responsible for Iran's generous pledges of aid
to Hezbollah.

Despite the Shi'a connection, Hezbollah's relationship with Iran
is based less on religious loyalty than on the benefits such an alliance
provides for each side. Secular strategic considerations are likewise the
backbone of Hezbollah's relations with Syria. While the leadership in
Syria is Shi'a and Allawite, Bashar al-Assad's generally secular approach
to governing is actually rather different from the approach Hezbollah advocates. Though not its own creation, Syria has historically used
Hezbollah as a way of projecting its influence; for Syria, Hezbollah is
a profitable investment vehicle, with returns coming in the form of
regional influence. After Syria withdrew from Lebanon, the country's
investment in Hezbollah became even more important. Without a
military presence in Lebanon, Bashar al-Assad relied on the Hezbollah
paramilitary to fill the vacuum left by the withdrawal of Syrian troops
from the Bekaa Valley. Hezbollah claimed influence over the Lebanese
government, and Syria claimed influence over Hezbollah and, by extension, Lebanon.

Having grown beyond its regional roots, Hezbollah's global network is tremendous. The group has cells in Latin America, Europe,
Africa, Asia, and allegedly in the United States. While the military side
of these cells often remains dormant, they are constantly fund-raising,
accumulating funds, and recruiting new members. Bombings of Jewish
sites in Argentina in 1991 and 1992—including the Israeli Embassy
and a Jewish community center—demonstrated to the world that these
far-flung sleeper cells can be activated almost overnight with devastating success.

Hezbollah became a household name in the United States in 1983.
On April 18 of that year, Hezbollah bombed the United States Embassy in Beirut, killing 17 Americans, and then on October 23, it

bombed the Marine barracks in Beirut, killing 241 Marines. The two attacks claimed 258 American lives, including America's top CIA official on the Middle East, Robert Ames. Prior to September 11, the bombing of the Marine barracks in Beirut was the greatest loss of life experienced by the United States at the hands of terrorists.

When I arrived in Beirut in June of 2005, Hezbollah's popularity was substantial in Lebanon, hardly what I expected for an organization labeled as a terrorist group. Even Maronites who despised the organization would tell me things like "I hate Hezbollah because they are the enemy, but I am happy they defend Lebanon," and "Even though they are the enemy, you must admit that Hassan Nasrallah [the leader of Hezbollah] is a very smart and charismatic man."

Hezbollah had always enjoyed popular support in impoverished Shi'a areas like Dahiye (South Beirut), Baalbak in eastern Lebanon, and much of the South of Lebanon. Hezbollah's ability to galvanize a strong support base is not surprising, given its virtual media monopoly in Shi'a parts of the country and its role as the dominant provider of basic goods and social services to aggrieved Shi'a populations throughout Lebanon. Hezbollah thrives in Lebanon because it has a large constituency of affiliates, who, while not part of the organization, describe themselves as a "nation that admires, supports, and recognizes Hezbollah."

Hezbollah, while undoubtedly a factor behind the Israeli withdrawal from Lebanon in 2000, waged a successful propaganda campaign claiming full credit for the return of southern Lebanon. This is a card that Hezbollah has used most effectively on those Shi'a who either live in the South or were forced to flee their homes in the South. For these youth, Hezbollah is viewed as a heroic force. They cast themselves as the principal organization filling the void left by a government unable to meet the country's socioeconomic challenges. The Shi'a communities are among the poorest in Lebanon, with the contrast of Beirut's wealth serving as a constant source of humiliation. They have also marginalized their principal rival Shi'a group, Amal. Historically, in particular in the mid-1980s, some support for Hezbollah was hindered by its rivalry with the rival Shi'a Amal Party. The evacuation of Israeli Defense Forces from southern Lebanon in 2000, the subsequent decline in Amal's popularity within the Shi'a community, and the alliance of Amal and Hezbollah in the 2005 parliamentary elections have brought substantial numbers of Shi'a formerly at odds with Hezbollah into their court. Hezbollah successfully transformed its image in Lebanon to one of an all-inclusive party promoting a concept of socioeconomic enhancement and resistance against foreign occupation. Politically, Hezbollah has managed to reach Shi'a outside of its traditional areas of support, gain popularity among some Sunnis and Druze, and even seduce some support from Christians, historically the group's staunchest opponents.

The support for Hezbollah that I saw in the summer of 2005 was nothing compared to that which followed the July 2006 war it fought with Israel. Shi'a who had been indifferent to politics found themselves passionately in Hezbollah's camp, and even portions of the Christian and Druze populations threw their support behind Hezbollah. For most youth it didn't matter what Hezbollah stood for; they simply wanted the bombing to stop. What transpired during the one month of fighting was a startling contrast to the prosperity they had enjoyed over the previous two years.

That day at McDonald's when I first told Hezbollah I was Jewish, I admit I was frightened. But I was surprised by an interesting paradox. On the one hand they were religious extremists, committed to the establishment of an Islamic republic, the destruction of Israel, and attacks on America. On the other hand, they were typical Lebanese youth: clubbers, barhoppers, and lovers of American fast food.

During the day, I heard extremist arguments and ominous rhetoric. They wanted to see Israel destroyed, they embraced suicide bombing, and they made no apologies for the long list of terrorist attacks undertaken in the name of Hezbollah. I expected that they went home at night and read extremist teachings and held radical conclaves. Hardly.

I would sometimes see these same young men out at the Beirut hot spots; sometimes they would acknowledge me, while at other times, upset at having their double life revealed, they would avoid me or pretend we had never met. These clubs were hardly religious centers or conservative in their atmosphere. The dance floors in most Beirut nightclubs are very small, catering instead to those who can afford tables and bottle service. The Hezbollah guys I would spot out at night usually crammed themselves into the overpacked dance floors, hardly cringing at the idea of having to pass through crowds of women on their way to the bar. These same Hezbollah partygoers ogled, rather than scowled at, the half-dressed women who danced on top of the bars showing off their latest fashions. Like most Lebanese youth, Hezbollah youth wanted to keep their daytime activities separated from their evening activities, and this meant that they didn't want people in the nightclubs to recognize them as Hezbollah. I never saw them out at hot spots in the predominantly Muslim West Beirut. I would only see them out in areas heavily populated with Maronite or Sunni party animals.

When I told Lebanese friends of mine that I had seen some of these youths out at the clubs, their responses reflected doubt. They rebutted that these are very religious individuals who do not drink and who do not do anything modern. Others would suggest that these guys couldn't have been Hezbollah, because true members of this organization would never let you know who they were. But what my friends didn't seem to understand was that these Hezbollah guys weren't there to plot a bombing of a Christian nightclub, or to kidnap Westerners;

they were there to party, dance, and even in some cases drink. Like everyone else—including other young firebrands from Amal—they were there to be Lebanese. It is hardly a secret that like Al-Qaeda, Hezbollah is also suspected of having sleeper cells in America. With 9/11 just four years in the past, the visual of what I saw in Beirut made me fearful that those thugs were in America "being" Americans at the same nightclubs that I frequent. This puzzling paradox highlighted the conflict extremist youth face between indoctrination and being a teenager.

By the time the Hezbollah youth reach university age, however, they have already received intense ideological training, learned to operate almost every major automatic weapon in Hezbollah's arsenal, and have been recruiting operatives for several years. For all intents and purposes, they have been working for the organization since they were children.

At age six or seven, a Shi'ite child is selected by either his parents or members of his community to begin indoctrination into the "Party of God." So, by the time they reach university age, they have been members of the organization for over a decade already. Not all members of Hezbollah will attend university. The ones who do are the future leaders. In the same way that CIA operatives work two jobs when posted abroad—one on the embassy staff and another in their cover position—Hezbollah operatives have the difficult task of acting as both student and operative.

For Hezbollah, dispatching their best and brightest to the universities is a foolproof plan. The students enter the university legally, and as a result, the organization is able to use society's educational institutions for its own manipulative objectives. Financial support from Iran, along with Hezbollah's own fund-raising capabilities, enables the organization to provide scholarships and funding to its future political operatives.

Students linked to Hezbollah are highly disciplined and well-trained. They have also completely infiltrated Lebanon's educational institutions. Even at the American University of Beirut, which is the most progressive and Western of all the universities in Lebanon and which had its president kidnapped by Hezbollah during the 1980s, the organization maintains a strong presence.

I was told by several professors and students that at the American University of Beirut (AUB) there were as many as 150 to 200 operatives from Hezbollah attending the university as students. In a university of seven thousand students, this is a frightening number—especially since Hezbollah's supporters were likely triple or quadruple that number, and considering the fact that many of the Hezbollah youth who attend AUB express passionate interest in studying engineering, physics, and mathematics in the United States.

Hezbollah students look no different than their peers once in the university. They attend the same classes, dress in the same manner, and are extremely cautious about their identity. Among Hezbollah students, roughly 70 percent enroll in the sciences, while the remaining 30 percent usually study some form of politics. The youth invited to become part of the *military wing* of Hezbollah are even more likely to blend into the student body: They are forbidden from revealing their affiliation to anybody. Those who are in Hezbollah's militia keep the secret from their friends, colleagues, and even in some cases their family. In the words of one Hezbollah party member I interviewed at a café in West Beirut, "You can't know if they are soldiers. He might pretend he is part of a nation and have a social life, but he might in fact be a soldier."

Among their peers, Hezbollah youth use a sophisticated and structured word-of-mouth network to spread the group's message. They spend a great deal of time on e-mail, reaching out not just to Shi'a students, but also to Sunni, Druze, and even Maronites. They pay close attention to the comments other students make in class and around campus, looking for any mention of a topic that they can use as an excuse to strike up an e-mail conversation and invite a potential recruit for coffee, lunch, or some other get-together to discuss the issues.

Hezbollah students seamlessly blend into university life. This can change instantly, however, at the order of Hezbollah's leader, Hassan Nasrallah. When Hezbollah calls on its operatives to join an initiative, its student members are so committed to the organization that they will drop everything to take part. It is sometimes the case, however, that these students can best serve the cause by staying in the university. One Hezbollah member told me on the Lebanese American University campus that if all members were called to jihad, they would have to take part; "taking part," however, may entail fighting the jihad on the university campus by disseminating information and launching a subtle campaign of propaganda. Hezbollah indoctrination is a cycle, as they try to get potential recruits to transform from sympathizer to supporter to member to possible suicide murderer.

Until that call to action comes, these students will rarely admit to being a member of Hezbollah the organization, instead describing themselves as part of Hezbollah the political party. It is important to distinguish between the two. Membership in the organization is reserved for a specific cadre of operatives: Shi'a men who have undergone necessary theological and military training. Outside of the organization of Hezbollah, the specific roles of these members are ambiguous and often unknown. But these men make up the core of Hezbollah: After all, despite its social, philanthropic, and political wings, Hezbollah is fundamentally a paramilitary organization with a military that dwarfs that of its host government.

One afternoon I met with five Shi'a students, only one of whom I had actually met on a prior occasion. His name is Bashar and I encountered him sitting among friends at the upper gate of one of Lebanon's universities. They were hanging out on a cement ledge, clearly enjoying themselves as their feet dangled just above the asphalt patio. It seemed like a nice summer afternoon for them: lounging, staring at girls, talking about the people walking by, and making jokes. There was a small crowd that gravitated toward them and others who looked their way, some evoking feelings of jealousy and others displaying a sense of envy. These were the cool kids. I timidly approached them and asked if they would fill out a survey.

"Sure, we will have some fun with this," Bashar said. We started talking, and I learned that they were all Shi'ites and all big supporters of Hezbollah. This wasn't because they told me but because they answered some of the questions on the survey out loud.

One of them read, "Do you see Hezbollah as a terrorist party?"

In a collective exclamation, they yelled, "Noooooooooooooooo," as if they were touting it with pride.

The same boy read the next question, "Do you see Hezbollah as an organization that represents you?"

Again, that collective exclamation, "Yessssssssssssss," this time followed with celebratory jubilation. I explained to them that I was trying to find a way to interview youth in Lebanon, and they were eager to give me their phone numbers to meet up. I guess I didn't picture members of Hezbollah hanging out on university steps, smoking cigarettes, and dressed in designer clothing. I had only seen images of them with black face masks, headbands with Arabic writing on them, and bands of bullets across their chests.

They filled out my surveys, but I didn't look at what they wrote until after we parted ways.

In one sentence, if the United States could change anything to gain the support of the youth, what should it do?

One of the kids had written, "America is the biggest imperialist and the only thing I want is to see America destroyed." Another survey read, "Nothing. We hate the American government, they support Israel and kill Palestinians." These words sent chills down my spine.

Following my arrangements with Bashar, we all met at a kebab fast-food restaurant near Bliss Street in downtown Beirut. It had that cafeteria feel to it, with the buffet-style servings and the plastic trays. It was filled with students, some studying while chowing on some kebab, others just socializing with friends and using food as the excuse. In the same way that I could smell McDonald's before even entering the fast-food joint, the smell of mass-produced beef kebab lingered in the air. But I wasn't fussy, because they were paying. The only people I recognized were Bashar, who was wearing a backward New York Yankees hat, and his friend, whose name I couldn't remember. The other three kids were new.

I sat down, introduced myself, and gave what became my usual pitch to his friends.

"I'm doing research on youth in the Middle East to try and make the world aware of how you all think and what is important to you. I have not come here to judge, but rather collect perspectives. . . ." And so on. This was my way of appearing amiable and disarming to them.

They were all business. No sooner had we finished introductions than they began speaking about the highly contentious Arab-Israeli conflict. As it turned out, three of the guys present were members of Hezbollah and the others were Shi'a supporters of the organization, meaning they were part of the Hezbollah political party. Mohammad was one of the political party members. He was big, but not fat. His hair was disheveled and bushy, which as I would later infer had likely resulted from the mere two to three hours of sleep he had had the previous night. He insisted on letting me know who he was, and by this I realized he meant a particular category of people.

"I am a Shi'ite from Dahiyeh, but I am not a member of Hezbollah," he explained to me. "Without Hezbollah I would not have seen my village. I am now twenty-one years old and I saw my country—my village—just from the year two thousand because it was conquered. So Hezbollah brought me home. We are grateful to them. Now, if we don't support Hezbollah politically and vote for them, they do not have the legitimacy they need to continue."

His friend Omar nodded in agreement. Positioned with his elbows on the table he explained to me how they view themselves vis-à-vis Hezbollah: "We are part of a nation that admires what Hezbollah did; we are a people who support, admire, vote for, and recognize the Party of God."

A third member of the group, Ali, introduced himself to me as a committee member of Hezbollah. This was a subtle way of letting me know he was actually part of the organization, although he wouldn't tell me in what capacity.

"Let me ask you this," he said. "If someone came into your house and murdered your sister in the middle of the night, what would you want to do to that person?" This was kind of a random question and certainly out of context. I wasn't exactly sure where he was going.

"What do you mean?" I asked.

"I mean, what would you want to see happen to that person?" Was he interviewing me? I thought about it for a minute and told him quite honestly, "I would want to see that person punished as much as possible."

"How old is your sister?" he asked.

"Twenty-six," I said.

There was a long pause. His face said that he had a point, but I had no idea what it was.

"In 1996, the Israeli military came to my house and shot my sister. Do you know how old she was? She was six years of age."

I didn't know what to say in response, so I waited for him to continue.

"You said you would want that person to suffer as much as possible, so you can see and understand why we want to fight against Israel. It is our right to seek justice."

He had put words in my mouth and tricked me into agreeing with him. He had me cornered. This was my glimpse at how Hezbollah recruits new members, how they sell their ideology, and how they make their points. Regardless of what one might think of Hezbollah—and there are certainly varying opinions—the operatives are strategic and well-trained in spreading their message. They can be very convincing to someone without knowledge and can be very manipulative to someone with knowledge. They always tried to pull this trick on me and it was surprising how often it worked.

We moved on to other issues. I asked them about the relationship between Hezbollah and the Palestinians. This was something I had been particularly curious about. Like Palestinian militant groups, Hezbollah had also directed much of its effort against Israel, yet while Palestinian groups were predominantly Sunni Muslim, Hezbollah was Shi'a. A Druze friend had told me that Hezbollah will never help the Palestinian groups because they are Shi'a and the Palestinians are Sunni; they will fear that the Sunni won't appreciate their support. There is no way that my Druze friend was correct. All I had heard from Shi'a and Sunni was a similar gripe against Israel. As a Jew, these sentiments would always make me quiver, but that was all the more reason to understand where their perspectives came from.

Ali fielded my question. He explained that as Hezbollah, he wanted peace in Lebanon, which he felt included the disputed Shaba Farms. Shaba Farms is one of the last remaining pieces of land that Hezbollah claims to be fighting for and undoubtedly the most significant in size and location. It is located on the border of Syria, Lebanon, and Israel, and Hezbollah has attempted to lay claim to the land as belonging to the Lebanese. In reality, Shaba Farms has been Hezbollah's excuse to continue its military expeditions. Ali said as Hezbollah, he will fight Israel over Shaba Farms, but it is not his responsibility to fight Israel over the Palestinian issue. After explaining this to me, he was careful to at least mention that he would support the Palestinians at the UN. I facetiously thought to myself, *That is so diplomatic of you,* but I hardly believed it.

Lacking confidence in Ali's answer, I pushed harder to figure out what the connection was between Hezbollah and the Palestinians. He sensed my skepticism and muttered something incomprehensible to his friend. He was either pissed off at me for not believing him, or he was frustrated that I didn't understand his answer.

One of the other boys spoke up. His name was Karim and he was the oldest of the group, but I thought the least articulate. He wore a tattered white T-shirt and ripped blue jeans. He looked like he had just crawled out of bed. His answer was a little more believable as he explained, "We as Hezbollah are not fighting for the Palestinians; we are supporting the Palestinians because they also defend their country, which is Palestine." Of course, Karim was careful not to give the details of what that "support" entailed.

I knew I could squeeze these details out if I just pushed a little bit, so this is what I did. Karim took the bait and explained that they might support them financially, but they will never send them soldiers. It made sense to me now. Thematically it appeared as though Hezbollah saw eye-to-eye with their Palestinian colleagues. They shared a common enemy in Israel, but their objectives, grievances, and struggles were different.

Ali chimed back in, explaining that it is not their pleasure to have peace with Israel and that most Lebanese don't want this. Karim had already made this point, but I think he didn't like someone else being the center of attention.

When I asked why they don't want peace with Israel, Mohammad, who up until now had been the quiet one, offered a fiery answer. "We can't have peace with a country that shouldn't exist. If we accept Israel, then we accept Zionism. Egypt did this and they fucked all the Egyptians. Peace with Israel will lead us to destroy ourselves." I am sure I looked aghast, because what do you really say in response to this? The

Hezbollah guys were big on examples. Ali told me a story about how in 1996, Israel attacked his village of Qana and killed not just all the children in his village, but also all of the UN workers there. While I didn't doubt that Israel had launched an attack in his village, I had trouble believing that Israel had used explosive teddy bears and had deliberately targeted women and children. What I didn't doubt was that he had heard something like this on Al-Manar Television, which is Hezbollah's media.

Ali asked me if I knew why Hezbollah has been able to fight against Israel. He wanted to remind me why, in his opinion, the organization would be here to stay. He doesn't believe it matters how advanced or modern the weapons are. In his Hezbollah world, they have an even more valuable weapon. This weapon, he explained, was not tanks, nuclear weapons, or airplanes. Instead, he argued, their strongest weapon is faith. I saw the others nodding in affirmation as Ali explained that the Hezbollah youth are willing to die just for the sake of killing Israeli soldiers because they know God is on their side. My reaction was not so much shock that they actually believed this, but instead a sense of tragedy that, growing up, they were probably never told anything different. They really did believe that killing Israeli soldiers would put them in God's good graces.

The Israel-bashing continued. I was used to this from other Lebanese youth, but the way Hezbollah talked about Israel was particularly violent. They always made it sound like self-defense: the suicide bombings, the kidnappings, the senseless rocket attacks; they believed that they were the victims. They felt constantly under attack by Israel and believed it was their duty to take them out at all costs.

The metaphors they used to illustrate their points were bizarre. At one point in the conversation Mohammad compared sexual harassment with being pro-Israel. He tried to reason that if you stand beside a girl and someone insults her, the natural response is to want to attack him no matter how big he is. OK, I understood this logic. But he then went on to suggest that Israel was the male bully and the Palestinians were the metaphorical girl being victimized. Besides being a strange analogy to draw, it didn't make any sense.

What would a conversation with Hezbollah be without a candid discussion about suicide bombing? Always feeling awkward to bring this up, I introduced the topic by suggesting that a lot of scholars and journalists have described this practice as immoral and contrary to Islam.

Bashar chose to field my inquiry. He suggested that as a people under attack, they have two options: sit down or go and fight. In his view, choosing to fight was a kind of suicide because you could likely die in battle. But he was careful to tell me that whether someone dies in battle or by detonating himself as a bomb, "We do not believe this is suicide because your goal is your country, your God, and your dignity."

Eager to get his point in, Karim added that Hezbollah strongly disagrees with the idea of using weapons on its own people. It still wasn't clear to me whom they viewed as *their* people: the Shi'a? Lebanese? Muslims? He explained that their people are the Shi'a and the Lebanese and recalled that even when they were fighting against their historical Shi'a rival group Amal, they did not employ suicide bombing. In a strange acknowledgment, he then went on to say that "we only kill ourselves for the special situation when we cannot do anything else against Israeli soldiers." He elaborated by describing how Israel has radars and weapons and all they have is their bodies and explosives. I didn't buy this, but I listened. It was difficult for me to believe that in all the years of conflict in Lebanon, Hezbollah had no other Lebanese blood on their hands. Armed with missiles and rockets as well as funding from Iran, the organization is the most substantial military force in Lebanon. And if they don't believe in killing their own, this seems to contradict the very idea of suicide bombing.

It is because of Hezbollah's known and diverse weaponry, rather than its capability as an organization that can employ suicide tactics, that make it especially dangerous. UN Resolution 1559 called for the disbanding and disarmament of all Lebanese and non-Lebanese militias. Hezbollah believes that despite the UN resolution, it cannot disarm. So long as it continues to believe it is the defender of Lebanon's borders and the militia for the Lebanese people, this is unlikely to change.

Feeling true to their duty, other members of Hezbollah raised doubts about whether or not Israel would stay out of the South even after they disarmed. They often explained that they are on constant alert because they must exist as a moving presence or Israel will attack them. His mention of the mobile presence is a key characteristic of Hezbollah. Its arms, offices, and stations are scattered throughout its territories. Its weapons are in the private homes of its members and supporters. All of its weapons caches are underground or clandestine. Hezbollah wants to create the aura of an unlimited weapons supply that potentially includes weapons of mass destruction (WMD), yet it wants the true nature of what it possesses to remain a secret. The reality is that the weapons are scattered in so many places that they themselves probably don't know exactly how much they have.

It all sounded very scary to me, with the potential for a minor border skirmish to escalate if the right buttons were pushed.

I heard from them time and again that their weapons are not for the Lebanese people and that they would not attack any Lebanese movement, only Israel, and only in self-defense. As the world would learn a year later, however, Hezbollah's tactics in its war with Israel would ultimately lead to the deaths of the innocents Hezbollah pledged to leave unharmed. I don't think that these youth realized that Hezbollah was in fact looking for a fight. If the Hezbollah youth were talking this way, then they were duped by an older generation that wanted something different than the protection of Lebanese borders. My instincts were right. The Hezbollah-orchestrated kidnappings that sparked the July 2006 war with Israel showed the world a militia looking for a fight.

This fight enabled the older generation to hijack the goals of their youth and quash any hope that a more progressive youth would drive the organization away from terrorist activity and into a role that would see them as an internationally recognized part of Lebanese politics.

At the fast-food lunch, I asked the group of beef-kebab-eating Hezbollah members how they felt about the world viewing them as terrorists. I thought they would be agitated by this question, but instead they sought to clarify that it wasn't the world, it was just America and its allies. He explained to me that they are also against terrorism, at which point he noted that Hezbollah is against Osama bin Laden and sees 9/11 as an example of terrorism. However, Ali, always eager to share his expert Hezbollah opinion, also noted that they do not view Palestinian Islamic Jihad and Hamas as terrorist groups, because they are resisting within a country that is rightfully theirs. From his standpoint, they simply want to go home to Palestine. Whether I spoke to Ali, or one of his Hezbollah colleagues, it was always the same focus on motives, rather than tactics. It was as if they believed that motives rendered even the most barbaric practices justifiable. Every time I brought up suicide bombing or targeting innocent civilians, their answer was always in the motive.

When I would return to Beirut from later trips to Palestinian refugee camps and Iraq, the Hezbollah members whom I had told I was Jewish several months prior over Happy Meals were all of a sudden less than cordial to me. They became totally unresponsive and I began to wonder why. In the past, I'd provided some of these Hezbollah youth with copies of my passport; admitting me to Hezbollah strongholds required official permission from the Hezbollah higher-ups. They had my name, place of birth, passport number, photo, and whatever else was on my passport. They also knew that I had studied at Stanford and at Oxford and that I was a Jewish American. None of this ever presented itself as a problem while I interviewed them. But when I returned to Lebanon from Iraq, these same Hezbollah members stood me up on several occasions, ignored my phone calls, and refused to respond to my text messages. They wanted nothing to do with me. The silence was actually ominous. My suspicions were confirmed when I received a cryptic text message from one of them indicating that they would not meet with me anymore. I wrote back, called, and talked to friends of mine who knew them. They wouldn't see me and they wouldn't give a reason.

I knew that I was now on their bad side. While I had felt safe around Hezbollah so long as they were cordial to me, knowing I had somehow pissed them off was a different story. Was it possible they had done a Google search and found the photo of me holding an Israeli flag at a 2002 protest at Stanford? Had they found out about my internships at the Department of Defense and the State Department, information that could also be obtained in articles written about me on the Internet? Or had they gone so far as to check with the Iranians, who would obviously tell them that I hadn't been allowed back in the country? I was curious, but I didn't feel like staying around to find out.

CHAPTER 8

STRUGGLING FOR DIGNITY

Before I left Beirut the first time, I met someone who would help me get to the Palestinian refugee camps, in particular the notorious Ayn al-Hilwah. The opportunity to visit a Palestinian refugee camp presented itself to me rather unexpectedly in Beirut. On one Thursday afternoon, I was eating lunch with a group of friends, mostly Sunni Muslims, in the cafeteria at the Lebanese American University. The cafeteria was like a food court at any American college, with a few minor differences: In addition to Snickers bars and hamburgers, a student at Lebanese American University could dine on chicken kebab. Four of us sat at a plastic square table, sharing stories about the previous evening. Each one of us had spent the evening at a different bar or club. Some had met girls, others had encountered exes, and one or two others appeared to have had too much to drink the night before. As we were talking, a rather heavyset and scruffy student approached the table to say hello to Juliana, one of my friends at the table. She stood up and they exchanged three kisses on the cheek, the standard greeting in Lebanon. She then gestured to me, and said, "Achmad, I want you to meet my friend from America."

He reached out to shake my hand and asked me if I was the American hanging out with some Hezbollah guys and others our age. When

I told him I was, he insisted that I must talk to *his* people. I wasn't sure who he was talking about, so I asked.

"The Palestinian people," he said, with tremendous pride. Almost immediately, he turned stern, and admonished me not to neglect the Palestinian people in my research and travels. I was already self-conscious about how I reacted when students told me they were Palestinian. I had made no effort to hide my religion and background at the universities and was actually rather forthcoming in offering the information. I saw opportunity in straightforwardness. Most of the Palestinian students in Beirut had never met a Jew; I felt a simple, genuine interaction could go a long way toward correcting popular misconceptions that Jews and Palestinians don't mix.

"You cannot write about the Middle East without talking to the Palestinians," he said. "The Palestinian people are integrated in all aspects of the Middle East and we have the greatest challenges of all. How can I get you to come and talk to my people?"

"I've had trouble getting permission to enter the Palestinian camps," I replied. Entrance permits to Palestinian refugee camps for inquisitive American students weren't exactly growing on trees in Lebanon. Though I had not yet actually looked into this in any depth, I wanted to convey my eagerness, as well as advertise my need for someone to facilitate my travel into the camps. "But if I can find a way to go, I'd be eager to speak with youth in the camps. Is it safe?"

Bypassing that specific question, Achmad nonetheless jumped at the opportunity to assist me. Like the youth of Hezbollah, like the Sunni, Shi'a, and Allawi youth that I had met throughout Lebanon, Syria, Iran, and Iraq, he wanted to open his world to me. I was moved by this. Youth are so frequently neglected by the media, their governments, and the West. I had once again found that even a mere demonstration of curiosity seemed to result in a young person's going above and beyond to help.

As we were talking, it dawned on me that there would be some real moral dilemmas I could face in this journey. I knew some of what I would hear would enrage me and that this would be as much an exercise in self-restraint as it would be a quest for knowledge. Would I lie about being Jewish if it meant ensuring my safety? I remembered what had happened to Daniel Pearl, the Jewish journalist beheaded in Pakistan, and really questioned my sanity. Daniel had very nobally chosen not to lie about being Jewish. The camps were bastions for propaganda and extremism. What if someone asked my opinions on Israel? I believe in a two-state solution for the Arab-Israeli conflict, but I didn't exactly think that sharing these views would resonate positively with Fatah, Asbat al-Ansar, and other Palestinian militants. Questions like these plagued me every night in the days before I left for Ayn al-Hilwah. Where was the balance between safety and morality?

Achmad assured me that he would take care of everything for me. He explained that he would spend the weekend arranging the details of my trip to Ayn al-Hilwah. I was placing a lot of faith in one kid I had just met, but for some reason his intentions seemed genuine. In the same way that I hoped people would trust me, I could see him reaching out in a similar fashion. He assured me that I would meet everyone that I needed to as well as his family. Achmad then asked me, "Did you know that we are the family of martyrs?"

I, of course, had no way of knowing that, but I recognized the opportunity at hand. When I asked if I would be able to talk to his family, he responded with jubilance:

"Will you be able to? You will stay with my family. You'll talk to my mother and we'll show you pictures of my brother who is a martyr. You will come and see where we live and the conditions we are raised in. When you see the young people in my town and in the camp, I think you'll be surprised at how different they are from what you see on television. I hope you'll come with me and when you return home you'll tell people the truth about the Palestinian people."

He explained that we would go to his hometown of Saida in southern Lebanon, the closest city to the Ayn al-Hilwah Palestinian refugee camp. Even before I met Achmad, Ayn al-Hilwah had appealed to me for several reasons. As the largest Palestinian refugee camp in Lebanon, it was home to some of the most extremist youth in the country, young men who boasted membership in militant Palestinian groups as well as international terrorist organizations linked to Al-Qaeda, but more than anything, I wanted to learn the perspectives of other segments of the 350,000 disenfranchised Palestinians living in camps throughout the country. I eventually visited several Palestinian camps in Lebanon, but Ayn al-Hilwah was the most significant, serving as a base of operations for several notable Palestinian leaders in Lebanon.

Achmad's home was the top apartment in an eleven-story building. He was proud to show me all the different rooms, the television, and all of their latest electronics. Outside one of the bedrooms, there was a string of drying laundry draped over a long wire. From the apartment window, there was a spectacular view of Ayn al-Hilwah. In the evening the sun set through the clouds, casting beams of light that formed a cage around the vast refugee camp. The walls were freshly painted, with photos of the family hanging crooked. In the corner of the living room, I found Achmad's mother sitting in a chair, her head fully wrapped in a head scarf and the TV blasting.

Traveling into Ayn al-Hilwah, even by invitation, was a risk. It harbored members of just about every single militant Palestinian group present in Lebanon. In particular, it housed the leader of the Palestinians in Lebanon and head of Fatah, Brigadier General Mounir Maqdah. Unfortunately, I had quickly learned that for every dangerous, extremist group in a country like Lebanon, there's often a group that's far scarier. General Maqdah and his followers were certainly dangerous, but they were not my primary concern. What I found far more threatening was the presence in Ayn al-Hilwah camp of Asbat al-Ansar, a primarily Sunni terrorist group with known links to Al-Qaeda and Osama bin Laden. The group, which has more than three hundred fighters, claimed responsibility for a slew of bombings throughout the 1990s. In 2003, they were behind a series of high-profile bombings of fast-food restaurants in various parts of Lebanon. And Ayn al-Hilwah was their base of operations. It did not calm my nerves when friends of mine in Beirut would joke that I might come back in a body bag. Even some of the youth I knew from Hezbollah told me to be careful, an admonition that left a truly bad taste in my mouth. When extremists are warning you about other extremists, you know you're taking a risk.

I believed that if I could find members of Asbat al-Ansar and talk to youth in Fatah—and manage not to get killed in the process—I would obtain two very useful perspectives from within the Palestinian community. I hoped that my apparent willingness to take the risky trip in the first place would win me respect and, more importantly, restraint vis-à-vis the militants. Talking to Palestinians was not difficult in Lebanon, but meeting and speaking with the extremists in Ayn al-Hilwah proved to be so, and was only made possible by the help of Achmad, who organized dozens of meetings and gatherings for me.

I wasn't exactly sure why I had to run, but at the moment, stopping wasn't really an option. In dangerous situations, terrified confusion can prove nearly as valuable as adrenaline. As my bodyguard yelled at me in broken English to keep running, I was propelled forward by little more than a sense that even the slightest hesitation would land me in a Lebanese prison—or worse.

Behind us, two soldiers from the Lebanese army, the de facto police force in Lebanon, chased closely, screaming in Arabic. I couldn't understand exactly what they were saying, but the message was pretty clear. If it weren't so chillingly real, the setting would have been perfect for a chase scene in a movie: We were weaving through the labyrinth of alleys that make up the border between the Ayn al-Hilwah Palestinian refugee camp and the Lebanese city of Saida. The alleyways were extremely narrow and the ground was of a rough dirt surface; enormous piles of garbage seemed like they had been strategically placed to impede my progress. I couldn't help but thinking that I'd stumbled upon a terrible third-world, life-or-death obstacle course.

Strings of electric cables formed a ceiling above the alleys. In this neighborhood, as in many other poor neighborhoods across the Middle East, the entire community shares electricity, Internet access, and cable television. The consequent splicing and resplicing of the wires— the means by which this community received and shared information with the rest of the world—formed the canopy above us.

With the Lebanese forces in hot pursuit, my bodyguard continued to yell. I had placed all my confidence in a man whose name I didn't even know, not the most reassuring situation in which to find oneself when fleeing from two screaming members of the Lebanese military. In fact, the one thing I did know about my bodyguard/guide/protector was that he had a handgun tucked into his blue jeans. But he had been appointed to me on the spot by Achmad as if he were the only available tour guide at some ancient ruins. As was often the case with casual displays of weaponry in this part of the world, his pistol was largely symbolic. If the moment came, it would be impossible for him to draw the weapon from his jeans and still fire with a clear shot in time to protect me. I knew it was naïve to assume his pistol offered any sort of real protection, but I was willing to take reassurance where I could get it. With the sound of the pounding boots of the Lebanese army in my ears, I had no choice but to follow my bodyguard.

After about six or seven alleys, the Lebanese soldiers stopped chasing, and I'd safely made my way into one of the most dangerous, lawless places in the world.

I was never clear on whether the Lebanese soldiers were trying to catch me or merely chase me into the camp. Though there was nothing to mark the spot, my unnamed bodyguard and I had clearly reached the point where the Lebanese soldiers drew the line between enforcement and containment. The Lebanese government, though claiming responsibility for all security-related matters in Lebanon, does not actually exercise jurisdiction over entrance into the Palestinian refugee camps. The militias—Fatah, Hamas, Palestinian Islamic Jihad, Asbat al-Ansar—control the camps, providing services and either maintaining or, as is often the case, disrupting order. The Lebanese military only contains the camps, keeping disturbances from spreading outside of the small but densely populated slums.

In Lebanon, there are twelve Palestinian refugee camps. The vast majority of these sprang up when Christian and Muslim Palestinians fled to Lebanon during the 1948 Arab-Israeli War. As Israel gained its independence, between 250,000 and 500,000 Palestinians fled their homes to set up what they thought would be temporary residence in Lebanon. When the Arab states suffered a devastating defeat during the Six Day War of 1967, it became clear that the Israeli state was only growing stronger and that the temporary residence that many Palestinians had envisioned in Lebanon had in fact become their permanent home. Between 1968 and 1969, the Palestinians demanded the authority to police their own camps. The guerrilla tactics of the Palestinian militants rendered the already weak Lebanese army ineffective, resulting in an agreement between the Palestinian Liberation Organization and the Lebanese government. Under the terms of what became known as the Cairo Agreement, Palestinian camps would be moved away from civilian centers and the Palestinians would be responsible for their own security.

The terms of the Cairo Agreement remain in effect. Each of the Palestinian camps in Lebanon polices itself, has its own government in the camp, and acts as a virtually autonomous entity. Out of necessity, I'd been willing to put my life in the hands of a bodyguard. This made me uneasy, especially considering the fact that he had offered his services as a favor to my Palestinian friend and was not receiving any money. I knew my guard was there to provide a false sense of security, but in the case of real danger, who would protect me in Ayn al-Hilwah? Neither of the two major groups that exercised influence in the camp—Fatah and Asbat al-Ansar—has shown much interest in distancing itself from terrorism. I wouldn't classify either of these groups as an ideal guardian angel for an American Jew.

It didn't help matters that there was no record of my entry into the camp; nobody knew I had been there. I was denied a permit to visit the camp and just days before I ventured to Ayn al-Hilwah, terrorists inside the camp were identified by the Lebanese government as the extremists who had carried out a high-profile car-bombing attack on the outgoing Lebanese defense minister, Elias Murr. The camp—never quite a picture of calm—was especially on edge at the time of my visit, with tensions between rival Palestinian groups escalating to dangerous levels. Days earlier, there had been reports of heavy gunfire in parts of the camp, the rumblings of a serious confrontation between rival militant groups.

The chase that brought me into Ayn al-Hilwah was exhausting. I stood next to my bodyguard on the side of one of the main streets of the camp. The dirt road was uneven and filled with ditches and holes. Cars drove by, but slowly and carefully; the streets were packed with refugees and the road was only a few inches wider than the vehicles driving on them. There were two-and three-story buildings along both sides of the street. In the camp, as in the alleyways outside, dangling electric wires formed a ceiling over the street. On every wall and every building, I saw pictures of either Yasir Arafat or Sheikh Ahmed Yassin, the late Hamas spiritual leader killed by Israeli Defense Forces in March 2004. As an American Jew, I was not very comfortable with this iconography; suffice it to say that there aren't many posters of Sheikh Ahmed Yassin in the Connecticut suburb I grew up in. The portraits of exalted extremists heightened my sense of anxiety and feelings of fear.

I tried making small talk with my bodyguard. Since we had just snuck into a Palestinian refugee camp together and I was counting on him to protect me in a highly volatile environment, I figured simple introductions seemed appropriate.

"What's your name?" I asked him.

"I am called Ayman," he answered, turning away. Apparently, Ayman was not one for small talk.

We stood in silence. Ayman would eventually become a friend, inviting me to his home, introducing me to his children, and showing off his collection of rocket-propelled grenades, AK-47s, Kalashnikov rifles, and pistols. He even placed his children on proud display with these weapons and made his daughter sing a song to me about Yasir Arafat. What I saw represented a tenuous bridge between Western youth and Middle Eastern youth. But at the same time, the scene was sickening, as the youngest boy, no older than three or four, began hysterically crying. The more he cried, the more guns were placed at his side, as if they were some kind of medicine or pacifier.

But as we stood there anxiously waiting on the side of the street, there was a vanishing gap between us. A black Mercedes pulled in front of us. The Mercedes had dark tinted windows and fancy rims on the wheels; it looked like it could have rolled out of a rap video. The window in front rolled down. It was my friend Achmad. He smiled at me. "I told you I had a way to get you in the camp," he said. It was only several hours earlier that I had expressed my frustration to Achmad that the local authorities had denied my request for an entry permit. He had assured me that I need not worry and that he had a plan. Riding around in a poor refugee camp in a black Mercedes hardly seemed like a "plan," but he then gestured for me to get in the car and said, "Let's go; we have many people to talk to today." The car took two quick turns and drove about two hundred feet before stopping. As it turned out, the black Mercedes with the tinted windows—like many other things I'd see that day in Ayn al-Hilwah—was more symbol than fact.

Achmad, Ayman, and I got out of the car and were greeted by a tall, powerful-looking man. He wore a white T-shirt with Arabic slogans and baggy army cargo pants. His face was youthful and though he could not have been more than twenty-five years old, his full beard and mustache gave the appearance that he was older. "Are you Mr. Cohen?"

I was less nervous at this moment than I had been in a previous visit to the smaller adjacent camp of Mia Mia. There, I was aggressively surrounded by a group of about fifteen to twenty young Palestinians. They were Hamas supporters, wearing T-shirts with a picture of the late Sheikh Yassin, and there were images of him on all the local buildings. They were in total control, some even holding chains. I knew they had no intention of hurting me, but their curiosity led them to inch closer to me. The conversation degenerated immediately into a group tirade about the United States and Israel. In the middle of this rant I asked the group what they would do if a Jewish person were to enter their camp and identify himself as such. A voice spoke up from the back of the group.

"We would cut his head off." They laughed; I cringed.

We kept our silence for a moment, all standing on the rough dirt road that weaved throughout Mia Mia. This part of the camp looked like an impoverished village, with metal-sheeted shacks lining both sides. The city of Saida is the only thing that separates the Ayn al-Hilwah and Mia Mia Palestinian camps from one another. From where I stood, I caught a glimpse of the low-budget housing that filled the city. Random cement walls, roadblocks, and garbage blocked the roadway from clear passage.

But my fear subsided as the conversation progressed. It became abundantly clear that not only did these young Palestinians differentiate between Jews and governments, but their earlier remark had been motivated by little more than a somewhat questionable desire to frighten me. Once I realized this, I took the risk of telling them the truth. I was with my Palestinian friend, and while he was just one person, I assumed he could intervene if things really got out of hand. I addressed my growing audience of Palestinian teenagers. I asked them if it would surprise them if I told them I was Jewish. There was a silence and then I heard a couple of the kids mutter something in Arabic. Though I hadn't explicitly revealed myself as a Jew, they could certainly draw that conclusion from what I had said.

They didn't respond with anger. They didn't threaten me. And they didn't cut off my head. But they were embarrassed. They knew I was a foreigner and they had just wanted to say something outrageous. While none of them said so directly, I know they valued the experience of having someone like me come in to listen, and I think they deeply regretted having used such harsh language. They talked to me about the needs in the camp and the lack of opportunities. I learned that in their classrooms there are not enough books to go around and sometimes the teachers don't even show up. They shared stories of their boredom and expressed a desire for more recreation. As I left, I received several hugs and shook hands with my Palestinian peers. As I walked out the entrance of my first Palestinian refugee camp, Mia Mia, I couldn't help but wonder whether or not they would be more careful with their words the next time someone from the outside came to visit. It reminded me in so many ways of my experience with the youth in Beirut. We are all young, but we are at the mercy of politics and longstanding hatreds.

The experience in Mia Mia was fresh on my mind when I was on my way to meet the genuine article: the military head of Fatah for Lebanon and the man in charge of Lebanon's largest Palestinian refugee camp. General Mounir Maqdah is the chief military authority over the

350,000 Palestinians residing in Lebanon. It was hardcore and frightening, but my recent experiences gave me courage.

With alleged links to Osama bin Laden, General Maqdah is notorious for atrocities committed against the Lebanese army and was given a death sentence in absentia by the Lebanese government. The Israeli government attempted a number of assassination attempts on him, most notably a 1996 missile attack on his compound, an event that he would later describe for me in detail. The death sentences did not stop with Lebanon or Israel. On March 28, 2000, Jordan's Security Court indicted General Maqdah on charges that he had provided military training to a group of Osama bin Laden's followers for future attacks against the Kingdom of Jordan. He was found guilty and sentenced to death in absentia.

There is no shortage of individuals, organizations, and governments interested in killing General Mounir Maqdah, and I had to be taken through a complex route to get to his compound. I was initially led by the serious bearded man, who wore a large automatic pistol strapped over his right shoulder. As with the chase into the camp, the whole thing felt strangely cinematic: going through secret passageways, passing through people's homes, turning sharp corners, and climbing through all of these different back routes. As we got closer to the compound, additional men joined us, each one brandishing a weapon (or two or three). By the time we arrived, there was a full-fledged battery. Once I realized they were in fact taking me to meet the general, I actually felt energized by the big fuss over my visit. It was just by chance that I had gotten the interview. Achmad came from a very prominent family in Ayn al-Hilwah and he knew the general personally. Several days prior to my visit, he had approached the general with the proposed interview.

The compound was not as large as I had anticipated, although it is possible there were parts of it I did not see. I didn't actually know where the compound was because they spent forty-five minutes taking me through a maze, spinning me around, putting me in cars, and doing all sorts of things so that I wouldn't know the general's location. But it was somewhere in the heart of Ayn al-Hilwah and not actually very far from where I'd started, as evidenced by a couple points of reference I had made note of when I first snuck into the camp. I was first taken to the general's private home. The house was extremely well protected and I saw armed men standing at every corner. Some wore yellow bands around their heads, emblazoned with the words *Allahu Akbar,* the Arabic script for "God is great." Others had the recognizable black-and-white checkered headbands, a common symbol of the late Yasir Arafat's Fatah Party. After walking by a half-dozen guards, I arrived at the general's porch. On the porch, there were two rocket-propelled grenade launchers that had been converted into flower vases, an ironic, if strangely fitting, metaphor for a group that claimed its use of violence was all in the name of a brighter, more peaceful future.

If I didn't know better, I would have thought the general was a decent man. He was friendly, willing to speak, and ceremoniously offered to give me tea. I had to remind myself that this man was allegedly responsible for the deaths of thousands of innocent civilians. This was a man who vocally and actively believed in, and subsidized, what Christopher Hitchens rightly calls "suicide-murderers."

We introduced ourselves and began the interview right away. I asked him for his opinion on the future of the Arab-Israeli conflict and he declared that a two-state solution was impossible. Throughout our interview, he also expressed respect and admiration for Hezbollah, Osama bin Laden, and Abu Musab al-Zarqawi. I remained cool but struggled to hide my true emotions. Showing my emotions at this point would be stupid at best. I wanted to kick him in the face, but I remained calm, nodded politely, and kept myself out of trouble. With regard to Al-Qaeda, the general remarked that "they have their own swords and their own strategies, but I hope their destination is to free Palestine. My destination is Palestine and anyone that is willing to help me, even Al-Qaeda, I will accept and work with them." I asked him if he thought Zarqawi was giving Muslims a bad name by decapitating innocent civilians. He did not denounce Zarqawi but instead cited a proverb that "everyone who is from their country has the right to decide and therefore, every Arab or Muslim has the right to defend their country if it is occupied."

I pressed him. "But don't you think this is excessive brutality?"

"Let me ask you this," he responded, "what is the difference between cutting by knife and cutting by bomb? Yesterday there was a bombarding by Israeli aircrafts in Gaza and the people who were killed were torn apart; their legs and heads and hands were all blown to bits. How is that any different than cutting off someone's head?" It was chilling to hear someone justify Zarqawi's actions. Even the Hezbollah fighters I spoke to condemned such action, stating that it was beyond extremism and gave Islam a bad name.

His answers, though shocking at times, were unremarkable. They were uniformly illogical, intolerant, brutal, and stupid. What I found more interesting was what the young men around him said to me after the general had left. I sympathized with these youth in some respects. Did they even know what they were doing, or was this the result of having grown up without an alternative?

After an hour into the interview, I asked him if some of the young militants, indolently strolling around the compound, could join in the conversation. He was amused by the request, but gestured for them to come over.

We all sat around a round plastic table on the general's porch. The group of boys looked like typical militants, with all the expected attire of headbands and weaponry. But they showed a childish excitement about being part of the interview, as if they thought this opportunity was uncharacteristic for them. The porch was more of a cement patio than anything, and it was a mere segment of the general's backyard. The only decorations I noticed, besides the plastic furniture, were a couple of vases, only some of which actually had plants growing out of them. Closer to the entrance to his home, but still on the porch, was some kind of a bazooka that had been transformed into a potted plant. The youth around the table had begun their military training at ten years old. At this young age, they began attending two types of schools, one for military service and the other to study the geography and history of their homeland. After six to ten months, they began their "military" training period: There, they learned combat techniques, as well as moral codes, obedience, and mutual respect for their fellow soldiers. They practiced with live bullets and used real weapons. I was shocked to hear that they trained on the same field that other kids played soccer on. Sometimes, they brought children as young as seven years old to the training, to help them become acquainted with—and used to—the weapons inside the camp.

One of the guys who spoke up in front of the general said, "We are street fighters; this is our army. Our training is designed to teach us army tactics, and street fighting tactics, but also it must be stuck in our minds and hearts that all Palestine is for us." When I asked them why they fight, the answer I got from each of them was a rambling, probably rehearsed tirade that focused on the Israeli occupation of Palestine and Israeli atrocities against Palestinians.

When the interview finished, the general asked his young fighters to escort me out of the compound. Away from the general and free to expand on the largely empty rhetoric they had felt compelled to give in his presence, they revealed that most of them do not feel any direct political connection with the Arab-Israeli conflict. They become active in it because that is what they are supposed to do; it is what they are indoctrinated to believe. Ultimately, however, their grievances revolve around topics far simpler than the Arab-Israeli conflict. They are unhappy with their lives, and they blame their economic and social hardship on Israel and America because the Palestinian leadership tells them that these are the sources of their grievances.

Immediately after the meeting, the young militants insisted on showing me a weapons arsenal. Weapons caches were not at the top of my sightseeing list, but I figured it was better that they show me the weapons than use them on me. They walked me into a cement room; when I walked in, what I saw resembled the background of the Iraqi hostage videos the world has become so uncomfortably accustomed to seeing on the news. The walls were a faint white, and the paint was peeling off. There was an old and filthy bed with a torn mattress that did not have sheets. Four large guns hung from the wall above the bed. Each of them was distinct from the others; one had a scope, others had large barrels. In one corner of the room, there was an old wooden cabinet. One of the youth reached into the cabinet and pulled out a vest and insisted that I wear it. Again, I rationalized that if I had to choose between terrorists using weapons on me and terrorists dressing me in weapons, I would certainly pick the latter. The next thing I knew, they had filled each of the pockets of the vest with handguns, axes, and grenades. They then removed several of the guns from the wall, placing one over my shoulder and having me hold the other two in my hands. As I became a human trophy case for their weaponry, I could not help but wonder how this would appear to someone back in the United States. Of course, this fear was slightly trumped by the fact that all of these weapons were loaded and there was a live grenade in my pocket. It was an odd moment. I was frightened, but realized that in a way, these were not so much gun-toting masked militants. Instead, they were broken souls with lethal toys that they had been forced to play with since a very young age.

It was as if me dressing in their weapons led them to believe that I had entered their world. I seized the moment and asked them bluntly why they had joined the movement.

Of the three boys I was with, the one standing closest to me answered. He had wavy hair and stubble on his face. His eyebrows were unusually large and he wore a light blue shirt. There was actually nothing about him that made him look like either a militant or a terrorist. His answer to my question did not reflect the call to nationalism that the general had explained or that they had described in his presence. Instead, he exclaimed, "What choice do we have? They try to create special programs for us to experience life outside of the camps, but we still face so many problems. We have no entertainment. We can study and some of us even study outside of the camp, but for what? We can't work, we can't find jobs; we get nothing for our hard work. We feel depressed because we cannot have the opportunity for success even if we try." This was very different from the bumper-sticker banter that they had spouted off around the general.

Another one of the boys spoke and looked at me with a sullen face and said, "Don't you think that we, too, would like to drive the nice cars in Beirut and be able to go out at night? But we can't because our lives are these camps. Inside here we are somebody, but out there we are refugees. We don't have rights."

The conditions in the camps are difficult and the lifestyle is humiliating. In seeking remedies for this humiliation they look to their elders, who tell them that the bad economy, the lack of opportunity, the inability to be part of the outside world, their lack of dignity, and the political oppression are all a direct result of aggressive Israeli and American policies. As the adult generations fight for a return to their homeland, it seems that many of the youth are fighting simply for a better life. And they look to the West as a model for that better life.

Even as we stood in a room filled with guns, knives, grenades, and other implements for killing, none of the boys expressed a love for violence. They instead revealed how difficult it is to grow up in an environment that precipitates humiliation and a loss of dignity. Despite their gaudy displays of weaponry and the ominous threat of physical violence that bubbled just beneath the surface, I could see that these youth were weak, and broken inside. They were not brave soldiers but fragile young souls with lethal toys. Lebanon is one of the most westernized countries in the Middle East, yet Palestinians feel like second-class citizens and are made to feel as if they are a burden on the society. The same boy who spoke of wanting to enjoy the nightlife of Beirut confessed, "We want to contribute to society, but we cannot do anything from the camp. At least if we fight, we feel as though we belong to something that is trying to bring about change."

I wondered if they were aware of how people in the West view them and as I had done with the Hezbollah youth, I asked, "How do you feel when people describe you as terrorists?" They did not seem upset by the question and actually seemed to think that it was fair to ask.

There was one boy who had not spoken until this moment. He had short black hair and broad shoulders. He had the face of a child, but like the other boys, the stubble on his face showed that he was much older. He explained, "We get used to the West, they cover one eye and see by the other. What they see is the violence, but they do not see the context. They don't see that we want to study and get jobs. They don't see that we use computers, and we enjoy movies. I don't think I have ever seen on CNN or BBC images of Palestinians playing the same sports as young people in the United States. Do you agree?"

He was right. The images we see on television frequently depict the small percentage of Palestinians who take up arms and fight. However, the struggle of hundreds of thousands of Palestinians who have peacefully tried to adapt to dire conditions inside the camp are rarely seen and their voices almost never heard. The media embraces the image of a Hamas soldier wrapped in a head scarf, brandishing an AK-47. The audience craves reinforcement of its image that Palestinian youth hold rocket propelled grenades instead of books. These images do exist and they are real, but they are the extreme minority. I nodded and said, "I think there is some truth to that." Upon returning to the United States three months later, I wasn't surprised to see numerous titles on the shelves of bookstores addressing this very issue of the media's misleading portrayal of the Islamic world.

"There is *a lot* of truth to that. You know we watch satellite television; we get that here in the camp. We fight because we have to, but people don't understand that. I think the United States government does not want to show these images of Muslims. They only want people to see images of fighting. If they want to call us terrorists, it does not matter to us anymore; we are used to it. If terrorism is going to school, playing football, and wanting to bring about change, then fine, we are terrorists. But I don't think that this is what they see when they call us terrorists."

With so few opportunities, Palestinian youth have all the free time in the world. However, times have changed significantly since their parents experienced the same dilemma of an overabundance of time. While the allure of the mosque and the extremist Islamist madrassahs remains, Palestinian kids today are also tempted by new alternatives. The Internet cafés, satellite televisions, and mobile phones have become their information mosques. While terrorists use these information highways to spread their messages, the inclination to use technology primarily for social and recreational purposes actually marginalizes the hostile messages. The youth have autonomy in what they choose to look at over these communications networks, and with every day of use comes increased exposure to new perspectives and ideas. The Google Age has allowed them to run wild with their curiosities as they delve into the realms of modern digital, audio, and visual communications networks.

The same day I met General Maqdah, I was also received by Fathi Abou El Ardaat, the leader of the Ain al-Hilwah youth union. He was not dressed formally, but instead wore black pants with a white-and-black button-down shirt that was ornate with a checkered pattern. His gray beard was thinly trimmed and his forehead was unusually high. In the corner of his office, he had erected the Palestinian flag. In the top corner of his office, I noticed photos of PLO president Mahmoud Abbas and the late Yasir Arafat that hung in adjacent positions. This was a different kind of meeting from the one I'd had with the general. There was no concealing the location, frisking, or Rambo-like display of terrorist weaponry.

Fathi was a particularly impassioned speaker who didn't waste any time. After introductions and his detailed summary of the Palestinian Youth Union's mission, he jumped to the topic of Palestinian suffering. In an almost scientific manner he informed me that there are four stages of suffering for the Palestinian student. I assumed he would focus on suffering at the hands of America and Israel.

Accompanying his words with careful gesticulations reminiscent of an orchestra conductor, he explained that the first problem is that the Palestinian has a difficult time continuing his studies and he is jammed in a class with too many students and no supplies. Making matters worse, he explained, it is difficult for most Palestinian students to pay school fees and receive the necessary attention in the classroom.

Fathi described the second stage of Palestinian suffering as the period after completing high school or university. He explained that there are no jobs for the educated, and without the job prospects a young man cannot begin to imagine finding a wife and building a family. He reminded me that the Lebanese government has regulations that deprive Palestinians the opportunity of working as doctors or engineers. He explained that while this is beginning to change, the Palestinian workers still do not get the benefits of health insurance, pension, and vacations. They are not protected.

As Fathi continued his explanation, he seemed to have forgotten about the other two stages of Palestinian suffering that he had mentioned to me. He had initially focused on what he perceived to be the priorities. Once I reminded him, he then went into the usual and expected tirade about the United States and Israel.

I found it very interesting that this is not what he had emphasized in our conversation. In fact, I'd had to remind him to mention the United States and Israel. The fact is, Palestinian youth are two generations removed from the days when they lived in their homeland. Most Palestinian young people do not expect to return home; instead, they are more pragmatic, interested in improving their everyday lives. They blame America and Israel by default, but they do it largely to maintain their sense of identity.

Fathi seemed to represent an example of someone in the older generation who had actually been impacted by the youth. Every day he surrounded himself with hundreds of young Palestinians and undoubtedly the transformation in that generation's mind-set had affected him. Perhaps he had a different perspective on violence than the general.

Just as I was on my way out of the camp, my slow stride was disrupted by a fight that broke out just in front of me. While I didn't know why the two boys were fighting, I saw that one was armed with an AK-47, while the other had only clenched fists. Recognizing the potential for escalation, some of their peers quickly stepped in to break up the fight. The dire conditions lend themselves to heightened tensions, and because so many youth belong to rival groups, it is not surprising that schoolyard quarrels often end with gunshots.

I continued strolling down the narrow alleyways that I had been chased through when I initially entered the camp. As I weaved through these alleys, I encountered a seemingly endless number of children who had gathered in large numbers to see me out. One of the girls proudly displayed a vine of grapes that she had acquired and asked me if I wanted one. One of the young boys gave me a high-five as he leaned against the cement wall. As I looked at their faces, I couldn't help but wonder: Will the cycle of humiliation never end? Will these children become yet another generation of Palestinian youth who find in a rocket-propelled grenade the antidote for their fractured souls?

CHAPTER 9

BABIES IN THE BA'ATH PARTY

SYRIA, 2005

Neither Iran nor Lebanon was without its challenges for me. Still, in both places I witnessed vibrant youth cultures that gave me hope. In Iran, where the government tries vehemently to suppress its population, young people find ways to express themselves and enjoy their adolescence. In Lebanon, the opportunities were minimal, but young people there brought about the first self-made transition to democracy in the Middle East. Even in Palestinian refugee camps, I found militants who showed me that despite indoctrination and military training, they were simply interested in making a place for themselves in society that gave them greater meaning than being unemployed in the slums of the refugee camps.

But Syria seemed different. Syria has long been one of the most nationalistic societies in the Middle East; indeed it is the birthplace of Arab nationalism. Only in Iran and Egypt is this nationalistic quality so deeply and historically entrenched. The concept of Greater Syria was one of the earliest expressions of this type of nationalism, which took off after the First World War. The concept called for Syria to exercise sovereignty over present-day Lebanon, Israel, Jordan, and even parts of Turkey. Driven in large part by this nationalist spirit, Syria competed with its ally and rival Egypt throughout the early part of the cold war for influence and leadership in the region. During this period, the Syrian people reveled in this nationalist spirit and were not the closed society that they are today.

In March of 1963, the shift toward totalitarian autocracy began. Just one month after a Ba'ath revolution in Iraq, revolutionaries in Syria proclaimed a new government under its Ba'ath ideology. The Ba'ath Party had been founded eighteen years earlier by Michel Aflaq and Zaki al-Arsuzi. Aflaq was a Christian from Damascus who had built a simple life for himself as a schoolteacher, and al-Arsuzi was a Sunni with the same background. Both had been radicalized by Arab nationalist sentiments during the Second World War and each had formed his own group. It was the merging of these two groups that led to the official establishment of the Ba'ath Party. The movement was largely secular and was intended to be a revival of Arab nationalism with a strong emphasis on socialist ideologies.

In this sense, Ba'athism was a deviation from and even a contradiction of the Islamist leanings of more extremist movements, most notably those of the Muslim Brotherhood in Syria and the Shi'a Islamist movements in southern Iraq. The Ba'ath movement centered itself around the concepts of pan-Arabism, and socialism, but also emphasized expulsion of foreigners from the Arab world.

When Syria unexpectedly suffered a crushing defeat in the Six Day War in 1967, the true reach of the autocratic leadership was put to the test. In November 1970, with the government weakened and the leadership vulnerable, Minister of Defense Hafez al-Assad undertook a bloodless coup in Syria that became known as the Corrective Revolution. After Hafez al-Assad seized power, it was not long before the system in Syria degenerated into a police state and eventually a totalitarian dictatorship.

*　　*　　*

Hafez al-Assad reigned from 1970 until his death in 2000. His rule was brutal and his totalitarian grip was firm. A simple man from an impoverished background, Hafez al-Assad rose to power through military opportunism. While president of Syria, he transformed the country into a cult of personality centered around himself. Opposition was forbidden, dissent was outlawed, and insubordination was punishable by death. There was no freedom of speech, assembly, or opportunity. While failing to achieve a degree of autocracy that was on quite the same level as in neighboring Iraq, Hafez al-Assad's regime ran a close second to Saddam Hussein's. Al-Assad viewed himself as the sole ruler and symbol not only of Syrian power, but also of the Arab world. He assumed the leadership role in the Arab world against Israel and exploited the Arab-Israeli conflict to project his commitment to Arab nationalism.

Domestically, Hafez al-Assad used fear tactics to keep his country united and the vision of Greater Syria alive. As a member of the Allawite sect of Islam, he ruled from a demographic that constitutes no more than 13 percent of the Syrian population. The Allawites are most similar to the Shi'ite sect of Islam, with whom they broke official ties in the ninth century. Forming a separate sect of Islam and basing themselves in Allepo, Allawites emerged as a parallel but not rival sect to the Shi'a. Al-Assad was constantly preoccupied with opposition from the Sunni, who comprise 74 percent of Syria's population. As a result, he tightened his grip on control, doing everything in his power to suppress the population, silence potential voices, and socialize the next generation of Sunni youth into a culture of fear.

As part of this culture of fear, Syrian youth have been taught to believe that democracy is dangerous and precipitates conflict. During the Lebanese civil war, the regime linked the violence in Lebanon with the concept of democracy. It is this linkage that has created yet another difference in the thinking between Syrian and Lebanese youth.

While the Lebanese youth associated democracy with American and Israeli foreign policy, young Syrians associated it with Lebanon and violence.

Whether they were part of the minority or part of the Sunni majority, Syrian parents instilled in their children the notion that if they looked throughout the Middle East, they would see that Syria was an anomaly. In the 1980s, Lebanon and Israel were at war, Iran and Iraq were at war, and the Syrian regime exploited these neighboring conflicts to remind the people that it held the key to their security. To some extent the parents became the agents of the regime, training their children to believe that it was best to keep their distance from politics.

In the early 1990s, the ailing Hafez al-Assad, who had a history of heart problems, announced his son Basil al-Assad to be his rightful successor. Preparation had been undertaken for Basil's ascension to power and the country had been decorated in posters proclaiming his capacity to rule. The planned succession was interrupted, however, when Basil al-Assad died unexpectedly in a car accident. Challenged with grieving over his son and maintaining an al-Assad dynasty, Hafez turned to his youngest son, Bashar, who at the time was working as an ophthalmologist in London.

The weakest member of the family and the least experienced in politics, Bashar al-Assad was groomed for the presidency beginning in 1994. After being rapidly promoted through the military hierarchy, Bashar ascended to the presidency upon his father's death in 2000. Bashar attempted to adopt the style of his father, but had neither the capacity nor the experience to replicate his firm grip on society. Instead, Bashar's hastened rise to power and inherent weakness offered a glimmer of hope in Syria. It created an opening for youth empowerment in Syria that saw a new era of expression and social indulgence that simply had not existed under Bashar's father.

While proceeding slowly, the youth in Syria are experiencing an awakening. For most of their lives they have lived in fear and have been socialized to go through the motions of life without ever questioning the status quo. They still live in some fear, but things are changing. Amid a highly nonsecular society that seems unfamiliar with democracy, the youth of Syria are beginning to embrace the progressive characteristics that are innate to youth around the world. While they are straggling behind youth in Lebanon and Iran, they are moving in the same direction. Under Bashar al-Assad, they have movement and avenues for expression that they didn't have even five years ago.

But still Syria was different. My introduction to the Syrian world largely came from two girls, and as we walked in the streets in the western city of Homs the stares came from all directions.

My ability to be subtle and keep a lower profile was not in my hands. I was with two Syrian cousins that I had befriended at a beach party several weeks earlier in Jiye, a small city just south of Beirut. I knew the girls were relatively liberal because I had met them at one of the wildest and craziest parties I went to in Lebanon; in fact, it was the same beach party that I had attended my second night in Lebanon. The girls had been hanging out by the bar, relying on nearby men to buy them drinks.

I was uncomfortable with the staring, but the cousins—Haifa and Maya—seemed to take some joy in being stared at. In Lebanon, women loved being stared at, too, but it was usually to show off their latest designer clothing. In Lebanon, women who wear the hejab are a minority and those who wear the full chador are an even smaller minority. For Haifa and Maya, dressing as Westerners ready for the nightclub was not about vanity. It was something of far greater substance. Like the girls in Iran, it was all about passive resistance.

And they really stuck out in Homs, an oil town known for the Sunni conservatism of many of its residents. The average women in

Homs are covered from head to toe in the full black nikhab and face covering, regardless of the excruciating heat.

The journey from Beirut to Homs was not long. I got a cab in Beirut, and three hours and ten dollars later I had made the journey across the northern border of Lebanon. The border was its own traffic jam, lined for several kilometers with eight-wheeled trucks waiting for their chance to cross. After caving to international pressure and withdrawing from Lebanon, the Syrian regime had tightened its borders to economically punish Lebanon. As I crossed into Syria, I could see the face of the Syrian dictator, Bashar al-Assad, towering over the border post as if he was keeping an eye on neighboring Lebanon. From the moment I stepped into Syria, I could feel the aura of a police state. The smell of fear was in the air. It was in the faces of the people and the diligence of the border guards.

Now I was in Homs, and Haifa and Maya were turning heads left and right. Given that Homs is a predominantly Sunni city, this wasn't surprising. In Syria, the Sunni may be the majority of the country, but they are subjected to the less conservative minority Shi'a that control the country. Haifa and Maya wore something different. Haifa wore a tight pink T-shirt that was nearly sleeveless. The shirt was short and reached just down to the belt of her Western-style blue jeans. Maya wore something similar, except her shirt was maroon instead of pink. Both of them wore a tremendous amount of makeup, giving their cheeks a rosy red coloring and accentuating their eyes. I was with two beautiful girls in a townful of burkhas.

These were strong girls. As we walked through the Old City and the Homs Souq, I watched them endure look after disapproving look. I watched elderly women yelling things at them in Arabic. Haifa and Maya represent a generation of Syrian girls who push the limit. They are glued to their satellite television, the Internet, and their mobile phone. Unlike their mothers, these girls have the access to know what they are missing out on. Society has changed and technology has opened their eyes in ways that their parents cannot begin to understand. They know what they have been deprived of. They watch Western movies, they hear stories, and some of it they witness firsthand in the underground nightlife. Knowing what is out there only sparks their curiosity. The girls insisted on showing me the few sites in the city—the mosque and the souq. It didn't take the girls long to open up to me, in large part, I suspect, because as a nonmember of their community I was safe. Maya told me about problems she was having at home and when I pressed, she explained that her father beat her. It was impossible to know how to respond; all I could tell her was that whether the laws of Syrian protect her or not, such abuse is wrong and she deserves better. These domestic violence stories always made me cringe and it was far too frequently that I heard about them.

Like their counterparts in Iran, Haifa and Maya deviate from the strict norms that the government and the older generations try to enforce in an act of expression. When Haifa and Maya walk among men and women who scowl at them for their perceived deviant behavior, it is a way for them to say without any words that the times are changing and they don't accept the status quo.

My new female friends were not anomalies. I visited almost every province in Syria and I always saw these same resilient girls. They stood out and they didn't have to speak; their message was loud and clear. Haifa and Maya are representatives of a generation of Syrian girls who reject the old way of life. They are deeply religious and believe in their Sunni identity, but they see religion as something largely private. While they may not see or believe in a separation of religion and politics, they would like to separate religion from their social and recreational activity. Most females in Syria do not take this to the extreme that Haifa and Maya did, but the vast majority behave differently when they are out of their parents' sight. The best chances for them to do this were in the Syrian nightclubs, where they could throw their hejabs in the corner as if it were a coatroom and dance the night away, forgetting at least temporarily about the society they come from.

* * *

In addition to what they see in the media and through the Internet, Syrian youth have been tremendously impacted by what they see in neighboring Lebanon.

Because Syria and Lebanon are comprised of the same ethnic and religious groups, however, it is easy to assume that the two are similar. In terms of population, Syria is nearly five times the size of Lebanon. In a country of nearly nineteen million people, Syria is more than 90 percent Muslim, of which 74 percent are Sunni. Yet Syria is actually run by the 16 percent of the population that is Allawi and Shi'a.

The Sunni population of Syria is notoriously more fundamentalist than the Shi'a and Allawi minority, whose political sentiments are based largely on strategic considerations.

Because of their small numbers, only 3 percent of the total population, Christians play only a minor role in national politics. In Aleppo, however, it is a different story. This northwestern Syrian city is more than 20 percent Christian, making it the second largest Christian population in the Middle East behind only Beirut.

Aleppo is Syria's second most populous city, but the Christians were not hard to find. There were communities located near the churches and when I walked through the old marketplace, I simply looked for crosses on the wall. The Christians share similar perspectives on politics and the government with the Shi'a and Allawites. Given the historic animosity that has existed between Christians and Shi'a Muslims in Lebanon, I was surprised to find such agreement right next door in Syria. Christian, Shi'a, and Allawi Syrians all have the concerns often found among minority groups, and none of them want to see their country transformed into a Sunni Islamic Republic, which many believe would be the likely result if the current regime were to fall. For each of these minorities, the current regime is likely to be the best deal they are going to get.

Unlike their counterparts in Lebanon, the Christian youth in Syria are a complacent minority. Other than the Allawite, who have benefited the most from the al-Assad regime, the Syrian Christians are arguably the group that offers the most support to the president. Such pragmatic support is not illogical, as Christians in Syria practice freely, enjoy what limited Syrian opportunities exist, and believe they have the protection of the president. When speaking of political reform, many young Christians, Shi'a, and Allawite in Syria argue that al-Assad has become less autocratic; as examples, they point to al-Assad choosing not to ban the Syrian Socialist Party and decreeing that the prime minister does not have to be a member of the Ba'ath Party. They are comfortable with this degree of choice, although most assert that they would still vote for Bashar. In the words of one Shi'ite student from the western city of Latakkia, "If there is an election between someone who we don't know and Bashar, for sure we will select Bashar because he is good for the Shi'a. We will vote him because we know that as a minority he will protect us."

Many Syrian Christians also believe that establishing Lebanese-style democracy in Syria would create a chaotic path to catastrophe for their community. Fearing the loss of minority rights to majority rule, Syrian Christians looked unfavorably upon the political standing of Lebanese Christians. I spoke to numerous Christian youth from Syria who had traveled to Lebanon and some who had even studied there. Over coffee with a young Christian in Aleppo, I was told, "Even though there are more Christians in the smaller country of Lebanon, we still feel like we are not safe and we experience great discomfort."

There is a popular belief held by Syrian Christians that if elections were free and yielded majority rule, the outcome would be a fundamentalist Sunni government that would oppress the Christian community throughout Syria. They fear what they describe as an "Iranian scenario." Although they dread a Sunni rather than Shi'a majority, their imagined loss of comfort is the same. This type of association of

Iran with backwardness was something I had first noticed in Lebanon. The youth of both these countries have the same fears and anxieties toward the regime as we do in America.

While these are the sentiments of most minorities in Syria, it is by no means universal to all of them. There are some who detest Bashar, there are some who want the Lebanese-style system, and there are some who support the Syrian Socialist Party. Oftentimes this depends on circumstance: whom they live near, the political sentiments of their parents, and the demographics of their town or city.

But most youth have been socialized into a society where they became accustomed to accepting the outcome without asking questions. For instance, while their neighboring Christians, Shi'a, Sunni, and Druze in Lebanon were fighting each other as well as enduring massive discrimination, Syrians watched carefully and came to value their own sense of relative security. Their conception of democracy was constructed around the situation in Lebanon and they came to accept what they perceived to be a safer status quo.

My Lebanese friends told me on several occasions that I needed to be careful in Syria. They told me that I would be followed around, monitored, and watched by Syrian intelligence. From what they described to me, I thought it would be just like my experience in Iran. But the vigilance was more discreet: I wasn't watched all the time, I never noticed myself being followed around, and it seemed—at least on the surface—as if I operated freely in Syria.

I had traveled to Homs with Maya and Haifa without any problems and took that as an indication that Syrian intelligence was unaware of my presence in the country. With this air of confidence, I traveled eight hours north to the northwestern province of Aleppo. The city is built around the ruins of the Aleppo citadel, the once proud fortress that protected the old city. The sheer size of Aleppo is most visible atop this citadel, and when it is time to pray the echoing sound of the call for prayer reverberates almost in succession from what must be at least several dozen mosques. The streets of Aleppo were intriguing, lined with shops of all varieties, and differently than other cities I had been to, there was something calm and orderly about this northwestern city. The roofs of shops and homes were covered with satellite dishes; every street corner seemed to be decorated with advertisements, posters of partially naked women whose faces had been replaced by the faces of American celebrities.

Later, as I stood near the famous citadel in Aleppo, two Syrian guys approached me and invited me to an underground gay rave. I didn't attend the party, but I asked them about Syria's gay community and how they organized raves. The boys explained to me that they walk through crowded markets and send out Bluetooth messages on their phone advertising gay parties, which they hold in abandoned buildings, people's homes, and even public parks. They dance all night and sometimes get several hundred people to attend.

By the end of my first day in Aleppo, I had met with a group of three young guys in a café, talked to a group of young Christians about what it is like to be the minority in Syria, and had the chance to speak with Sunni, Shi'a, and Allawi youth in various parts of the city. That night, I went to bed surprised at how easy it had been to talk to people and how fortunate it was that I wasn't being followed.

Back at the hotel, around ten-fifteen P.M., the man at the front desk told me over the phone that I had a visitor. My guest was about forty years old, he had a full beard, and his nose was nothing shy of gigantic. He was also extremely fat and seemed to waddle rather than walk. He introduced himself as Rashid and said he had been asked to "tend" to me for the evening. I should have been angry at this, but my confusion led me to be more curious than anything else. He wore a suit and a tie and looked very official, and I was tired and not thinking straight; so when he asked me to come with him, I followed. I still found the whole thing more peculiar than scary. He hadn't told me anything about himself and was kind of weird and evasive when I would ask questions.

We got in his black Land Cruiser, with its fine interior and leather seats, and we drove for a while down some narrow streets. At one point, Rashid sideswiped a car, cracked its mirror, and kept going. We were in what appeared to be the older part of Aleppo. The cobblestone roads were too narrow for two-way traffic; every time we saw a car coming from the opposite direction, Rashid would put the car in reverse and back off the street until the car had passed. After about fifteen minutes of driving, we arrived at our destination. It was what appeared to be a rather elegant restaurant. The crowd looked highly sophisticated. The men all wore suits and the women were adorned in elaborate head coverings. The restaurant had an indoor/outdoor feel to it, with plants growing from the floor and a semiopened rooftop. Despite the elegance of the restaurant, the air was filled with overlapping clouds of smoke that emanated from the flavored tobacco pipes on each table. It was fairly late at night, but when we walked in, we were seated in our own private section of the restaurant. What was going on here? Who the hell was this guy?

He ordered a nargilah, or hookah as it is also known, and asked me if there was anything I wanted to drink. What if he was going to poison me? I'd seen the movies; I asked for water. Rashid then pulled three cell phones out of his pocket and put them all on the table, as many people in the Middle East do. But why did he have three?

"So what is your plan in Syria?" he asked me. "Who are you meeting with while you are here?"

I told him the same thing I told the Syrian Embassy in London: that I have always been interested in Syria's ancient history. In what was my standard cover, I explained that I had been an archaeology major as an undergraduate.

He sat and nodded his head. His phone rang and he spoke for a bit. I didn't understand any of it, but it sounded like official business of some sort. His questions then became both stranger and more direct. "Who have you spoken to since you have been here? What is your business in Syria? How much do you know about Syria?" It was all very ominous. I realized then that I had been followed earlier in the day. My behavior would have aroused suspicion: I had lingered around the schools in Aleppo, wandered the marketplaces, and chatted with people in the public venues, interviewing young Syrian students about reform and what they wanted for Syria. Though I was eventually taken back to my hotel, this late-night dinner with "Rashid" was Syrian intelligence's way of sending me the message that I was not operating as freely as I wanted to believe.

Syrians in the northwestern province of Aleppo had been relatively open with me, but this was more a tribute to the city's demographics than anything else: The relative diversity of Aleppo lent itself to pro-gressiveness. As I traveled back down south to Sunni cities that I had skipped over when traveling from Homs to Aleppo, I found a very dif-ferent scene. I visited a number of Sunni towns and cities in a journey that would lead me to the Sunni city of Hama.

I took several detours on the way to Hama, in part to see more of the country, but also because some of the world's most spectacular historical sites were situated between Aleppo and Hama. Among these sites are the famous Apamea gates and more than seven hundred "dead cities" from various periods of ancient Syria. Most are comprised of portions of churches, schools, courthouses, and homes. Locals, mostly Bedouins, had moved into some of the ruins, using parts of them to store sheep and goats. The dead cities are a remarkable testament to the Byzantine Empire, and some date back as far as 4000 B.C. The ruins ranged from magnificent arches and temples, to a couple pieces of limestone half-buried in the dirt. Some of the structures were easily recognizable, while others could have been a granary or part of a cemetery. There were no guidebooks to this place; it was miles and miles of seemingly endless village rubble. The structures were poorly preserved and I always proceeded gingerly, never really sure if a snake would come out of a hole or a brick would fall on my head. I went to as many of these lost cities as I could, but after a while, they all started to look the same and climbing over ancient homes, mosques, and churches grew tiresome and repetitive.

I had been to Jumayi, Serjilla, and Duvia, but everyone had kept talking to me about Al-Bara, which, in addition to being the largest of the dead cities, was also the most historically significant. My increasingly bored driver, who had already taken me to several of the cities, seemed tired of making these trips in the blistering heat, but when I offered him a bit more money, he seemed more than happy.

As we pulled into a cul-de-sac, I asked if I could leave my things in the car. This was really stupid of me, as these "things" included my computer, my books, and my notes. But I thought I would be right back.

"Barja baad saa," I told the driver. I would be back in one hour.

"OK, just one hour. Otherwise it is more money," he reminded me. Everyone was always trying to squeeze me for an extra few hundred Syrian pounds here and there.

At first glance, the ruins of Al-Bara were not particularly striking. It looked more like a bunch of rocks buried in vines, trees, and shrubbery. There was no clear passageway to walk through the ruins as there had been in the other dead cities, of which Al-Bara is both the most extensively preserved and also the largest. Its six square kilometers all look mostly the same and unlike the other dead cities, one can really lose one's bearings when inside. The city's history is rich and eerie, dating back to the fourth century A.D. Al-Bara once stood as one of the most significant cities along the trade route from the northern city of Antioch to the southern gateways of Apamea. The city was of particular value because of its rich and arable land that enabled its Eastern Christian inhabitants to cultivate it into a major center for olive oil and fine wines.

Al-Bara initially endured the turbulence created by Islamic invasions, but eventually it succumbed to the Crusaders in the eleventh century. Al-Bara became a notorious base for Crusader attacks in western and central Syria. In one of their most infamous campaigns, the Crusaders launched a horrific cannibalistic attack on Ma'arat an-Nu'aman in 1098. Tales of their brutality and consumption of the victims led potential victims to fear them until they were driven out twenty-five years later.

I continued to push deeper and deeper into these vast ruins. But when I stopped to place my camera on a rock to use the self-timer to take a photo of myself in front of a small pyramidal structure, I suddenly realized I couldn't remember where my driver was. I had walked in so many directions and turned around so many times that I had become hopelessly disoriented. I had already been gone for at least an hour and even when I stood atop an elevated surface, I still could not see my driver anywhere.

At first I didn't become too concerned because I assumed I would find my way back, but hours went by and I could not. I finally came across a paved road and was able to flag a man down on his moped. He was young, probably nineteen years old, and he wore a red-and-white checkered Kaffiyeh scarf. He was definitely Sunni. He could sense that I was concerned and in my broken Arabic I asked for his help. He gestured me onto the moped and we were off to find my driver.

He took me on a hazardously fast motorcycle ride throughout the six square kilometers of ruins as we drove over dirt paths, paved roads, and even small rocks in some cases. But after about an hour, we still had not found the driver.

This young man seemed like he would have helped me all day, but he decided that before going on, we should take a break to get some tea. We drove out of the ruins into the neighboring village until we reached a tea shop, which I would later learn was owned by his brother. I figured we had bonded on his moped, so I thought I might as well ask him a bit about politics. Up until this point, I had had a difficult time getting a lot of the Sunnis to open up to me in Syria. They was so different from Lebanese Sunni, who were eager to rant and rave about their politics. But my unnamed driver was with me in the middle of nowhere in some random tea shop. Perhaps he would be more candid with me.

We chitchatted a bit. I would ask him questions like "What do you think of Bashar al-Assad?" and he would give me benign answers that revealed very little. I didn't want to risk offending the only person who could help me find my way to my driver, but I decided to be frank with him. Because he looked so young, I felt a certain level of comfort with him. I was actually surprised to hear that he was in fact twenty-five years old.

I mentioned to him that it seemed Syrians didn't care much for talking politics. He explained that this is the Syrian way. He didn't elaborate, so I pushed him a bit. He sipped his tea a couple of times. Then he told me why Syrians live in fear.

His name was Mazen, and his family had originally been from the Sunni city of Hama. Mazen was the youngest looking twenty-five-year-old I had ever seen. Hints of a beard offered some veneer of age over his baby face. His eyes were piercing and large, but with his skinny neck, the kaffiyeh scarf he wore on his head made his face look minuscule. My ears perked up when I heard him say "Hama," because it was my next destination after the dead cities.

Mazen explained that he was three years old when the Sunnis began living in fear. He told me that Hama has an eerie silence to it and made sure I understood why.

One of Syria's largest cities, Hama has had a dark and a tumultuous relationship with the al-Assad regime. In the late 1970s and early 1980s, Syria entered into the Lebanese civil war, first on the side of the Maronites and later on the side of the Muslims. Dissenters in Syria blamed the Syrian government for squandering its resources and military on a war in neighboring Lebanon. Creating greater pressure on the regime, it was also at this time that Syria was rumored to be providing funds to the Partiya Karkerên Kurdistan (PKK) rebels in southern Turkey. These two external endeavors led to a rise in the outlawed but popular Muslim Brotherhood. Founded by Hassan al-Banna in 1928, the Muslim Brotherhood is a predominantly Sunni extremist organization that began in Egypt and soon spread all throughout the Middle East. With Syria weakened by its entanglements abroad and growing domestic opposition, the Muslim Brotherhood claimed new members each day.

Sporadic terrorist activities by the Muslim Brotherhood against government sites in Syria soon escalated into more destructive attacks on Syrian infrastructure. At the beginning of the summer of 1980, the Syrian government announced that anyone found to be holding membership in the Muslim Brotherhood would be punished by death. On June 26, 1980, in response, the Muslim Brotherhood staged an assassination attempt on Syrian president Hafez al-Assad. While al-Assad survived the attack, his bodyguard was killed and he became extremely paranoid in the months that followed.

For several months, there was an escalation of state arrests of prominent Sunnis and reprisal attacks from the Muslim Brotherhood that eventually led to an all-out Sunni insurrection in February 1982. Sunni extremists, led by the Muslim Brotherhood, declared the city of Hama de-Ba'athified and took over government buildings.

Hafez al-Assad was enraged that his totalitarian grip seemed to be slipping to extremists. He would not stand for it. His brutal response, though directed at the Muslim Brotherhood, would leave a scar on the entire Sunni population of Syria. Beginning on February 2, 1982, al-Assad ordered the shelling and destruction of the predominantly Sunni city of Hama. The city was leveled and those who couldn't escape were murdered. In the end, the regime killed twenty thousand people, mostly Sunnis.

News of what had happened in Hama spread like wildfire. Sunnis all around the country became fearful that their own cities might be attacked next. The few Sunni political groups that existed went dormant. Hafez al-Assad took the opportunity to remind the Syrian people what would happen if his politics were questioned. Hama became his way of evoking fear, his empirical evidence that he would not tolerate dissent, in particular from Sunni extremists.

"I was only three years old when it happened, but I remember," Mazen said. "And I remember the years that followed in even greater detail."

I could hear the emotion in his voice; this was clearly hard for him to talk about. "From that moment on, we were told that politics are to be ignored and that we should not think about these things."

I finally understood why Syrian Sunnis were apolitical to the point of total disengagement from the public sphere. Ultimately, this overwhelming majority of the population had been intimidated into accepting the same skewed interpretation of Syrian politics that kept their Shi'a, Allawi, and Christian countrymen so docile. Instead of confronting the fear and repression perpetrated by the al-Assad regime, Sunnis choose to look next on the other side of the fence and delude themselves into believing that the grass is most certainly not greener in Lebanon. Like most Syrians, the Sunnis have been conditioned to look at the economic and sectarian troubles in Lebanon and blame politics and democracy as the root causes of these problems. Sunnis living in Syria would often joke with me that "the problem with Lebanon is every ten people is a political party."

I wanted to ask Mazen more questions, but I really needed to find the car. We had lost track of time and I was now almost two hours late for my driver. The only thing I was banking on was that since I hadn't paid him anything yet, he would take the risk and wait for me. There was so much going through my mind. All of my things were in the car, so I was worried about losing my computer, camera, and belongings. Part of me also felt guilty that the driver would think I had scammed him. More than anything, I felt so helpless and lost. Those moments in the ruins when I didn't know where I was and the uncertainty of how I would get back to my driver had made me afraid. This was still a country I didn't understand.

I wondered if it might help to draw a picture of the area where my driver had parked. After all, this had worked when I was searching for the synagogue in Iran. This idea largely arose from the fact that I was having a really difficult time explaining what I meant by *cul-de-sac*. I drew a picture of the cul-de-sac where we had parked and a small triangular ruin that I remembered seeing near the pavement. This was now the third time in my travels throughout the Middle East that I played Pictionary.

I must be pretty good, because Mazen seemed to know exactly what I was describing. We got back on his motorcycle and he drove very fast down hills and through the ruins. I thought we could easily crash—and at moments thought we certainly would—but Mazen seemed to know what he was doing. His head wrap kept getting in my face as we were driving, and it was probably better that I couldn't see anything.

After fifteen minutes of barreling through the dead city at breakneck speed, I could see my driver's car in the distance. I screamed his name three times, and finally, and luckily, I heard a beep from his horn as if to acknowledge that he heard me. I was relieved. I offered Mazen money for his help, but he wouldn't accept. I kept trying to say that it was a token of gratitude, but he wouldn't take money.

He looked at me, shook my hand, and said, *"Shukran, habibi."*

I didn't understand why he should be the one to say thanks when he was the one who had helped me—and I told him as much. He explained that life in Syria is difficult and there are virtually no opportunities for young people to talk about their dreams and their hopes. Mazen was thanking me for having shown an interest, for having cared enough to ask. He was saying thanks for listening.

These words were very powerful and reminded me simple and even brief human interactions can transform opinions.

I wondered what Hama was going to be like. Mazen's story was chilling, and having seen his eyes tear up as he told his story gave my visit more gravity. But I had one more stop before heading to Hama. I came to the small Sunni town of Al-Marrad on the way to Hama to say farewell to my driver. From Al-Marrad I would have to find my own way and a new driver. The town had very little going on besides a small marketplace. This wasn't the traditional souq that I had seen; instead, it was a very primitive marketplace with blankets instead of shops. Al-Marrad's main street was a poorly maintained dirt road, and judging from the stores I saw on my walk, this was a very impoverished and traditional community. Even the mosques were small and unimpressive, especially compared to the grand mosque that I had seen in Aleppo or the shrines that I had visited in Homs. They almost looked like miniature models of a real mosque.

I'd been to Afghanistan and seen women in the burkha, but I have never seen people so covered in my entire life. The women in this town wore a full black chador and revealed nothing, not even the hands, which were covered with black gloves. Even their eyes were concealed by the black cloth that completely covered their faces.

Had it not been for my conversations in Iran about hejab, I never would have understood where this came from. I supposed that in Al-Marrad this was what women—or the men who forced them to wear this attire—viewed as modest. No matter how much I had been told about the concept of covering, I had trouble accepting such an extreme approach. It just looked uncomfortable and demeaning. I tried to talk to three different women but was ignored each time. The third time, I was spotted by three young guys playing backgammon at the Al-Marrad version of a convenience store. They were laughing and one gestured me over.

They looked a lot more comfortable than the women, as they sat in their pants, short-sleeve shirts that I could see through the thin fabric of their robes, and sunglasses. And unlike the women, they were willing to talk to me. I told them about Mazen and this seemed to really open them up. They explained to me that living in a small but religious town like Al-Marrad, they could be more vocal because the intelligence units spent their time in the cities and they tended to stay away from the most religious pockets of Syria. Syrian intelligence weren't worried about a small town with dirt roads and minimal infrastructure as posing much of a threat to the establishment.

They were young and each wore a long white robe over his clothes and a red-and-white checkered kaffiyeh attached to his head with two black rings. They explained to me that in Syria, politics is taboo.

"What we care about is Syria, we are Syrian," one of the boys said to me.

"And what do you want for Syria?" I asked.

He explained that they don't want what they see next door in Lebanon. He described Lebanon as a place with too much democracy and too many political parties. But reform was something that this group of boys wanted. They were not opposed to democracy, but they didn't want too much of it. Instead, they asserted that reform is something that must come slowly.

I asked them how they felt as Sunnis in a country ruled by Shi'a and Allawite. I was making assumptions that Syria and Lebanon were similar and they called me out on this. Syria has a far deeper nationalist identity than Lebanon and one of the boys explained that "Shi'a, Sunni, Allawite, Christians, we are all Syrian brothers. We are Syrian first and Sunni second." Like many of the Iranians I spent time with, Syrians believed in country first, clan second.

Hama was not like the historical graveyard that Mazen had described. In fact, it looked quite the opposite, lively and with a carnival feel to it. There were tons of street venders in Hama, selling everything from kebab and popcorn to sweets of varying kinds. The streets were overcrowded with other venders as well, but the scene looked less like a market and more like a tag sale. People drove like lunatics and just watching everyone cross the street made me nervous, especially when there were kids. At one point it took me at least fifteen minutes to cross a roundabout, never really certain of the traffic pattern to safely walk. The city's action was located along its river, which is adorned with wooden bridges and twenty-foot water wheels. The water wheels are magnificent, towering over the city as if they were skyscrapers. Like a little kid, I marveled at their size. On both sides of the river, kids could be found doing the same.

While Hama didn't resemble a city ridden with trauma, talking to people revealed the existence of certain scars. People in Hama did not want to talk politics. They pretended to know nothing and have no opinions.

In the main park in Hama the setting was calm with women eating ice cream, kids playing soccer, and the shadow of the water wheels casting an almost metaphorical darkness over the whole scene. It was actually hard to imagine that this was the same place that just a few decades prior had been leveled by Hafez al-Assad and turned into a graveyard.

There were some kids around my age playing soccer, so I walked over and asked if I could play too. They immediately wanted to know where I was from and I told them America.

They laughed a bit, indicating what they thought of my likely soccer skills or maybe at the simple fact that I was American. But I'm a pretty nice American and a very good soccer player and I showed off my moves in the park. There were about ten of us and we played for over an hour. They asked me to lunch and I gladly accepted. We sat around a table at a traditional Syrian kebab restaurant with family-style portions. It was the typical fast-food kebab joint with a large leg of meat spinning around on a metal bar. There was something unappetizing about watching my food move around on display and then seeing the butcher slice off parts of it to give to my new friends. As we chowed on our lunch, a crowd of children gathered outside with their faces pressed against the restaurant window. Every time I made eye contact with them, they would run away laughing, leaving only their face prints on the glass, only to return again within seconds.

I asked them what they did for fun and one of the boys, who had a shaved head, said, "I think you will be surprised to hear this." He pointed to a group of completely covered girls, some of whom even had their entire faces covered, and said, "Do you see that over there? Some of those girls, if you are out at the nightclubs, you won't even recognize them. They will dress completely differently and won't even wear head scarves."

"Sometimes we go out to the clubs and the girls wait outside the door with their hejab, and then as soon as they get inside, they remove it," another one of the boys explained to me. I later saw this in a Damascus nightclub, where there was a pile of hejabs in one of the corners of the venue.

I moved to touchier topics and asked about their thoughts on the regime.

One of the boys, who I distinguished from the others because of his unibrow, told me that, differently than Lebanon, they don't care about politics in Syria. He explained that in Lebanon if you ask a young person even two years old, they will identify with a political affiliation. Always eager to distinguish between Lebanon and Syria, one of the other boys noted that they don't want to leave their country like the

Lebanese. They want to live, work, and die in Syria and even if things don't change, they are still going to stay and work. Whatever question I asked, they always found a way to remind me that they were Syrian. One of them explained that even though they are all Sunnis, some of them believe that Syria should be an Islamic Republic, while others don't. But he also reminded me that these differences don't matter because they are all Syrian.

I asked them how careful they needed to be when talking about politics. One of the boys began answering me while his mouth was half-filled with a lamb kebab and said that before, they never used to speak about politics, just girls and sports, because it was safe. Now, they talk about girls and sports because it is more interesting conversation than politics. Again, drawing the parallel with Lebanon, the same kebab-eating boy highlighted the fact that Lebanon is rampant with political parties. He reminded me that in Syria there is only one *real* party, which is the Ba'ath Party, and if one doesn't like the party, then that is only to be talked about in the home.

I wanted to know if they thought Bashar al-Assad was changing things for the better. One of the boys who had been silent now spoke up and told me that things are changing. He explained that while the president is doing his best to change Syria, he still cannot do it very well because of all the mistakes of the past fifteen to twenty years. He continued by explaining that the principals in the Ba'ath party made mistakes that cannot be changed in just two years. The idea that Bashar is doing his best, that reform is moving, but slowly, was very popular among Syrians. They almost seemed to think that reform has been a success, which it clearly has not. It was not that these kids had drunk the Kool-Aid; instead, they were seduced by façades of reform. When I asked them what reforms they have seen, the boys started listing cheaper cars, less expensive mobile phones, greater access to satellite television, and more Internet cafés. These short-term fruits embodied reform for a group of young Syrians with way too much time on their hands.

I asked them about larger reforms, but all I got was a little more detail. Instead of cheaper cars, this time they explained that before Bashar, the tariffs on cars were 255 percent, but now they are only 40 percent. Bashar al-Assad was seducing these youths into thinking that the cheaper cars were synonymous with legitimate reform.

Young Syrians are patient with reform and even content with it in some cases because Bashar al-Assad has shrewdly appealed to what youth care about in the short run. They are enamored of cheap cars, accessible mobile phones, unlimited satellite television, and the spread of the Internet, and they associate all of this with greater freedom and opportunity. Meanwhile, private banking, education, and social reforms remain stagnant. These are the reforms Syria needs for the future, but when I spoke to most Syrian youth, they hadn't really made the distinction between short-term gains and long-term needs.

These guys did mention some changes that could have passed for steps toward reform. In prior years, for example, one could not be in politics without being a member of the Ba'ath Party. Though this has changed, Bashar al-Assad has not quite allowed for multipartyism. Instead, he has permitted small political parties to take part in a symbolic competition.

The youth also seemed to believe that the regime was less focused now on Ba'athist indoctrination. One of them explained to me that in school he used to have to learn about Ba'ath ideology, for instance the pronouncements of Hafez al-Assad, but now the curriculum has changed and they no longer have to learn about the laws of the party or the ideology. The same boy also told me that in earlier years, Syrian students used to have to learn about the military, about fighting, how to bear arms, how to load and reload, how to unjam a weapon. But, again, they no longer have to do this.

I asked them to identify the greatest problems they face in Syria. Without hesitation, one of the boys pointed to the educational system. The others nodded in affirmation and different voices explained that there are virtually no educational opportunities in their country. While they love their country and don't want to leave, they feel compelled to travel to Lebanon or Dubai so that they can get the education they need to come back to Syria and make something of themselves. They don't believe the world will accept a Syrian degree. They are probably right.

One of them explained that they desire a more open society, but the others pushed back and said that they fear too much freedom because they see what is taking place in Iraq. This was not surprising, given the spread of the Sunni insurgency to the Syrian border.

These kids didn't seem to believe in demonstrating or protesting to achieve change. When I asked them why, they again went back to the same car example, explaining that they never protested for cheaper cars. Instead, they believe that their patience was rewarded.

I moved to my last subject and asked them what they thought of America. As had been the case everywhere else, they emphatically asserted that they love America and its culture. They want American products and they even like going to Lebanon just becaue there is more American influence there. They have Coca-Cola and Pepsi, they have McDonald's, and their clubs play American music. But they viewed the United States government as something different. They saw my government as far too close to Israel and seemed to think it was out to destroy Islam. They were emphatic about this, but like most young kids in the Middle East, their justification was not rooted in facts, but instead bumper sticker slogans that had been inculcated upon them by extremists.

CHAPTER 10

THE ROAD TO MESOPOTAMIA

SYRIA, 2005

My journey to Aleppo, Homs, and Hama barely scratched the surface of Syria, but I needed to get back to Beirut. I had a multiple-entry visa that would require me to register with the Syrian government if I stayed much longer, so my plan was to come back after a few weeks and make my journey to eastern Syria, where the Salafist militants allegedly had crossed over from Iraq. I was low on cash and I wanted to give myself the option of turning away at the last minute, so I opted to go by car.

I passed some time gallivanting around Beirut as usual and then prepared myself for a long journey. My plan was to travel from Beirut back to Hama, across Syria, drive up the Iraqi border into Turkey, and eventually make my way into Iraq. With 90-percent certainty that I would chicken out of the Iraq stage, I threw my laptop and small suitcase all into a shared taxi at Charles Helou Station in Beirut and began my journey at six A.M. The journey out of Lebanon was a two-hour trip that I had already made five or six times. It still amazed me that it only cost ten dollars to go from Lebanon to Syria by taxi (a two-hour drive), but it cost fifteen dollars to drive from one side of Beirut to the other (a twenty-minute drive). It made traveling to

Syria a rather frequent occurrence for me. The only catch was that for such a cheap cost, I was expected to share the taxi with as many people as could fit. Sometimes this was one or two other people, while other times it was four in the backseat. A year later, when war would break out again between Israel and Hezbollah, I heard from friends that it cost almost six hundred dollars to take the same trip out of Lebanon.

It was just after dawn and barely light out. In the distance, I could catch a glimpse of the Mediterranean. We were going north, away from the sea and onto the road to Mesopotamia—modern-day Iraq. I was anxious but tired; I would have slept through the entire ride if my rest had not been repeatedly interrupted by the woman smoking cigarettes next to me.

Just a few days before I left, some of the Hezbollah guys that I knew tried to convince me not to go to Iraq. They told me that I was crazy for wanting to go to Iraq and one of them even suggested, "If you come back from Iraq without a head, don't say we didn't warn you. These people are crazy." While such warnings had already come from family, friends, and colleagues, Hezbollah's really caught my attention. When Hezbollah thinks that something is unsafe, well, it's probably not that safe. But I figured that when I got to the border with Iraq, I didn't have to cross. Deep down, I think I believed I would actually turn away at the last minute. I would certainly have time to make up my mind: in order to get to Mesopotamia, I had to travel across Syria, up the Syrian-Iraq border, through Turkey, and down into northern Iraq. There was much to experience beforehand.

As was usually the case, I had to wake up from my nap when we arrived at the Lebanese-Syrian border. At the border, I saw the usual scene of trucks lined up for miles, probably waiting for days, before crossing. When Syria had been pressured into withdrawing its troops from Lebanon in March 2005, it did so with great reluctance and at great cost to Syria's economy and prestige. The Syrian withdrawal from Lebanon coincided with American government pressure for Syria to do a better job securing its borders. While the United States wanted the Assad regime to secure its border with Iraq, the Bashar al-Assad regime in Syria used the opportunity to shut down its borders with Lebanon to economic traffic. While some traffic was let through, commercial trucks were left sitting at the border, sometimes for weeks on end. Border crossings have become like gigantic parking lots, with literally miles and miles of trucks not moving an inch. With Lebanon's economy already in shambles, the commercial lockdown of the border has come at great cost to the Lebanese, yet another source of widespread Lebanese hatred for Syria.

Fortunately only commercial vehicles were being held up. It was actually rather easy for me to get to the Lebanese-Syrian border. In fact, this was my third time going to Syria in the past two months and I had never run into any trouble at the border, but this time was different. My passport resembles a small book. It is thick and well-worn and often raises the eyebrows of officers, guards, and stuffy bureaucrats. I was even once asked upon arrival in Stockholm if Burundi was a real country. The immigration officer at the Syrian entry point was focused on one page of my passport and asked me, with a cocky and stern look, why I had gone to Israel.

I was puzzled. I had been to Israel in 1990, but this passport was issued in 2001. There were no Israeli stamps in my passport, the presence of which would immediately result in my being denied entry to Syria. I had deliberately avoided taking a trip to Israel before I traveled to Lebanon and Syria, precisely to avoid this predicament. *"Maruuhit Israel,"* I told him (I hadn't gone to Israel).

He didn't seem to believe me. I shrugged and put my hands to my sides; I had no clue what he was talking about. He pointed to a stamp in my passport and I leaned over to look. He was pointing to my multiple-entry visa for Ethiopia. He had mistaken the five-sided star on the Ethiopian stamp for a Star of David.

"This is for Ethiopia, not for Israel," I said. He still looked confused, so I drew a picture of a Star of David alongside the five-sided Ethiopian star to demonstrate the difference. He was finally convinced and he allowed me to proceed.

Syria, like most Middle Eastern nations, does not recognize the State of Israel. They do not take kindly to even the smallest reminder—like a stamp in a passport—that Israel does in fact exist. Such willful ignorance is not limited to border crossings. I was once at the Virgin Megastore in Beirut, browsing DVD box sets of *The West Wing*. They had the first and third seasons of the popular show, but the second season was conspicuously absent. The saleswoman told me that the store was forbidden from selling the second season: The word *Israel* had been uttered too many times in those episodes.

Such restrictions are government posturing and Middle Eastern youth know it. Even the most vehemently anti-Zionist youth I met would express frustration at living next to a country in which they had never been allowed to set foot. As one Hezbollah student told me, "I don't want to go to Israel to fight or destroy it. I just want to see what it is like. I grew up only twenty kilometers from the border, and still I have no idea what it is like there." In fact, when you ask a lot of young Lebanese what language they would like to learn besides English, many of them suggest Hebrew. This is even more so the case among the Shi'a from the south, the area bordering Israel.

The charade at the border had been a colossal waste of time and I actually got the impression that the other people in the taxi were irritated with me for holding up their journey. Too tired to address the awkwardness with my traveling companions, I just went back to sleep.

I had probably dozed off for about an hour when I woke up to the sound of singing. It was my taxi driver; in his voice, each word that he sang grew louder and was dragged out longer. It sort of sounded like "Hava Nagila." Then I heard the words:

Hafez!
Basil!!
Bashar al-Assad!!!

It got louder and more celebratory:

Hafez! . . .
Basil!! . . .
Bashar al-Assad!!! . . .

Now the taxi driver wasn't the only one singing. The older lady who had been smoking in the back also joined in. They were clapping and smiling. I didn't know what else to do, so I joined in. My Syrian traveling companions were literally singing the praises of the brutal al-Assad dictators, and it was chilling to see their pictures on every street corner, their decals on every taxi windshield, and billboards glorifying their mythical achievements and disgusting brutality.

The taxi dropped me off in Homs again, the same predominantly Sunni city that had been my first introduction to Syria several months earlier. This time I didn't stay long. I hailed another taxi and asked to be taken to Palmyra, or Tadmor, as it is known in both Arabic and its original language of Aramaic. Three hours from Homs and 250 kilometers northeast of Damascus, the ancient city of Palmyra stands in the center of Syria. The site being adjacent to perhaps the largest oasis in the Middle East, it is not hard to imagine why the ancient Romans chose it to construct the eastern flank of their empire.

They built Palmyra as a center for tax collection, a stopping point for trade, and a protection fortress for the eastern front of the Roman Empire, and two thousand years later much of what once stood here remains. I spent two full days walking through the ancient columns, exploring the amphitheater, and wandering around the rock tombs. It was a massive desert, except instead of cacti growing out of the sand, there were gigantic columns of limestone whose blocks fitted tightly together in a perfectly symmetrical pattern to form archways. In every direction I could see a different feature of the city and it became fun to decipher the varying historical functions of what I saw. Even when the city seemed to end, as indicated by smaller columns and fewer ruins, I could still see the large rectangular rock tombs erected out of the sand. It never ended.

When I stood before those magnificent ruins in Palmyra, it became easy to see how Syrian young people, looking at their history, are overtaken with a sense of pride. There are thousands of ruins scattered throughout Syria. Even granted an entire lifetime for the purpose, one could not see them all. Considered by some to be the most spectacular ruins in the entire world, Palmyra is filled with intact columns, arches, coliseums, temples, churches, and a variety of other structures. To young people, the ancient ruins in the Middle East are more than just tourist attractions. In Syria and Iran, young people would always refer to my desire to see these sights as admirable; my young friends praised what they saw as my interest in understanding their cultural pride. In Iran, it was about seeing Persepolis; in Syria, Palmyra; in Iraq, the ancient citadels; and in Lebanon, Baalbak.

While I was in Palmyra, a young man approached me on a camel. He couldn't have been older than seventeen, but he told me that he spoke nine languages. When I asked him where he had learned them, he explained, "from the tourists." But the place was empty. He explained to me the frustration of being Syrian: knowing what treasures the country possesses and wanting to share them with the world, but having no visitors.

The city of Palmyra was filled with interesting shops. Some of the stores were designed for tourists, with Syrian artifacts at hiked-up prices. These were not the blanket shops of Al-Marrad. There was a whole row of stores, much like a main street in any busy and developed town. While some of the stores offered artifacts and clothing, there was also no shortage of tea shops, places to smoke flavored tobacco, and restaurants. As I walked into one of the shops, my eyes immediately zeroed in on a small but ornate Quran, protected by an intricately designed metal case. It stood with its majestic allure on a fancy silver stand. After bargaining on the price, I was told by the young shopkeeper, "Be very careful with this, it is very special. Make sure you take care of it and show it respect." He then picked it up, kissed it, and said a prayer. I asked him if he would mind showing me some of his favorite passages. And so began an afternoon-long lesson on the Quran. We went through dozens of passages, as I listened to him explain what they meant and the various ways that they could be interpreted.

He was very knowledgeable and clearly well-read in the Quran. He didn't boast about his religious commitments, nor did he emphasize how deeply pious he was. I have found in my experiences in the Middle East that those who feel the need to brag about their religious commitments are often those who are either new to their faith or not well-versed in its teachings. I met so many young people throughout Lebanon, Iran, Syria, and Iraq who claimed to be deeply pious, well-read in the Quran, and scholarly about Islam. When I would ask them to show me the location of a passage in the Quran, however, many of them didn't know where to turn. Despite an oft-stated commitment to Islam, most youth in the Middle East have never read the Quran cover-to-cover. Instead, they rely on others to tell them what it says. Such reliance on oral education highlights the importance of the mosque and the cleric they choose to follow. Religious extremists employ this method to find new recruits. While this structure of religious education is not exclusive to the Middle East, this reliance on intermediaries to interpret all religious doctrine has provided an opening for dangerous extremists to hijack Islam. I was amazed at how many youth believed—often incorrectly—that the words of the extremist *marja* (clerical leader) they followed were verbatim from the Quran.

After a few hours going over passages in the Quran, he asked me why I was so curious to learn about Islam. It was as if he hadn't expected me to care, let alone sit with him for hours going over the text of the Quran. I explained to him that for a student of the Middle East, understanding Islam is essential. He looked at me perplexed and then said with astonishment, "I didn't think anyone in America would ever want to learn about Islam." He shouldn't have been surprised by this. I actually found it refreshing to see someone sitting with a Quran and pointing out passages, rather than regurgitating rhetoric that had been distorted by individual interpretation. It wasn't quite critical thinking, but it was a step in that direction. I asked him where he got the impression that an American would never want to learn about Islam, and without hesitation he proclaimed that America hates Islam, and wants to destroy the religion.

I hated hearing this because I knew it wasn't true. Yet he seemed so firm in his conviction. I didn't try to argue with the young shopkeeper; but I reminded him what the American government had done for Muslim victims after the tsunami and the assistance the United States provided to Iranians after the earthquake in Bam. I told him about Bosnia and about how important our own Muslim population is in America. Like the other young people with whom I'd shared these examples in Lebanon and Syria, he had a difficult time responding. He stuttered a bit. "Well, maybe in those events the United States did something, but . . ." He trailed off.

Before we parted ways, I decided to buy a kaffiyeh from him. It was the typical Syrian head wrap, designed with red and white checkers. He placed it on my head and rested two black woven rings on top so as to hold it in place. After carefully adjusting it, he pulled back to admire his handiwork. He then shook my hand and said, "Now you look like you are from Syria."

As was my usual tactic, I found some random guy on the street willing to drive me farther west. He had been lingering around Palmyra, perhaps looking for work. He made it easy to find him because he actually approached me with the offer of a cheap excursion to one of the rock tombs that I had been too lazy to walk to earlier that day. In the blistering summer heat, I always looked for an excuse to cut my walking time and he had a big pickup truck that made it all seem like an adventure. His name was Raja and he was tall, with a full beard and dark skin. He wore long pants and a collared shirt every day we were together, but his head was always adorned with a scarf. Raja was originally from Deir-e Zur, but had passed through Palmyra for business, or rather hopes of business. Like so many other young adults, he was simply looking for a way to make a living in Syria. He had tried handicrafts, rugs, and even tea; now he was hoping to make some money by leveraging his pickup truck as a taxi service.

We were heading in the same direction, so he offered me a good deal. I told him I wanted to visit several nomadic communities that were off the beaten track and then continue on to Deir-e Zur. Other than that, he knew very little of my plans. As I ventured farther into the eastern Syrian province of Deir-e Zur, where the influence of insurgent Iraq had supposedly meshed in a dangerous manner with an already fundamentalist political environment, I was looking for anything that might evoke a friendly response. He kept telling me, "Don't worry, my friend. I will take you to do and see all that you want and when we get to Deir-e Zur, you will meet my family and see my friends. You will see the real Syria." So we headed out together. I had now made it halfway across Syria. I was a third of the way to Iraq and more than a little anxious about the rest of my trip.

I rode in the back of Raja's white pickup truck with my head wrap blowing in the wind. It was so refreshing and I cherished every minute that the wind relieved me from the living sauna of Syria in July. I still had every intention of continuing northeast to Turkey and then down into Iraq, but at this point, there was no need to explain that to Raja.

While I was planning to enter Iraq through the north, I figured it might also be interesting to cross the Abu Kamal border and try to get to the ancient southern city of Babylon.

Not aware where he was ultimately taking me, Raja took me deep into the Palmyra Desert so that I could meet some Bedouins. Having spent three months living with the Maasai in southwestern Kenya, I had my own impression of what the nomadic lifestyle was like. I expected a simple lifestyle: no running water, no electricity, no technology. I expected apathy about politics and a visible rift between the Bedouin nomads and the rest of Syrian society.

I was right about one thing: The Bedouins did live in the middle of nowhere.

Raja and I drove to a point where roads ceased to exist. Consequently, we didn't seem to be going anywhere. All I saw in every direction was desert. Every once and a while, I would see a small shrub as I sat up from the back of the pickup truck, but the sight was certainly not worth the sand blowing in my face. It was never clear to me how Raja navigated. It should have been lonely, as there was literally nothing anywhere in sight. But it wasn't. I felt peaceful and without a worry in the world. For the first time in Syria, I didn't feel as though I was in a police state. For once, I could focus more on being overheated than of being followed. There was no Big Brother watching me, no images of Syria's dictators past and present; it was just me, Raja, and a bunch of sand. This must be why the Bedouins prefer the desert lifestyle.

As we continued on through the desert, I thought back to a trip to Africa. In March of 2003, I had driven through the desert of Mali on my way to Timbuktu. In the smoldering heat and without any water, my car sank in the desert. Nearly passed out from heat exhaustion and scared about how I would get out of the situation, I was rescued by Tuareg nomads. They took me into their tents and sent the children out in the middle of the night to dig the sand away from the car so that I could leave in the morning. But this felt different. Getting stuck in an African desert was no picnic, but being lost less than two hours away from Iraq's war-torn Sunni Triangle was nothing I wanted to experience.

But the car didn't sink, we didn't have to be rescued, and the driver found the Bedouins that I had been looking forward to meeting. The nomadic Bedouins may be a small portion of the population and exercise little influence over politics, but they cover a vast region of Syria and are one of the most important symbols of Syrian culture. Traditionally associated with nomadic migrations that took place between the fourteenth and eighteenth centuries from the Arabian Peninsula, many Bedouins settled in the Levant, bringing their traditional pastoral ways with them to the vast deserts of Sinai and Palmyra.

There are roughly one hundred thousand Bedouins living in Syria, but the vast majority of them have settled into the town and city lifestyles; the predominantly Sunni Bedouins are one of the great symbols of the Middle East, yet only a small percentage continue to live as nomads. These days, it is more common to see Bedouins driving pickup trucks and running small businesses than herding sheep. Most of the Bedouins who choose to maintain a nomadic existence can be found scattered throughout the Palmyra Desert, where we were.

When we arrived, the Bedouin encampment was almost as I had pictured it. There were three white cloth tents that stood alongside one another: Each was held up by ropes that were staked down in various directions, and the tent itself was held down by a collection of sandbags. It was windy in the desert, so much so that those wearing veils seemed to use them more for protecting their faces from the sand than for religious purposes. Not far from the tents, the Bedouins had erected fences to shelter their livestock. I saw water storage containers and there was a separate tent for the kitchen.

I wondered how anyone could possibly enjoy a life out here in the desert. It was so secluded from everything. The youth who live in these nomadic communities seemed to have no form of recreation and no way of getting an education. The setting would have looked simple and stereotypically nomadic, if it hadn't been for one small thing. The Bedouin nomads might have chosen to live in the middle of nowhere, but they were connected to events not only in Syria, but around the world. No, it wasn't through telepathy; it was through satellite television.

I saw a gigantic satellite dish in the sand that was almost as large as the Bedouin tent it seemed to have wires leading into. When I was living with the Maasai, people had televisions and cell phones, but they didn't function, they were decorative. These dishes had wires and cables.

The head of the household next to the dish was a man named Ihab. He wore a black cloak and had a thick beard and big bushy eyebrows. He was very amiable and introduced me to his six children, the oldest of whom was seventeen. I sat with them on a gorgeous Bedouin carpet, the pattern mixing bright blue and yellow colors, with a darker red and brown. Within moments, one of the young boys in the household brought a large metal serving tray with five or six smaller plates. Each plate offered a different dip or snack. As I examined the plates I saw a creamy white sauce, which turned out to have a bitter taste. In one of the other dishes, mixed spices and oil created a rough orange dip; and in another plate was a mixture of greens, olives, and white chunks that resembled tofu, but that were in fact a bitter cheese. Just as I was wondering why they had brought dips and no food, another young boy peeked around the corner and emerged out of hiding with a bowl of pita bread, making the formula complete.

As we ate we talked politics and about Bedouin culture, but to be honest, I was completely distracted by my curiosity for the television. Just after Ihab had explained to me how during the elections, the government provides transport for the nomads to come to the local towns and vote, I asked him, "Can I see your TV?"

He laughed and with an obvious air of pride led me through the separation in the tent to show me his television. The TV was fully functioning and I saw another wire leading from the television out to a round generator that rested, like the satellite dish, in the sand.

Two of the women in the household were gathered around the TV, watching what I was almost positive was Al-Jazeera or something like it. I asked Ihab how many channels they got on the television, expecting him to say three or four. He shocked me when he said nine hundred. I was bursting with questions, but the first one to come out was how they pay monthly cable charges out here in the desert. He laughed at this question and explained that they just pay a hundred dollars at the beginning for the satellite dish and the cable box. After that, they don't pay anything. Admittedly I was a bit jealous, a hundred dollars and unlimited cable. Not a bad deal.

Ihab did not have the only household with a satellite dish. I saw numerous dishes throughout the desert and I also heard stories about the Qashquai nomads in Iran with similar setups. While I didn't actually see it myself, I'd also read articles and heard eyewitness accounts of some nomadic communities in Syria that had solar panels outside of their tents.

I still had questions for him. "What do you do when you move?"

"Do you see those mules over there?" I looked at where he was pointing and then turned my head back to listen. "We tie the satellite and the generator to the mule with rope."

These nomads were connected. A great deal of the hatred toward America in the Middle East is often attributed to a difficulty in reaching people. What I realized from the nomads in Syria, however, is that there is not a problem of access. Satellite television was the most prevalent technology I saw in the Middle East. It existed in the Palestinian refugee camps, in private homes, in shared facilities, and apparently even in the nomadic deserts. The cost was minimal, the access was tremendous, and especially in the slums, cable was often spliced as many as five to eight times between families.

When nomads in the middle of the desert have upwards of nine hundred channels, lack of access cannot be said to be a problem for those outlets trying to reach Middle Eastern audiences. But those same nomads—like so many others in the Middle East—are glued to Al-Jazeera, Al-Manar, and Al-Arabia, three traditionally anti-Western networks. Changing their preferences is going to be more difficult than giving them access.

Ihab's children, however, are a different story. The very idea of channel-surfing excited them and even if they didn't speak the language, they would watch non-Arabic channels. For them it was about something new, increased access to diversified perspectives. The youth embrace variety far more than the adults, because they have a better understanding of a technology that gives them choices. They were born with choices.

After watching television with Ihab's family, Raja and I visited a number of other Bedouin settlements. From there, we saw the other side of Bedouin culture, the nonnomads. These Sunni people were warm, hospitable, and interesting to talk to. What I didn't realize at the time was that this would not be representative of the larger Sunni population I was about to meet. Where I would go next was a different story.

As we moved farther east, Syria became stranger and stranger. I began to see scowls rather than friendly grins, and people met me with hostility rather than amiability. The dialect of Arabic also began to change, and it just didn't seem that I was welcome anywhere. My driver and I had an amiable relationship, but our interactions were about to get awkward and uncomfortable. He still didn't know I was American and as far as I was concerned, there was no reason to tell him. What I didn't realize was that as we moved closer toward the Syrian-Iraqi border, there would be checkpoints. After only thirty minutes of driving, we reached the first of these checkpoints, where I was asked to present my passport. My driver reached out his window to the back of the pickup and I handed him my passport. As soon as he realized I was American, our relationship began to sour.

I could tell that he was pissed that I hadn't told him I was American. Rather than trying to ameliorate the situation, however, I simply asked him how long it would take to get to the Abu Kamal border with Iraq. He told me it would take two to three hours and then immediately asked with an air of suspicion why I wanted to know. I explained that I was planning to eventually go to Iraq through Turkey, but it might be interesting to enter through Syria. He looked appalled and the car actually slowed down as he turned his head to respond.

He began making the argument that things weren't safe in Iraq and that it was not a place to travel, but I persisted. He stopped answering me and we didn't speak again until we got a flat tire almost an hour and a half later. Ironically, it was right next to a sign with an arrow pointing toward Iraq. I asked him to take a picture with me in front of the sign and he refused. He didn't want to be in it. As we replaced the tire, I asked the driver if he would mind taking me to Iraq.

His tone was almost angry. "I told you; you shouldn't go there!" I asked if I could change his mind by offering more money, but he didn't budge. He reiterated his same point and stood firm in his refusal to take me there. He became both defensive and neurotic, telling me that he didn't think it was even possible to cross the border into Iraq and then asking me to promise that if I did make it into Iraq, I wouldn't tell anybody that I knew him or that he'd driven me.

Once the tire was fixed, I climbed into the front seat of the pickup truck. We drove in silence for a little while before he once again reminded me that he didn't know anyone in Deir-e Zur and there was no point in mentioning his name to people. This was in stark contrast to when I'd met him and he pawned himself off as the socialite of eastern Syria. His comments were particularly odd, because he'd told me earlier that he was from Deir-e Zur. He could see I was confused and questioning his level of truthfulness. In an effort to remedy the situation, he contrived the story that the name he had been given was not what people called him. He explained that he went by his father's name, which was Khalid, and assured me that where he was from they would not know any "Raja." We reached another checkpoint and stopped just before the metal spikes that a guard had placed in the road. My driver had said he didn't know if it was possible to cross into Iraq, so I figured I would ask the guard. I sounded like an inquisitive tourist, except I was just a few hours from the Sunni insurgency. Nonetheless, the guard answered that it was possible to cross from Abu Kamal, but I would need a visa to enter Iraq. Raja, or Khalid, or whatever my driver's name was at this point interjected, and demanded the guard explain to me why this was a terrible idea. The checkpoint guard seemed amused and, with great delight, clenched his fist and gestured a decapitation by sliding his thumb across his throat. It sent chills down my spine but was music to my driver's ears. He now seemed to be waiting for me to give in and give up on Iraq.

But I didn't say a word. We hadn't been more than five minutes past the checkpoint when he pulled his truck to the side of the road. He was confronting me and explained that he would drop me off just before Deir-e Zur, using the excuse that there was too much traffic and he had to deal with replacing the tire. He was making excuses. Before I had mentioned Iraq, he had no problems with anything. But now he didn't even want to be associated with me.

Given the controversies and attention surrounding the porous border between Syria and Iraq and given how many insurgents were allegedly hiding out in Deir-e Zur, I wasn't surprised that he had concerns. He was concerned about traveling with an American in the car. If they thought I was CIA, they might think he was helping the United States and then that could put his life in jeopardy. Or maybe he was concerned that if he proved to know anything about the border or took me there, the United States might think he was a friend of the insurgents. Either way, he felt that any association with an American going to Iraq would be bad for him.

Through my experience with Raja, I got my first glimpse of what I was about to encounter in Deir-e Zur. Raja or Khalid or whatever his name was now dropped me off at a roundabout just before the bridge leading to the city center. Before I gathered my belongings and went to find another taxi, he said to me again, "Remember not to tell anyone how you got here or that you know me. I am just a taxi driver." But that wasn't true. He had already told me he was from the city. He knew what kinds of people were living between Deir-e Zur and the Iraqi border. His paranoia was frightening.

The city of Deir-e Zur rests right along the Euphrates River at the bank of the southwestern part of ancient Mesopotamia. The famous civilization was comprised of the Fertile Crescent, the arable land that rested between the Euphrates River in the south and the Tigris River in the north. Deir-e Zur has historically been an important farming city and a trading center for business between Syria and Iraq.

The city of more than 133,000 people stirred controversy immediately after the 2003 United States intervention in Iraq. Reports began to surface that Sunni insurgents were crossing into Syria through Abu Kamal and settling in Deir-e Zur. I had heard from a number of people that there was actually a substantial number of insurgents who were either hiding out in Deir-e Zur or had assimilated in an effort at career change.

Its contemporary significance was not the only reason I was interested in traveling to Deir-e Zur. During the Armenian Genocide in 1915, the Deir-e Zur province of Syria was the scene of horrific death marches and mass executions of Armenians. Today, there are caves filled with skulls as a reminder of what happened.

I got into another taxi after parting ways with my driver. Within five minutes, I arrived at my hotel in Deir-e Zur. Everybody was rude to me. At the hotel they gave my blue passport a look of disgust. I really felt like I stood out. People would whisper about me and follow me around. It was not by any stretch of the imagination a comfortable place to be. I spent a few days in Deir-e Zur, exploring and trying to strike up conversations with people. Hardly anyone was interested. On my second day in the city, I hailed a taxi at one of the city roundabouts.

I wanted to see the famous ruins of Dura Europa, which was home to Syria's oldest synagogue, and the ancient city of Mari, which was an old Mesopotamian city. I negotiated a price with the driver that he agreed on, but by the time we left the city center and had gone halfway to Dura Europa—a ninety-minute drive away—he doubled the price. I was furious and I refused emphatically. He abruptly stopped the car, turned around, and pulled over.

"If you will not pay, then get out of my car!" he screamed at me. I was in the middle of a long road with nothing else around me, so I didn't have much of a choice but to give in to my driver's extortion. The rest of the ride was hostile and uncomfortable. The glove compartment of the car had been concealed by the seat in front of me, but when I glanced over it, I saw something appalling. It was a decal of Osama bin Laden, with Arabic writing that I recognized as "Death to America." I wanted to get out of the car and I prayed that there would not be a checkpoint; I didn't want to think what this driver might do if he realized I was American.

We arrived at Dura Europa. I had heard so much about it but, at first glance, was unimpressed. It just looked like two mud walls. Because I was paying my driver to wait for an hour and I was desperate to get away from him, I agreed to pay a hundred Syrian pounds for a motorcycle ride through the ruins. I was glad I did, because on the other end of the vast archaeological site was the most spectacular view of the Fertile Crescent that I saw in all of my travels. I sat on the back of this motorcycle with a Sunni man, who comfortably drove me to the old synagogue, told me the story of its history, and was extremely friendly.

When we got to a lookout point of the Euphrates River I asked him why my driver had a decal of Osama bin Laden on his dashboard. He told me that my driver is one of the foreigners.

When I asked the Sunni man what he meant by that, he explained that "he came from Iraq." He left it at that and wouldn't give me any more information, but I inferred that this guy had been an insurgent. As our travels continued, I saw that everywhere we went, people treated my driver like a foreigner. Despite my being an outsider as well, people seemed to take my side. When I really wanted to stir up hatred for him, I would tell people about his decal of bin Laden. This was a great way to get people on my side, because nobody wanted to be associated with bin Laden or Al-Qaeda. Even their fellow Sunnis viewed the Iraqis who had come into Deir-e Zur as harmful to the community. To begin with, Syria and Iraq had been historical enemies. More important, the Syrians had come to resent the lack of security and the international scrutiny that had resulted from Iraqi Sunni infiltrating Deir-e Zur.

From the hostile province of Deir-e Zur, I went by taxi to the northeastern Syrian town of Qamishli, which was my last stop before heading to Turkey and on to Iraq. Qamishli had been a historically peaceful town. The city of two hundred thousand people is a remarkable mix of Shi'a, Sunni, Christians, and Jews. It also has a substantial Kurdish population that has been harshly suppressed by the Syrian regime; there is a long history of Kurdish oppression in Syria, which has continued into the present. After repeated hostility in Deir-e Zur, this quiet village was a great place to relax for a few days before I put my life to the test again.

For sixty dollars, I was able to catch a ride from the Syrian-Turkish border all the way to Ibrahim Khalil in northern Iraq. The whole trip took five hours and I spent most of the time wondering what would happen once I got to Iraq. I will never forget when I first saw those large gates at Ibrahim Khalil after crossing from Habur, Turkey, into no-man's-land. This was it. The border area was chaotic, as lines of people waited in a gathering area in the middle of several hideous cement buildings. The place was swarming with children lugging large coolers on their backs trying to sell cold drinks. Given that the place felt like a sauna, I'd imagine business was good for them.

I had been told by experts that going through Habur, Turkey, was the safest way to enter Iraq, but the extent of that safety was debated. Some said I was walking into a death sentence, while others suggested that I would be fine. But nobody denied the existence of a risk.

By the time I got to the Iraqi border, I was sweating bullets, both from the unbearable heat and my nerves.

I prepared myself to enter what I thought would be a war zone. As I stood before the Ibrahim Khalil border post in the gateway to the Iraqi Kurdistan Region, it did not look like the Iraq I had seen on television. The border was peaceful, surrounded by gorgeous green hills in the distance. Just in front of me I saw a small blue sign that said, "Welcome to the Iraqi Kurdistan Region." I took a photo with my Turkish driver and then he left me.

Before I arrived, I had been promised escort by the Kurdistan Democratic Party. I really hoped this would work out, as I was now all alone and without a car on the border between Turkey and Iraq.

I could hardly breathe, partially because of the excruciating heat but mostly because I was sandwiched between two rather large Kurdish men on a short wooden bench. Surprisingly, the Iraqi border was less chaotic than others I had been to, and despite the fact that it was in truth the entrance to a war zone, it was a pleasant calm. One of the men beside me had defined and cartoonlike features. His head was covered in a tightly wrapped cloth and he wore baggy gray pants held up by a stylish Kurdish cummerbund. We were both curious to speak with each another. I wanted to ask him about Iraq, and he just wanted to know what I was doing there. I noticed him glancing at my American passport.

Just as I began to zone out, he asked me if it was my first time in Iraqi Kurdistan, to which I replied that it was. The fact that he could offer me one of my first perspectives of the region animated him. He adjusted his turban and looked right at me. I don't think I have ever had someone stare at me with such a direct, focused gaze. If he hadn't been so friendly and well-intentioned, I might have found it somewhat abrasive. He told me I would love Iraqi Kurdistan and then asked me what had brought me to Iraq.

I explained that I had come to Iraq to meet Kurdish youth and get their perspective on how they felt about politics, democracy, the war in Iraq, and the United States occupation. Before I could finish, he interrupted. His eyebrows wrinkled as he looked at me sternly and told me, "It is not an occupation. It is liberation." Wow, I thought, FOX News must really be popular in this part of the country.

I extended my hand. "My name is Jared." I didn't know how else to respond. I had not expected to hear this while I was in Iraq, let alone have it be the very first thing said to me.

"I am Safeen," he said proudly. Our conversation was cut short as I heard my name called loudly from inside the customs office. It had been brief, but this interaction with Safeen led me to believe that much of what I would see in the Kurdish part of Iraq would differ from my initial impressions of a country at war.

I was escorted to one of the offices of the Kurdistan Democratic Party, where I found myself sipping tea and relaxing on a comfortable couch. Within minutes there were several Kurdish officials there to greet me. They had known I was coming and had been expecting me. It was at this moment that one of the officials sitting in front of me took his blue Nokia cell phone and placed it on the table. He pushed it toward me and said, "You should call home."

CHAPTER 11

IRAQIS WHO LIKE US

IRAQ, 2005

The Iraqi Kurdistan Region was physically breathtaking, and with each turn in the road came an even more magnificent landscape. When I first crossed the Tigris River into the Fertile Crescent that once harbored the world's most magnificent civilization, it was easy to bask in the glory of the Mesopotamian fantasy.

Besides the picturesque setting, just being in Iraq was enough to sustain a feeling of constant excitement, and I wanted to photograph everything and anything. This was a feeling I hadn't experienced since the first time I went to the Democratic Republic of Congo. Back then, I was collecting dirt in film canisters, taking pictures of fences, and relishing everything about being in such a place. My driver laughed as I took pictures of objects as banal as signs and cones on the side of the street; he even opened the sunroof so I could stick my head out and get clearer shots. In the first fifteen minutes alone, I photographed an advertisement, a truck, and other trappings of the peaceful, everyday life that I hadn't expected to see in Iraq.

"I think you are very happy to be in Iraqi Kurdistan," my driver said to me with an air of pride. He was a member of the Kurdistan Democratic Party and he seemed very proud to be driving me. He was slender and he wore a suit that was far too big for him. I think he either thought I was older than I was or that I was a representative from some important organization. It was doubtful that he knew I was just a graduate student who had wanted to go to Iraq.

"Yes, I am," I said. "It doesn't seem dangerous here. Is it safe for me to stick my head out the window and take pictures?"

"Here in Iraqi Kurdistan, everything is safe. You will feel most welcome." After these reassuring words, we did not speak much. There were a lot of smiles, but his English was minimal and he spoke Kurdish, not Arabic. I found that people in the Iraqi Kurdistan Region often downplayed their knowledge of Arabic. During the time of Saddam Hussein, they had been forced to speak Arabic instead of Kurdish, making memories of this language all too reminiscent of the Ba'ath Party. Though they are Muslims like most people in the Middle East, the Kurds are not Arabs; their status as an ethnic minority is of far greater significance to them than religious identification.

Consisting of the northern third of Iraq, the Iraqi Kurdistan Region contains high-value oil fields in Kirkuk and strategic borders with Syria, Turkey, and Iran. Home to some of Iraq's most aesthetically pleasing landscape—large canyons, gorgeous mountains, and impressive waterfalls—many of the Sunni and Shi'a from other parts of the country come to the Iraqi Kurdistan Region on tourism. The waterfalls at Geli Eli Beg, the famous natural wonder once depicted on the Iraqi dinar, are among the region's most popular sites for Sunni and Shi'a from other parts of the country. The Bexal Waterfall is another popular destination, where Iraqis from all over the country come to enjoy the riverside bazaars, outdoor cafés, and magnificence of the view. Once known primarily for their beauty, the resorts of the Iraqi Kurdistan Region have become popular refuges for those who can afford to take extended vacations from the sectarian violence that plagues the rest of Iraq.

The Iraqi Kurdistan Region is by no means home to the world's largest Kurdish population, but the Kurds living there are the most pro-American and pro-Israeli people in the Middle East, possibly even in the world. I was not so naïve as to assume that the Iraqi Kurdistan Region represented the whole of the Republic of Iraq. I knew that the overwhelming praise for the American government and its undertaking in Iraq was unique to the region; things were most certainly different in the Sunni Triangle in central Iraq and in Moqtada al-Sadr's Shi'a stronghold in the south. But the "amount" of support and love for America and Americans in Kurdistan was still surprising.

At the time of my trip in northern Iraq, there was an insurgency in the Sunni-dominated center of Iraq that had killed forty-five Americans in just the last ten days of my trip. There also continued to be violence in the Shi'a south, including the shooting in the head of one Western journalist. When I was in the north, however, I saw no hint of an insurgency. Instead, I saw signs of democracy, freedom, and liberty; I saw a thriving culture of socially and politically entrepreneurial youth who had carved themselves a place at the table.

The modern Iraqi Kurdistan Region dates back to the aftermath of the Ba'ath Revolution in 1958, when Iraqi Kurdish leader Mullah Mustafa Barzani returned from exile to establish the Kurdistan Democratic Party (KDP). Three years later, Barzani led a revolution for self-determination and autonomy of the Kurds. The violent revolution lasted until 1971, when the Iraqi Kurdish leaders reached an agreement with then Iraqi vice president Saddam Hussein. The agreement promised the Kurdish people of the north autonomy, but Saddam failed to hold up his end of the bargain. As a result, life changed very little for the Kurds and by 1975, the agreement wasn't worth the paper it was printed on.

Since the Kurdish Revolt, the shah of Iran had been funneling money into Iraqi Kurdistan to help destabilize Iraq through the Kurds. Needing to find some way to cut off the Iranian funding to insubordinate sections of northern Iraq, Saddam sought to rid himself of the Kurdish predicament. Preoccupied with the need to consolidate his power and pressured from the West, he met with the shah of Iran to draft the 1975 Algiers Accord. Under the terms of the Algiers Accords, Iraq would hand over the Shatta al-Arab region of Iraqi Kurdistan to Iranian control and Iran would in exchange effectively cut its funding to the Kurds.

No longer challenged by a Kurdish revolt that had Iranian money—which in those years meant American money as well—behind it, Saddam moved back into northern Iraq and began "Arabizing" the Iraqi Kurds. For Kurds, this was a brutal lesson in realpolitik, one they would never forget. Despite their overwhelming support for the United States, the Iraqi Kurds consider the 1975 Algiers Accord the first chapter in a saga of abandonment by the West.

The Kurds were in sustained revolt for almost the entirety of the Iran-Iraq War, but Saddam used the violence of the conflict as an opportunity to use excessive brutality against the insurrectionists. During the war, massive amounts of Kurdish land were destroyed, as the eastern flank of Iraqi Kurdistan became a battleground that would take years to repair. I visited several of these cities, and they looked as if they had never quite recovered.

Almost three years after the Iran-Iraq War ended, Iraq was once again at war. In August 1990, Saddam invaded and annexed Kuwait, Iraq's small, oil-rich neighbor. Within six months, the Iraqis had been driven out of Kuwait by American forces. As the war ended, President George H. W. Bush publicly encouraged Iraqi Shi'a and Kurds to rebel against the apparently vulnerable Saddam Hussein. Drawing on Bush's rhetoric for motivation, the Kurds staged a rebellion in the north, while the Shi'a responded with an uprising in the southern cities of Najaf, Karbala, and Basra. His encouraging words of support notwithstanding, President Bush chose to remain on the sidelines for both uprisings, with bloody results for the Shi'a and Kurds alike.

As the Shi'a attempted to oust the Ba'ath government from southern Iraqi cities, Saddam's forces initiated a brutal crackdown that left thirty thousand Iraqi Shi'a dead. The Kurdish uprising met equally violent resistance but was nonetheless successful in its ultimate objective. During the 1991 Kurdish uprising, the statues of Saddam Hussein came down, the posters and murals were defaced, and the Kurdish flag with its pronounced sun in the center replaced the Ba'ath Party flag. Kurdish autonomy became a reality as United Nations Security Council Resolution 688 declared the Iraqi Kurdistan Region to be a safe haven for the Kurds. The UN Resolution was carried out by Operation Provide Comfort, where the Kurds were encouraged to come back from Iran, Syria, and Turkey to a newly autonomous Kurdistan region under the protection of a UN no-fly zone.

While the Kurds were relatively protected from Saddam by the UN no-fly zone and Resolution 688, the early years of Iraqi Kurdistan were not easy. With the common enemy appeased for the time being, the tensions that had been simmering between the KDP and the Public Union of Kurdistan (PUK) began to surface. These tensions were exacerbated by new economic and political challenges. While autonomous, Iraqi Kurdistan was still technically part of Iraq and therefore also subject to the UN embargo that followed Iraq's invasion of Kuwait. In addition to withdrawing all of his troops, Saddam had also withdrawn all funds and resources, contriving his own domestic embargo on the newly autonomous region. This led to economic strangulation on both the international and the domestic fronts. Making matters worse, the Kurds had been banking on acquisition of the oil-rich city of Kirkuk, but Saddam was not so anxious to relinquish control of this important city. Without oil money, central government revenue, or the opportunity to attract international investment, the Kurds were left with mere customs and border taxes as their primary source of public revenue. Meanwhile, the KDP and PUK feuded over resources and territory and the political tensions escalated into an all-out civil war. The violence got so bad that KDP officials actually appealed to Saddam to intervene in the civil war, and the Iraqi dictator happily sent thirty thousand troops to seize PUK areas.

By 1997, with Saddam reestablishing a foothold in Iraqi Kurdistan and the conflict expanding to include Turkey, it became clear to both the PUK and the KDP that if the conflict were to continue, the only losers would be the Iraqi Kurds. After a ceasefire agreement was reached, American secretary of state Madeleine Albright helped broker a deal that led to de facto reunification of the Iraqi Kurdistan Region. Ultimately, the disputes between the KDP and the PUK were internal and political; in reality, the rival parties had the same approach to the Kurdish national question and ideological differences between the groups were insignificant.

United and autonomous, Iraqi Kurds continued to live in fear until March 2003, when Saddam finally fell. While Saddam had withdrawn his troops from the Iraqi Kurdistan Region, he had continued to sponsor terrorist attacks against Kurdish establishments. Saddam was a malevolent threat to Kurdish autonomy; only the end of his regime would bring peace and comfort to the Iraqi Kurdistan Region.

On my first day in the Iraqi Kurdistan Region, I was excited to explore. Still not fully aware of the extent to which Iraqi Kurdistan was a world removed from the turmoil in the rest of the country, however, I was cautious. For my first few days in Iraq, I took taxis everywhere—even to cross the street. Taxi drivers laughed at me when I would pay them five dollars to go fifty feet, but they didn't complain.

In those first days, I kept waiting for something to frighten me. Where I expected to stumble upon insurgent training grounds, I found kids playing soccer; where I foresaw hatred toward Americans, I found individuals who wished to embrace me. This was not the Iraq I had seen on the news. Then again, how frequently is the Iraqi Kurdistan Region actually given attention in the mainstream media?

I began my exploration of Iraq in Arbil, the regional capital of Iraqi Kurdistan. The city, believed by many to be the oldest inhabited city in the entire world, was surprisingly urban, consisting of busy markets, a vibrant downtown, and a tremendous citadel that dates back to 7000 B.C. Once one of the most important cities in ancient Mesopotamia, Arbil fell under the control of various empires and modern regimes, ultimately evolving into the capital of the Iraqi Kurdistan Region. In front of the ancient citadel stood a shrine of one of the city's former leaders, as if the rock statue of this spiritual figure were guarding the walls of the ancient city.

I learned that the ancient city was comprised of three quarters: Takiya, Topkhana, and Saray. The walled city, or the Qalah of Arbil, as it is known, has "witnessed all epochs of Mesopotamian history and prehistory from 7000 B.C. until the present."* In 705 B.C. it became not only the religious center of the Assyrian community, but also the primary source of water for the region. Its magnificent twenty-two-kilometer aqueduct was one of the most impressive structures of its time. Today, however, the Qalah is a dirty and run-down community for some of the poorest people in Arbil; the citadel is home to as many as five thousand Iraqi Kurds, who continue to struggle in a quest to rebuild the lives they lost under Saddam Hussein.

It was isolated, with garbage-strewn streets, and sheltered from the new developments of the city center. It was an Iraqi slum located within an ancient treasure. Yet as I'd seen in Iran, Lebanon, and Syria, even the slums in the Middle East are connected to the world at large. Amid the squalor and poverty, I saw street children walking around with cell phones and I saw satellite dishes on top of every single home.

I asked a couple of people to explain to me how these homeless children could afford a cell phone. They told me that groups of children share a single phone. Obtaining old cell phones is neither particularly

---

*Displayed on a sign in front of the Qalah of Arbil.

expensive nor difficult, especially since there are young "businessmen" who steal them from the crowded markets and then sell them for a cheaper price. The only challenge is obtaining the SIM card to make the phone work, but several of these poor young people will pool their resources to buy one for their shared phone. In truth, these street children don't really have anyone to call. Then again, that is not what the phone is for. It is about having something modern to play with; it is about having something that they have control over. It is a toy for them and a way to learn. As soon as one of these boys gets a SIM card, he immediately learns new tricks with the phone and learns its features; he is free to explore new avenues for communication. Despite the limits of their own lives, these kids know how wide the channels of communication span. They are free to dream of another world and another life.

And now that Saddam was gone, satellite television was not only legal but also readily available. The standard price was a hundred dollars for a thousand channels, similar to the rate in Syria. If one were a good bargainer or found a good black-market distributor, it was possible to do better. There were also several young men who had made a nice career out of programming satellite dishes for their technologically inept elders.

Young people in the Iraqi Kurdistan Region loved their satellite television. They watched everything from Al-Jazeera to CNN, BBC, FOX News, and all the major stations from Saudi Arabia, Iran, and Lebanon. And of the thousand channels, I think at least a hundred must have been pornography. In the words of one Kurdish couch potato, "We went from a life of prison to satellite. Now we look at everything, X-rated films, American movies, this is all new to us. It is a shock for us. It is like jumping from the sauna into a cold pool. Imagine, before all of this, fundamentalists would kill people for watching a movie or going to a bar."

People in Iraq never turned their televisions off. When they weren't at home, their television stayed on. When they ate dinner, the television blasted. Even when they had guests over, their television stayed on. Even at the most formal dinners I attended at people's homes, the television never went off. For these Kurds, television is a symbol not of wealth but of freedom. A television that never goes off serves as a reminder to these once oppressed Kurdish people that they can think whatever they want and that they are free from the ruthless grasp of the Ba'ath Party.

I also saw a ton of Internet cafés in the slums of Arbil. They are springing up all over northern Iraq; young people there certainly have enough time on their hands to become acquainted with using the Internet. The mechanisms of civil society and democracy may be in place in Iraqi Kurdistan, but the economy remains too slow to provide young people with jobs. Consequently, many of them spend hour after hour on the Internet. I learned more about new programs on the Internet from Iraqi youth than I had from friends at Oxford. They taught me how to use messenger services and Internet phone services I had never even heard of. What I had already heard of, they showed me how to *really* take advantage of.

The Arbil slums were an interesting place to see the far reach of communications technology, but I found most of the people there to be rather apathetic about politics. Now that the Kurdish civil war is over, they don't bother much with politics. As for the war in Iraq, well, it might as well be taking place in another country.

My next stop in Arbil was Salahaddîn University, the Iraqi Kurdistan Region's most famous educational establishment and one of the best in Iraq. Founded in 1968 and originally located in the eastern Kurdish city of Sulaimaniya, Zankoy Selaheddîn moved to Arbil just over a decade later and has grown into an internationally recognized university with eighteen different colleges. There were a few notable buildings that really gave the university its character. I wasn't exactly sure of their function, but they were beautiful stone structures. There was a contrast between segments of the university that looked brand new and parts that seemed dilapidated and as if they hadn't been refurbished in over a decade.

I explored the university, looking for young Iraqi Kurds to talk to. As I asked around for the office of the university president, I encountered a student who seemed eager to speak with me. His name was Omar. Despite the blistering heat, he wore long pants and a long shirt buttoned all the way to the top. He conducted himself in a very professional manner. This is something I would notice about Kurdish youth: They have very adult mannerisms and they take themselves very seriously. Many will put on a shirt and tie just to go to the market or run an errand.

We made small talk about the heat, but soon turned serious. He asked me how I found Iraqi Kurdistan and where I was from. I asked him to describe the atmosphere in the Iraqi Kurdistan Region immediately after September 11. He explained that while people in the Sunni and Shi'a parts of Iraq believed September 11 was the punishment from God, the Iraqi Kurds felt the experience and the grief was shared because they, too, had experienced suffering at the hands of Saddam Hussein. Initially I was confused, because Omar was making a distinction between the Iraqi Kurdistan Region and the Republic of Iraq. I would learn that most Iraqi Kurds do not see themselves as part of a larger Iraq; being part of Iraq has always been a temporary acquiescence for them, an unfortunate detour from a road that will ultimately lead to an independent Kurdish state.

Eager to get the Kurdish reaction to the sequence of events that followed 9/11, I asked about popular perceptions after the United States went into Afghanistan. Omar paused for a minute and then, after letting out a sigh, explained that at first they felt safer in Iraq, but not long after the liberation from the Taliban began, many Al-Qaeda fighters fled Afghanistan and set up camp in Tawela and Biyara where they collaborated with members of the extremist Sunni group Ansar al-Islam.

After chatting with a couple dozen students and getting a sense of what I would need to see while in northern Iraq, I had the chance to sit with the president of the university, Dr. Sadiq. Dr. Sadiq's office had fancy rugs and couches and an elegant desk. He had neatly combed gray hair and wore a dark gray suit and bright orange tie. There was an air of confidence about him; I could tell that he was proud of the university and what he had contributed to its success.

Dr. Sadiq had a tremendous amount of confidence in the students of Selaheddîn University. He described them as innately political, channeling their considerable activism and spirit into student unions, demonstrations, civil society organizations, and other ambitious endeavors. With an air of pride, he predicted that it is the students who will bring about the reforms in the Iraqi Kurdistan Region. His premonition didn't surprise me, as these students today are learning about democracy and shaping their modern identity around what this means to them. As a result, young people are active in getting involved. In Arbil alone there are at least 183 nongovernmental organizations, some of which are a couple of guys sitting in a garage, but many of which are legitimate organizations. These youth are very ambitious. They have a vision, they love their country—Kurdistan—and they have a developed sense of citizenship. As a result, they believe that in order to be good citizens, they must embrace the idea of democracy. For young Kurds, embracing democracy is synonymous with making a contribution. In this supposedly prosperous part of Iraq—where unemployment is as high as 60 percent—youth have the free time to channel this ambition toward volunteering and civic entrepreneurship.

I had been invited to the Iraqi Kurdistan Region as a guest of the Kurdistan Regional Government. I initially had concerns that such hospitality was a ploy for me to be a mouthpiece for the Kurds, but this was not the case. I talked to whomever I wanted and if I needed help, the government was there to provide it for me. They didn't interfere at all; in fact, they seemed eager to hear my findings on the youth. The foreign minister said to me on a number of occasions that the youth are of vital importance and that the government wanted to fully understand their needs and their thinking. So before setting out to meet the young people building Kurdistan's dynamic civil society, I took advantage of the access I had been granted and paid a visit to the minister of human rights. I wasn't quite certain what was in the portfolio of this ministry, so Hachem, an aide to the minister, offered to show me.

Hachem was in his mid-twenties and his desk was decorated with the Kurdish flag, as well as the flag of the Ministry of Human Rights. He sat in front of a large, modern computer monitor. He told me to come over to his side of the desk so he could show me some of the ministry's work. As I huddled with him around his brand-new Dell computer monitor, he reached into a box and pulled out more than twenty DVDs. He popped in the first one and told me that it was called *Crimes Under Saddam* and was designed to show the brutality of punishment under the former Iraqi dictator.

As we went through image after horrific image, I thought I was going to be sick. The images and videos Hachem showed me were eerily reminiscent of what I had seen at the Yad Vashem Holocaust Museum in Israel and the Holocaust Memorial Museum in Washington, D.C. I watched three young people with their hands tied behind their backs get thrown off the top of a three-story building; the torturers then picked the bodies up and did it all over again. I watched repeated beatings, firing squads, and whippings. I watched a man get his hands surgically removed for dealing in American currency. I watched tongue amputations take place as punishment for speaking out against Saddam. I watched the Fedayin al-Saddam sit a man next to another man who had already been blown up and place an explosive device in his pocket; the man's last words were, "Is this how I am going to die?" I watched executioners make four or five tries to decapitate a man, finally using a smaller hand knife and violent sawing gestures to complete the task; I saw the killers then hold the severed head up in the air.

Hachem wanted me to see what Iraqi Kurds had lived under before the Kurdish uprising in 1991, and what the rest of the Iraqis had experienced up until Saddam was overthrown. After we'd made it through the first batch, Hachem pulled out about twelve more DVDs, and we watched all or part of each of them.

When one sees the torture, brutality, and barbarism to which they were once subject, and one compares that horror to the peace and hopefulness of present-day Kurdistan, it is not difficult to understand why they look so kindly upon those they view as responsible for deposing Saddam's murderous regime.

Of all the images shown to me by Hachem, the footage of Halabjah had the greatest impact on me. On March 16, 1988, just one day after a combination of Iranian and Kurdish forces seized the eastern Iraqi city of Halabjah, Saddam Hussein and his trusted general "Chemical Ali" gassed the city, killing approximately five thousand people. Many of these were women and children. I watched video footage of people running from the chemical gas and of children frozen by the poison. I heard tapes of screams and saw skin melt off people's faces. I watched children with their hands in the air and mothers holding on to their daughters. It was all so horrible.

The March 1988 gassing of Halabjah was part of a larger campaign by Saddam Hussein against the Kurds of Iraq. The Kurdish youth in Iraq today were born into the most brutal phase of Saddam Hussein's Anfal Campaign, a period in which Saddam didn't discriminate between innocent civilians and soldiers, or between men, women, or children. Beginning in 1978, but taking on its most organized and brutal form in 1987 and 1988, Saddam's Anfal Campaign still torments the youth of the Iraqi Kurdistan Region, whose earliest memories are of running from Saddam's troops. At the order of Saddam Hussein, more than five thousand Kurdish villages were emptied and more than two hundred thousand people were arrested, many of whom either disappeared or were killed. Among the most brutal of these campaigns was the extermination of eight thousand Barzani tribesmen. Many of the mass graves that were uncovered during Operation Iraqi Freedom provided evidence of Saddam Hussein's Anfal Campaign.

The latter phase of Anfal offers the mostly deeply embedded images and horrific memories for young Kurds. In February 1988, the final year of the Iran-Iraq War, Saddam Hussein launched the first of what would be eight major Anfal operations. As the Iranian forces, aligned with Kurdish forces, gained positions on the periphery of Baghdad, Saddam sought not only to quash the encroachment, but also to punish the Kurdish people, who he believed were both insubordinate to his regime and inherently inferior to the Arabs who ruled Iraq.

While the Halabjah massacre is the most notorious of the Anfal campaigns, Hussein also orchestrated extermination campaigns in Garmiyan, Koi Sanjaq, Lesser Zab, Bahdinan, and Bazi Gorge. In most of these cases chemical gasses were employed by the Iraqi army and women and children were not spared. After six months and eight campaigns of Anfal operations, it is believed that as many as two hundred thousand Kurds, including many women and children, were brutally slaughtered. Just three days after arriving in Iraq, I had the opportunity to visit Halabjah. The journey was nearly five hours from Arbil. I drove across Iraq, visiting Sulaimaniya and other towns and cities on the way. Given the notoriety of Halabjah, I expected a big city. Instead, it is a quiet, melancholy village, a living ghost town. It reminded me of the Rwandan town of Murambi, which I'd visited in December 2002. The bodies of some of the sixty thousand people massacred in Murambi during the 1994 genocide were littered around the classrooms they died in. I felt the same pervasive, profound sadness in Halabjah.

As I drove into the city limits, there was a billboard that read "Welcome to Halabjah." Depicted on the billboard were images of dead babies and gassed Kurds. All of Halabjah was a reminder of what had happened on that fatal day in 1988. There were monuments comprised of mortar shells; there was a cemetery with five thousand tombs commemorating the victims. In the center of the city was a large monument to the gassing of the Kurds; posted next to it was a giant blue sign that read "It's not allowed for Ba'aths to enter." Although the Kurds have had virtual autonomy since the 1991 uprising, there always remained a fear that Saddam Hussein could come back in; the Ba'ath presence still lingered at the periphery of Kurdish life. The youth in the Iraqi Kurdistan region believe that with Saddam out of the picture, they are now one step closer to their dream of Kurdish independence. Whether or not this is true is yet to be seen, but young Kurds give the United States credit for taking Saddam out of the picture.

The trauma, pain, and stories of brutality of the Anfal campaigns are still deeply embedded in the minds of Iraqi Kurds. For older generations, Anfal was the darkest of a prolonged period of misery, brutality, and fear under Saddam. For the younger generations, it represents what they have been trying to get away from since their childhood. In fact, each time I met a young Kurd in Iraq, the first two things he or she would tell me about were the Anfal Campaign and how Kurdistan was different from the rest of Iraq. These two issues form much of the Iraqi Kurdish youth identity. And when they spoke of Anfal, I noticed a lot of similarities with the youth of Iran. Both had experienced brutal violence and trauma at the earliest stages of their lives and both want change, but not at the expense of violence and instability. I suspect this aversion to danger and chaos is one of the main reasons why the Kurds have so warmly embraced the American presence in Iraq. While battalions of soldiers landed in Iraqi Kurdistan, the fighting has taken place in the Sunni and Shi'a regions of Iraq. In fact, the Kurds take tremendous pride in the fact that Americans parachuted into the north because it was a safe entry point for them into Iraq. The few military campaigns that did take place in the north, most notably the eradication of Ansar al-Islam from the northeast, were welcomed because they actually made the region more stable.

Ansar al-Islam, the Supporters of Islam, is a Sunni terrorist group with a strict Sunni Islamist interpretation of Islam. It was established in December 2001 as the union between two extremist Kurdish groups: the Islamic Movement in Kurdistan and the Soldiers of Islam. Led by Mullah Krekar, Ansar al-Islam based itself in the northeastern part of Iraq and fortified villages along the border with Iran. Within weeks of coming to power in the region, the group began cleansing the northeast of all cultural relics, shrines, and artifacts and all residents were forced to convert to Islam, with harsh punishments for those who refused. The group's methods were brutal; they engaged in torture, mutilation, and decapitation.

The membership of Ansar al-Islam included numerous fighters who had fought against the Soviets during the 1980s in Afghanistan. With alleged links to Al-Qaeda, Ansar al-Islam has received funding from Osama bin Laden and also created a safe haven for notorious terrorist leaders infiltrating into Iraq, most notably the late Abu Musab al-Zarqawi. The group also allegedly had ties to Saddam, and for American war planners, Ansar al-Islam was the link between the Iraqi dictator and Al-Qaeda.

In 2003, following the American intervention in Iraq, the American government helped Kurdish forces root out Ansar al-Islam. Though the operation was successful, most of the Ansar al-Islam fighters escaped into Iran and eventually found their way back into Iraq, where they have since joined the Sunni insurgency. While the insurgency has taken place largely outside of the Iraqi Kurdistan Region, the few attacks that have managed to penetrate the heavily guarded territories of northern

Iraq were believed to have been carried out by remnants of Ansar al-Islam. When I visited the former Ansar al-Islam towns of Tawela and Biyari, I expected to encounter fundamentalist populations. I had been to Afghanistan the previous February and found that even after the Taliban had left, their influence remained: The people were reserved, and many women still wore the blue burkha. But neither Tawela nor Biyara was like this.

Tawela was the more northeastern city of the two, tucked into the base and hills of a natural border between Iraq and Iran. The surrounding hills were cluttered with shacks along the cliff, and every single house, regardless of its size or location on the cliffs, had a satellite dish. The central market was situated around a mosque adorned with a turquoise dome and four tall, thin minarets. After Zarqawi came to Iraq, this mosque was his first place of worship.

Despite its link to the infamous leader of Al-Qaeda in Iraq, Tawela wasn't a fanatically religious city. I saw a group of boys listening to Western music on a boom box. There were girls walking around only marginally covered. Everybody whom I met in this former extremist outpost was peaceful and hospitable.

For the Iraqi Kurds, Ansar al-Islam was the last nuisance in a string of violence that had plagued their region. They have now developed a community that is relatively safe, democratic, and egalitarian. Politically speaking, there are few, if any, places like this in the Middle East.

Even so, social and recreational progress is moving at a far slower pace. Iraqi Kurdistan doesn't have the same wild and crazy parties found in Iran and Lebanon; it doesn't even have the submissive but quietly insubordinate Sunni youth population found in Syria. Having been to Halabjah, having heard the stories of the civil war, and having visited Biyara and Tawela, I understood some of the reason for this docility. The Iraqi Kurdish youth have had a horrifically violent and turbulent upbringing. Iran had the Iran-Iraq War, Lebanon had the civil war, and Syria had Hama, but Iraq was somehow different. Saddam Hussein's totalitarian grip on society, which for the Kurds lasted until 1991, was of a different breed. They grew up socialized into his cult of personality and brutality. As a result, the first decade of their lives was emotionless, uniform, and void of free thinking. In the words of one Kurdish student from Arbil, "Before the uprising, the Kurdish people generally were exposed to the Ba'athists; they could penetrate the brain of everybody. After the uprisings, the phenomenon of the Ba'athists vanished. This has completely changed the way of thinking for the Kurdish people. Our new ideology embraces, rather than hides, the concept of Kurdistan."

As satellite television, mobile phones, and the Internet are taking over, Kurdish youth are beginning to question long-standing cultural norms, particularly when it comes to the treatment of women. This is a new process: It was only in 2002 that honor laws were outlawed in the Iraqi Kurdistan Region. Honor law is a common understanding in the Middle East that if a female does something to dishonor her family—adultery and premarital sex are common crimes—any male in the family has the right to kill her without legal consequences.

As I'd seen and heard at the university, young Kurds are becoming active in creating a civil society. They are eager to start civic and civil organizations, some with greater backing than others. I encountered some youth organizations with offices, nice furniture, and computers; others were little more than a couple of guys sitting in a dark shack. The level of civic activism in the Iraqi Kurdistan Region is inspiring. We all could learn a thing or two from their dedication.

The most impressive group was the Kurdistan Student Union. I expected the students to be wearing shorts and shirts. But when I walked into the Kurdistan Student Union, I was embarrassed. I was wearing track pants, a T-shirt, and Birkenstocks and everybody else was dressed as if they were going to the office. Many of the boys wore jackets and ties, and all wore collared shirts and dress pants; the girls wore long dresses or skirts with nice blouses.

The Kurdistan Student Union was established in 1953. The union is headquartered in Arbil but has eighteen branches in the region. There are even branches in Mosul and Baghdad. There are no socio-economic requirements to join; the group boasts an official member-ship of 158,000, but youth from around the Iraqi Kurdistan Region often involve themselves in Kurdistan Union activities. The mission of the Kurdistan Student Union is to serve as a youth lobby to the Kurdistan Regional government. On a more basic level, the student union is designed to bring young people together so that the gen-eration may speak with a strong, united voice. The union runs or sponsors athletic clubs, newspapers, magazines, discussion groups, political groups, Internet sites, and even television programs. It is ar-guably the most progressive and influential youth lobby in the entire Middle East.

The Kurdish students are proud of the place in society they have earned. The president of the union told me that "in our history we have a lot of student victims who sacrifice themselves for the sake of their country. As you see there are many politicians, famous Kurd-ish politicians and leaders of the Kurds, that were members of this union, including Jalal Talalbani, the president of Iraq, and Mr. Bar-zani, the president of Iraqi Kurdistan Region." He reminded me of my friend Ruzwana, who had served as president of the Oxford Union and would always note that seven British prime ministers had begun their illustrious careers in this office as well. The students of the youth union were duly proud of the group's history and present-day influence on Kurdish affairs.

During that first meeting, I sat with about twenty members of the union in a gigantic room. I still felt uncomfortable about my attire, but I hoped they wouldn't notice or acknowledge the difference. As I was pondering this question, a group of youth walked in with a television camera and said that they were going to film the meeting for the student television network.

Where it exists in the Middle East, youth media is very influential. Young people don't trust politicians and they don't trust the older generation. They do, however, trust one another. I was told by Kurdish students in Iraq that they didn't watch Al-Jazeera, Al-Manar, or CNN; they instead relied on their own student media.

As I stared at the camera, one of the students sitting next to me made a comment, "I see you dressed smart for us." He was hunched over and his thick mustache made him look much older than his age. He wore a yellow-striped shirt and pants. Everyone gave an uncomfortable chuckle. Was he insulting me or just being funny? I started to apologize, but I was quickly waved off by the student union president, who told me my underdressing wasn't a big deal.

I began my questioning by asking whether as a youth organization they felt engaged by the government. One of the students explained to me that they have an excellent relationship with the government and expressed a firm belief that as a student union they were shaping events in their country. He wore light pants and a white T-shirt with a couple pens in his pocket. He looked like the kid in the front of the classroom. He was referring to the drafting of Iraq's first constitution, which was taking place at the time. The constitution was on everyone's mind. With Saddam Hussein gone, what role would Kurds play in the new Republic of Iraq? Would the Kurds be part of a federalist system? Would they maintain their autonomy? What positions would they get in the new government? All of these questions were unanswered and the Kurds were on edge. The students were fully in tune with the issues.

"The government has seminars and workshops with us so that we can give our input," the young man continued. "Even on the issue of the constitution, the government notices that the students are a sensitive part of the nation and that we need to be consulted." Youth empowerment was very important to these students. In Iran and Syria, the youth hadn't embraced their role as the majority of the population. In Lebanon, the youth had experienced their influence during the Cedar Revolution, but their role as a political influence was still nascent and not entirely united. But in the Iraqi Kurdistan Region, the youth understood their role, embraced it, and utilized it. Through their own effort, self-realization, and trial and error, young Kurds understood how to be influential. They united, expanded, and honed their message. They learned the politics, the needs, and the methods for making their voice heard. It was an example to be followed. I was intrigued and wanted to know more.

I asked the group what they do if they want to influence their government. This time, the student union president answered. His name was Bahar. He wore thick glasses, a blue dress shirt with short sleeves, and a striped pink tie. He described several ways that they influence the government, noting media, the Internet, and formal letters as their primary mode of advocacy. The letters particularly got my attention and I asked them if the government ever responds. I was surprised to hear that the government actually does respond to these letters. I heard stories of ministers coming to their seminars and engaging in roundtables with the youth. The students admitted that sometimes the conversations are useless in terms of substance, but do present them with an opportunity to remind the ministers that if they neglect the youth there will be consequences. He told me the story of a letter they wrote about a need to change the school curriculum. After months of waiting for a response, the student union organized a demonstration to show their demands to all of Iraqi Kurdistan. In the end, the curriculum was changed.

More than anything else, the students want to be a presence. They want their faces on TV, they want their rallies in the streets, and they want their opinions published. These students are very strategic; they pick and choose their battles. With all of the larger questions that the government is facing, the students are aware that issues like school curriculum cannot be responsible for bogging down a still-forming government. Aware of the potential for easy but meaningful victories, the young people push for reforms on apparently marginal issues. When they win, it is a display of their strength. It is an incredibly effective tactic.

The government wisely uses the student union as a way to keep this majority demographic engaged. In Iran, Syria, and Lebanon, the disconnect between youth and their governments leads to rumors and discontent that get exacerbated by word-of-mouth networks. In Iraqi Kurdistan Region, the student unions and the government have a mutually beneficial relationship. The students know what is going on and can properly channel their demands, and the government moderates a potentially disruptive portion of the population.

I asked them what they want for the future. I looked around the room, waiting to see who would answer. I noticed that the girls never spoke; they didn't even look like they wanted to speak. Not surprisingly, another one of the male students spoke up.

Their aim was clear; they wanted a Kurdish state and described this is as the overall aim of the Kurdish people. But they also stated that this aim will never be a reality without America standing behind them. The students proudly described how fourteen years of self-management and self-administration has been accomplished by the Kurdish people. They saw themselves as one of the world's best experiments ib self-made democracy.

Kurdish youth often referred to themselves as a "successful experiment." They look around their neighborhood, including their own country, and they see violence, corruption, and autocracy. They see their peers either in quiet submission or rebelling quietly and underground. When they look at themselves, they see something different and they are proud of this.

It is this pride in what they have achieved since 1991 that makes Kurds hesitant to view themselves within the larger Republic of Iraq.

Iraqi Kurds are among the most democratic people in the entire Middle East, but there is one thing about Kurdish society that deviates from this democratic momentum: Young Kurds do not want to be part of the Republic of Iraq.

They tore down their statues of Saddam Hussein in 1991, they've already had their civil war in the mid-1990s, and they've already had their first elections. Joining the Republic of Iraq is, for many Kurdish youth, a setback, a return to the past. This point came up often, so I asked them, "What does it mean for you to have a Kurdish president of the Republic of Iraq?"

One of the students, a young man named Havîn, jumped right in to say that while they are pleased the president is Kurdish, this is not the most important thing to them. Pressed further, he confessed that the current political situation leaves them no choice but to be with the central government. However, this is not what they ultimately want, which is independence and their own Kurdish state. Havîn paused for a moment to take a sip of his orange soda, and then spoke again. He seemed optimistic about the prospects of an independent state, almost too confident that this would happen.

After hearing repeated claims that they wanted their own state, I asked why they had no interest in being part of a unified Republic of Iraq. One of the students, a rather articulate and well-dressed boy named Qeşem, suggested that it is not natural for them to be part of Iraq, but this is the wish of the neighboring countries and the international community. He expressed a fear that as a minority group, the Kurds will have their future determined and shaped by the larger Arab demographic. Qeşem and his peers believed this to be an ominous legacy of the Ba'ath Party and felt that the Iraqi people still view society through the Ba'athist lens.

Qeşem then reminded me that the Arab nation, the Arab parts of Iraq, are part of a larger Arab nation, but the Kurdish part is part of the Kurdish nation. The Kurds want the authority to work with the establishment, but not be forced into a situation where they are required to work with the religious and Islamic ummah. From the Kurdish perspective, they have their own flag, they have a parliament and government, and they have experienced self-administration for fourteen years. With all of these things, they believe it only makes sense for them to eventually have their own state. Qeşem reminded me that they have lived and died for this right, telling me, "We have a river of blood and victims that led to the success of the Kurdish experiment. Now that we almost have it, we don't want to relive history."

Qeşem had touched on the fundamental contradiction of contemporary Kurdish political culture: Young Kurds were adamant about being prodemocratic, but they were wholeheartedly against majority rule. They wanted Iraq's wealth equally distributed among Kurds, Sunni, and Shi'a and they wanted a commission independent of the parliament to be in charge of this disbursement. It was important to them that the Shi'a not control the nation: One student warned that "America should take care of this point that the authorities should be equal among the nations. America must not give the rights of one nation to control another nation. We are a land of Kurds, Arabs, Turkomen, Shi'a, Sunni, and Christians." Most of these youth looked down on Sunni and Shi'a Iraqis as primitive in their thinking because they have only recently come to know life after Saddam.

One of the other impressive student organizations I encountered was the Kurdistan American Society, or KASFA. The goal of this civic group was to connect young Kurds to the outside world. Such an organization is significant: Rather than helping young Kurds move to the outside world, it seeks to make Kurdistan *part* of the outside world, integrating the young population into a global civil society. Unlike in most of other parts of the Middle East, young Kurds don't want to leave home. They see the Iraqi Kurdistan Region as a success story and they want to be around to benefit from the fruits of their accomplishments. They want to invest in Kurdistan, they want to be part of it, and they want to enjoy the freedoms they have. This mentality completely changes the psychology of the youth. The high level of seriousness among the youth is probably directly related to the fact that they see themselves as professional brokers in every aspect of Kurdish life.

The young leaders of KASFA expressed sympathy for Jews in Israel and appreciation for the American government, two stances rarely found in the Middle East. Revealing their sophisticated understanding of international politics, however, the young men made clear to me that their support was primarily practical: They knew that Americans and Kurds (and to some extent Israelis) shared common objectives and, more immediately, common enemies. They were well aware of the American abandonment in 1991, and recognized that most transnational alliances were based more on shared missions than on any sense of unconditional loyalty. They know that the United States has use for Kurdistan, and they know that they have use for the United States. And though this mutual affection may find its roots in realpolitik, the Kurds are indeed Iraqis who like us.

There was noticeably less partying in the Iraqi Kurdistan Region than in other parts of the Middle East I had been to. Their social gatherings are more tame and conservative, at least the ones I saw. An academic friend of mine had put me in touch with the boys of KASFA, who, in addition to sharing their NGO with me, also insisted on planning what they described to me as a typical Kurdish evening. While the events began at sundown, the preparation started long before that. After I met with them one afternoon for a typical interview over a can of orange soda, the two founders—Honar and Aram—insisted that we needed to go to the local market. Honar was in his late twenties. His head was shaved and he had a very round face. He had one of those pushing-young-adulthood bellies and a big smile. His colleague Aram was a bit taller, darker-skinned, and had a stylish part in the middle of his head. He sported some scruff, but on the whole, he was fairly clean-shaven. Both of them dressed in khaki pants and collared shirts. This seemed to be the Kurdish youth uniform.

We hopped in a taxi together and within ten minutes arrived at the market in downtown Arbil. From the road, it was difficult to see the sheer size of and congestion in the souq. But peering into the market through a narrow open way, I could begin to see we were about to enter into organized consumer chaos. As we walked through the busy rows of shops, which looked more like organized tables, I began to ponder why we had actually come here. Honar and Aram seemed to be on a mission, which I soon learned was a quest to find me Kurdish attire for the evening. As we navigated through the crowded shops and tables of clothes, watches, utensils, spices, and other knickknacks, we finally arrived at a place that looked like a store, as it actually had a door and walls. It was a clothing shop with different color clothes on gigantic rolls. The shopkeeper took my measurements, cut me some cloth, did some sewing, and gave me what seemed like a Kurdish kit. There was a head wrap, a gray shirt, large gray pants that looked like they were for a five-hundred-pound man, a random long piece of cloth, and a red-and-white string. Honar and Aram went with me back to my hotel, told me to come down at seven P.M., and asked me to bring my "Kurdish kit" to the hotel lobby, where they would help me make my transformation.

I became impatient and insisted on trying to dress myself. I had seen enough traditionally dressed Kurds with their baggy pants and cummerbund at stomach level to assume that I knew what I was doing. Confident that I had pulled it off, I walked down the stairs from my hotel room to the lobby. Almost in unison, the entire hotel staff—dressed in their cleanly pressed white dress shirts with extra starch and black bowties—burst into a fit of laughter and flocked toward me. They clearly felt I was a disaster or the Kurdish version of a fashion nightmare. I was like a race car in a pit stop as a whole crew of hotel staff fixed me up.

Honar and Aram were impressed when they saw me, but they were unaware of the frenzy that had preceded their arrival. They intended for the evening to be a surprise and took me thirty minutes outside of Arbil to the town of Salahaddîn.

There was no hot spot as I had expected. This was not an underground party and it was not a street party. Instead, it was Aram's home. He lived in a small white house, decent-sized, with a large cement patio and large windows. Aram led me inside and showed me to the dining room, where, rather than being one of many individuals dressed in Kurdish attire, I was alone in this. The children—Aram's brothers and cousins—loved it and got a kick out of taking my head wrap off my head when I wasn't looking.

This was a different kind of dining room. There were no tables and no chairs. Thin and faint white curtains concealed the one window in the room. The only furniture was a small wooden stand with a fifteen-inch color television with the sound blasting. But it wasn't Al-Jazeera or a local prayer channel; it was Nic Robertson reporting for CNN from Baghdad. Ten of us sat around a white sheet that was virtually covered in oversized portions, bottles of soda, and utensils. This was a feast.

There were over a dozen bowls of food, each with a mixture of something a little different. There were rice dishes, lamb, beef, kebabs, greens, and assorted vegetables. Some of the smaller bowls had a white creamy yogurt, while others had dip that looked more like hummus. This was enough food to feed a small army.

The substance of our dinner conversation began with an elaborate description of all the fine dishes I saw on the white sheet. From there it quickly moved to the Iraqi insurgency, but mostly because I probed them on this. It wasn't that they were reluctant to talk about the violence in the Sunni region, but they didn't view this as anything that had to do with them. As far as they were concerned, this was an Iraqi problem and they were Kurds. They view cooperation by integrating themselves into the Republic of Iraq as a mere formality. We exhausted this topic and after enough conversation, there is only so much you can get out of a people who don't identify with what is going on in their own country. So we talked about Kurdish music, and the kids around the table played me their favorite tunes.

Traveling to the Iraqi Kurdistan Region was like traveling to an oasis of peace and stability in the middle of a bloody war zone.

CHAPTER 12

WAKING UP IN THE INSURGENCY

IRAQ, 2005

Leaving Kurdistan, I drifted off to sleep in the car. Even in the hours before the sun has risen, the scorching heat of the Iraqi desert is unbearable. During the summer, just breathing is a difficult task. Still, it didn't take me more than five minutes to fall into a deep sleep. My visit to Iraq had been fruitful and less dangerous than I had anticipated and I was satisfied with the trip. For once heeding the severe travel restrictions imposed by the American government, I had shown rare restraint and avoided the war zone that most of Iraq had become. Though traveling alone throughout the Middle East is never without its anxieties, I was able to sleep soundly, knowing that I was as safe as I'd been in months. When the afternoon heat finally woke me a few hours later, I blinked open my eyes and tried to focus on the Ibrahim Khalil border between Iraq and Turkey. There was one slight problem: It wasn't there.

I had entered Iraq at this crossing, but now I saw nothing around me that resembled the route I had taken to Iraq, and was planning to take out. I no longer saw the beautiful hills of the Iraqi Kurdistan Region. The buildings were dilapidated and there was a turned-over and burnt-out car on the side of the road. These were not typical sights for northern Iraq. It looked like a war zone, the Iraq I had so wisely avoided visiting. I leaned to the front seat to ask the driver where he'd taken me.

It was then that I realized that I was alone.

I've been in a lot of dangerous situations before, but something about this one really scared me. It was nearing 130 degrees and I was alone in what appeared to be a war zone in the middle of Iraq. If I'd known then that I was actually in the heart of the Iraqi insurgency, I would probably have had an anxiety attack.

In my last ten days in Iraq, forty-six American soldiers had been killed throughout the country, with a significant portion of those fatalities occurring in the Al Tafal Region southwest of Mosul. In addition to this, an American journalist in Basra had been shot in the head and killed during that same period. If Iraq was unsafe to travel for soldiers and journalists, what did that mean for me, a twenty-three-year-old unarmed American Jew?

Fortunately for me, I was tired, disoriented, and willing to convince myself that I was jumping to conclusions about my location. But the danger of the situation became immediately apparent when I stepped out of the car to stretch my legs and look around. On a cement wall, I could see a defaced painting of the former Iraqi president, Saddam Hussein. Just east of the defaced image, a tattered old Ba'ath flag flew high above a local checkpoint. No longer under the protective banner of the Iraqi Kurdistan regional government, I stood staring at the standard of the new Republic of Iraq. I had no idea where I was.

I knew that I had fallen asleep in Kurdistan, expecting to wake up when my driver had arrived at the Iraq-Turkey border. Instead, I was alone, somewhere in the heart of Sunni Iraq. The only thing that kept me from giving in to utter dread and terror was the irony of the situation: After years of recklessly putting myself in harm's way, I'd finally acted responsibly and somehow ended up in the most dangerous situation in which I'd ever found myself.

I was suspicious of every person who walked by. The Kurdish government was no longer protecting me and there was plenty to be afraid of: As not simply an American, but as an American Jew, an "entrepreneur" could make a nice chunk of change by telling insurgents of my location. Once captured by insurgents, well, I'd seen the horrifying videos too.

Fearful of everybody, I didn't want to talk to anybody. But I had to know where I was. If I didn't get out of Iraq and safely to Syria or Turkey, I could be killed. Frozen in terror, I could do nothing but watch as a middle-aged man walked slowly by, eyeing me suspiciously.

He wore a long, dirty white robe and had a large, full beard. His face was wrinkled, especially around his nose and eyes, which were squinting at me from beneath particularly bushy eyebrows. He wore a white head scarf kept in place by two woven black rings. He was also almost certainly not an insurgent. The bucket and metal tool he carried identified him as an average workingman.

"Shu ism haida medina?" I asked the man.

"Al-Mawsil," he answered in an almost unintelligible voice.

I was in Mosul, the most dangerous city in one of the most dangerous countries in the world. There was literally no other city he could have named that would have been more terrifying.

I knew then that I needed to make myself invisible—and fast. I had no time to panic, to remember that I should have been hundreds of kilometers away, peacefully crossing from Ibrahim Khalil in Iraq to Habur in Turkey. Some horrible twist of fate had brought me to Mosul, and I needed to accept that and figure out how the hell I was going to get out of the Iraqi insurgency alive.

My first thought was that the driver had abandoned me and would be returning with insurgents. This type of setup was not especially rare, and I wasn't paranoid to expect the absolute worst: namely that I had put my life into the hands of a man who had just as quickly sold it to terrorists who would pay for the opportunity to torture and kill a Jew from the United States.

I had two equally unpalatable options: I could look for a friendly face in one of the least hospitable environments in the world, or I could continue to trust the driver who had brought me there and then disappeared. Dizzy and nauseated from fear, I managed to think straight long enough to figure that running and hiding were mutually exclusive, and that if I ran, it would probably be much harder to hide once I got to wherever I was running to. So I hid.

What followed were the longest forty-five minutes of my life.

I walked back to the car and pulled the rusty handle. I curled up in the back to lie down so that nobody could see me from the outside. Unfortunately, the car was parked at a rather busy intersection in the outskirts of Mosul, and I was on display for whoever happened to pass by. The road was lined with shops selling everything from chewing gum to tires, and the dirt side streets were trafficked by a steady stream of consumers, pedestrians, and shopkeepers. Every so often, I would see someone peering directly into the car to look inside.

As I sat there—an unarmed American on display in the middle of the Iraqi insurgency—my imagination ran wild. Every time I saw someone on a cell phone, I wondered if they were calling insurgents to tell them about the idiot American just waiting to be kidnapped. When people came to look into the car, I wondered if they would rob me or worse. Strangely, I found the prospect of having my wallet and passport stolen more terrifying than imminent bodily harm. The prospect of being stuck in Mosul without any means of escape was a nightmare whose ending I couldn't even begin to imagine.

Every time I made eye contact with one of the passersby, my heart stopped. So I closed my eyes, praying against all odds that I would somehow fall asleep, and maybe even wake up safe and sound in Turkey. But if my fear wouldn't keep me awake, the temperature would. It must have been at least 140 degrees in the car, and I had no water. Overheated and dehydrated, I was slipping into a state of delirium beyond terror.

I began to flashback on the past year and wonder whether all of this was really worth it. Here I was—crouched in the steamy backseat of a rusty car, hiding from enemies whom I wouldn't recognize until it was too late—and for what?

It then occurred to me—in the midst of all the self-pity and paranoia—that the fear I was experiencing probably represented only one-tenth of what Iraqi youth must feel on a daily basis. This realization alone was enough to keep me going; through the staring faces and the vigilant eyes, my suspicion began to subside. I had a momentary sense of calm, or at least something approaching calm.

I had been in compromising situations before, with Shi'a extremists and Sunni Palestinian militants. The Sunni insurgents in Mosul, however, were of a different sort. In comparison with the extremists I had come into contact with in Iran, Lebanon, Syria, and the Palestinian camps, those in Iraq were an entirely different breed. Being a researcher, a student, or any other identity would not protect me with these thugs. If I was caught, I would likely die in a brutal and horrific manner. This was my fear in Mosul. At the time I could not have envisioned how the situation would degenerate. I was there in August 2005, but just six months after my journey through northern Iraq, Sunni insurgents bombed the twelve-hundred-year-old Shi'ite holy Askariya shrine in Samarra. The attack on this symbol of Shi'a Islam led to terrible sectarian violence as the Shi'a sought reprisal and a series of back-and-forth attacks brought the country to the brink of civil war. The brutality of this slaughter was horrific and inhumane, with decapitations, senseless bombings, and even the use of drill bits to torture victims. It was a horror to come that would have at the time seemed unimaginable.

In my time in the Middle East, I had learned that extremism exists on a continuum, that there is a broad spectrum of views, methods, and goals for these groups. While Hezbollah and Hamas employ brutal terrorist tactics, most notably suicide bombing, they view themselves as some form of a resistance movement. In Iraq, the insurgents reject the entire international system and use Iraq as their primary front without any clear objective. It would have been overly paranoid to imagine myself being taken hostage and decapitated by Palestinian militants; there was no reason not to fear this very real possibility in Mosul. I was in a playground for lawless insurgents, ideological hijackers motivated by little more than rage and bloodlust.

As it turns out, clumsy Americans are not the only ones who live in fear in this part of Iraq. Sunni youth in Iraq are for the first time in their lives experiencing life as a minority—without the protection of Saddam Hussein and his cadre of Sunni loyalists from Tikrit. While many Sunni youth secretly despised Saddam, they also took for granted the comfort and opportunities that they enjoyed relative to the Shi'a and Kurdish populations. Now, they were terrified to walk in the streets; their futures were suddenly cloudy, even foreboding. The insurgency was happening in their own backyard and the hijacking of Islam by their fellow Sunnis had made their social and political situation in the new Iraq precarious at best. I saw in them a growing helplessness, not unlike the tragic impotence I saw among Palestinian youth. They didn't have the luxury that Kurdish youth have to write letters, print protests, and demonstrate. They live each day as it comes and have to focus on staying alive. Stability is all they have room to ponder; this was not a youth population that seemed empowered to play a role in shaping their future. They didn't know what to do: If they could leave Iraq, many would. For the majority caught between rejecting the insurgency and ensuring their own safety, however, life in Mosul is a devil's bargain.

Before I knew it, I heard a knock on the passenger-side window. It was the driver, unable to get in the car. I had locked all of the doors. He smiled at me and nodded his head, gesturing for me to open the door. He appeared to be alone, so I obliged. I immediately saw that he had two large red jugs in his hands. They were filled with what appeared to be gasoline. I started screaming at him in English. "Where the hell did you go? You just leave me on the side of the street in Mosul? Do you have any idea how dangerous that is?" I yelled. He listened and nodded politely. He had no idea what I was saying. I stopped screaming. I asked him where he had been the past forty-five minutes and the absurdity of his answer almost made me laugh. He had left me abandoned in Mosul so that he could walk to buy black market gas for nine cents a gallon so that he would not have to pay the actual twelve-cents-a-gallon price. He had put my life in grave danger for what probably amounted to thirty-six cents. I had at least a hundred times that amount just in souvenir currency for family and friends. Despite my driver's total lack of common sense, I couldn't really press the issue. I'd already been in uncomfortable situations with drivers in Syria near the Iraq border, and I figured that I had no other choice but to make the best of my driving companion for a tour of the Iraqi insurgency.

Cheap gasoline explained why he had disappeared, but I still didn't understand why we'd ended up in Mosul when I hadn't had to pass through this horrific place on my way into the country. His answer to my inquiry was either naïve or reckless, I wasn't really sure. He had chosen the most direct route out of Iraq, totally disregarding the danger of driving an American through the heart of an insurgency. This detour to Mosul wasn't an accident: It had always been his plan to cross into Syria through the very borders that insurgents were using as hideouts. The route he had planned made us susceptible to roadside bombs and ambushes; the border crossing he had chosen was not guaranteed to be open to Americans. I happened to have a multiple-entry visa for Syria, but my driver didn't know that. Syria does not just issue visas on the spot and I seriously doubted that my driver would stand by my side as I found some way either to head back or to expedite the process. That's not just a reflection on my driver; it would have been unreasonable to expect favors at such a dangerous border. Either this man had no sense of risk or he really needed to get to northeastern Syria in a hurry. His choice of route was risking not only my life, but his, as well. If insurgents or other hostile characters saw him driving an American—even a civilian unaffiliated with the armed occupation—they would have assumed he was working with the U.S. government.

And even if our car was not spotted by insurgents and ambushed, just driving on the road in the Sunni part of Iraq is a suspenseful and terrifying experience. Roadside bombs are unsophisticated, cheap, and extremely prevalent. I had heard stories of bombs made from cell phones, plastic bags, masking tape, and gunpowder. I winced every time our car approached garbage on the street, while the driver blithely barreled along. Each slight bump set my heart pounding.

The hour alone had been miserable, but the next several hours were unbelievably excruciating. Ironically, the only thing that made me feel even remotely safe was the fact that I was not in a convoy, fancy car, or Humvee; instead, I was in a white Toyota Camry, clearly on its last legs. What remained of the paint on the car hinted that it had once shone a bright white. The Toyota symbol, while still recognizable from the two-thirds of it that remained, dangled off the back of the car. The front windshield had a huge crack and the right side of the car had a bullet hole in it. The tires, while themselves intact, rested on a wheels that were of varying designs and colors.

The inside of the car was in worse shape than the exterior. The seats had significant tears in them and the mechanics of the dashboard were visible, with wires shooting off in all directions. The glove compartment had no door, but a small handgun that had previously been in the driver's possession fit perfectly inside. There were no speakers on the doors and there were random papers and documents thrown about the car.

I found some very slight comfort in the thought that even if insurgents did spot the car, I would be able to hide from their sight, and they would probably not view the vehicle as suspicious: It would just be another piece of junk traveling up and down the road from Mosul to Rabea'a, our destination at the Syrian border.

Still, the comfort was slight enough that I was doing my best to remain as hidden as possible. I had managed to fit myself into the small area between the backseat and the front seats, curling myself in a ball below the windows. While curled up in the back of the car, I took my computer case and placed it over my face and neck. If the car got shot through the windows, I would lose my hard drive instead of my life. I then took my passport and notebook and placed it over my chest. As a child, I had used sofa cushions and pillows to build forts; now, only a few years later, I was fashioning bulletproof vests out of books. Fear can make you do frivolous things when in need of reassurance.

After about twenty minutes in this position, I started to move back up to the seat, but quickly crouched back down when my driver gestured that it might be a good idea to stay there. I guess he was aware of the danger we were in. Without any other options, I reluctantly placed faith in the fact that he must have known what he was doing.

The drive seemed to take forever; to this day I really cannot recall how long we remained on the road from Mosul to Rabea'a. Despite his apparent recognition of the danger we were in, the driver stopped three or four times to say hello to people he knew along the way, mostly in local side shops; he even stopped to have teas. At one of the stops, he turned to me, still sandwiched between the front and back seats, and politely asked if I wanted anything.

Throughout this entire hellish day, it had taken all the restraint I could muster not to strangle this man who seemed a bit too nonchalant at the risk he was taking with my life. If I didn't know better, I would have thought he found my fear entertaining, a little bonus beyond what I was paying him. His total disregard for both of our lives infuriated me, and my anger grew each time he pulled off the road to chat with a buddy. I decided that if I saw American troops, I would get out of the car and seek their assistance. By this point, being embedded in a war zone with troops in active combat seemed more appealing than being stuck in the backseat of a shitty Camry with a man who was totally uninterested in either my or his own safety.

As angry as I was at the driver, I was angrier still at myself. All things being equal, I had gotten myself into this mess. After all I'd been through—all I'd seen and done and lived to tell about—I could lose my life because I'd fallen asleep on the way to Turkey.

When we finally did come upon American troops, the car almost got shot. While sandwiched on the floor of the car, I saw a three-vehicle American convoy coming down the street. The trucks looked like gigantic pickup trucks with machine guns on the back, protected by three shields. As the convoy approached, I noticed the American soldiers turning the machine gun toward the car. There is a de facto law that has been established in the occupation that when the American troop convoys come down the road, cars must move off to the side and allow them to pass. The widespread use of suicide attacks by moving vehicles had forced the American troops to enforce the regulation by shooting to disable the engine of a car if it did not move for the convoy. My driver was slow to respond, and only moved off the side of the road at the last minute. Seeing how nervous he was, I realized that this had actually been a fairly close call.

After more driving, we finally reached a long line of traffic. I was happy to reach the border, but I now had to deal with an entirely new set of fears.

Once again, my driver left me in the car as he stepped out to talk to people. While he socialized, I hid; this was the charade that we had employed throughout this truly miserable day. As we got closer to the front of the traffic, I saw that there were several American troops manning the border. I can recall very few moments in my life when I felt this kind of relief and patriotism.

I jumped out of the car and walked quickly and excitedly toward the Rabea'a border. I had forgotten that I looked ridiculous: I was wearing oversized and baggy gray Kurdish pants, homemade Kurdish

Kalash shoes, a blue Banana Republic T-shirt, dark sunglasses, and a backward blue Etnies hat. I approached the first soldier I saw. He was dressed in the full army gear, wore a helmet, and held on to a large gun that was strapped to his shoulder. He was youthful, probably late twenties, and had a thick mustache.

"Hi, how are you? Sir, I have a bit of a problem—" I began.

"Are you American?" he interrupted to ask.

"Yes, sir, I am."

Shocked, worried, and, not least of all, curious, he exclaimed, "What the hell are you doing here?"

"I fell asleep in Iraqi Kurdistan and woke up in Mosul."

"You drove from Mosul?" he asked, as if this was the most ridiculous thing he had ever heard.

"Yes, I did. Was that a risk? I mean, I know it's a risk, but how dangerous is it?" I stammered.

"Well, do you see me? I am standing here with a gun. Do you see the other soldiers around? They have guns. You are in a war zone. This is an insurgency," he stopped, eyeing me again. "Seriously, what the hell are you doing here?"

"Can you help me get safely across this border?" I pleaded.

He gestured me over to his superior, an older-looking man who stood roughly twenty feet closer to the border.

Just as I was leaving, the first soldier asked me, "What state are you from?"

"I'm from Connecticut. You?"

"Texas," he answered.

Just before walking away, I looked at him and said, "Thank you for your help. I want you to know we all appreciate what you guys are doing here."

He looked at me as if he did not believe what I was saying. His response reflected the low morale of so many young American troops.

"Yeah, right," he said. "But thanks anyway."

I didn't know what to say. I do have the utmost admiration and respect for our troops in Iraq, men and women often younger than myself risking their lives for their country and for the Iraqi people.

I walked over to the other soldier and greeted him the same way. He asked for my passport, which I happily presented. He looked at me and said, "You're American," as if this was a surprise to him. "What are you doing in Iraq?"

I explained to him, "I've been doing research on youth and how they think about democracy. I was supposed to go out through Kurdistan, but I fell asleep and woke up in Mosul."

Shocked, he looked at me.

"Man, you are crazy! You really shouldn't be here, I mean for your own safety. This is really crazy!"

He handed me my passport and told me where to go to get it stamped. In the distance I could see the Syrian border post with pictures of the late Hafez al-Assad and President Bashar al-Assad. It became very clear how unsafe I felt in this part of Iraq when I started to fantasize about the safety I would feel in the neighboring Sunni villages, heavily populated with fundamentalists and assimilated insurgents.

As I walked toward the immigration office, I saw my driver once again. He had caught up and reassured me that we were continuing on together to Qamishli. He, of course, just wanted to make sure that I was still paying him and not jumping into the arms of the American soldiers at his expense, but I told him I still planned to go with him. He seemed relieved and told me that he would be waiting with the car as soon as he got through immigration. I was very amiable; the comfort I felt from being in the midst of American troops made me instantly less bitter toward him. Strangely, I felt a sense of camaraderie with him, like we had made it through hell together.

The soldiers at the immigration office were really excited to see a fellow American. They were genuinely curious about what I had been doing and, strangely, really liked hearing the story of how I had ended up in Mosul. The morale among this group seemed high, and even while they expressed frustrations over continuous deployments and a lack of recreation, they seemed to believe in the larger cause. I watched them energetically go about their border operations, which included conducting interrogations and maintaining order.

One soldier, a large kid from Arkansas, was particularly eager to speak to me. His name was Dan and he was about my age. Dan grabbed a plastic chair for me and told me to wait in the shade while the Iraqi immigration officers processed my passport. For some reason, the Iraqi officer was particularly aggressive with me and even at one point pushed me out of his way with some force. Dan saw this happen and screamed at him, "Don't touch him like that again!" I really felt good, like I was being protected. After the day I'd had, the sense of safety and comfort made me almost giddy.

I shared a cigarette with the soldiers. I heard about their families and their various stories that had brought them to Iraq. They asked me a lot of questions about the status of sports teams, what new albums were out, and how people in the United States were viewing the situation in Iraq. It was a very special moment for me. I'd interacted with the military before, but mostly to talk policy with officers at the Pentagon. Here, on the Iraqi-Syrian border, I was interacting with my peers, enlisted soldiers who were carrying out a truly dangerous mission with great courage and mental strength. I admire them tremendously.

After getting my passport stamped, I walked through the no-man's-land toward Syria. I was not going to die in the insurgency! All of my fear had been left at the border. As I turned around and looked back at Iraq, I saw a gigantic cement structure that towered over the border. At the top arch of the structure, black capital letters spelled, WELCOME TO RABEA'A GATEWAY TO IRAQ. In the middle was a picture of Iraq, filled with the red, white, and green Iraqi flag. Like the flag, the picture had three stars in the white stripe, with the Arabic writing *Allah Akbar*, for

"God is great." As I glanced at this sign, I couldn't help but look back positively on my time in Iraq. While my last twenty-four hours there had proven terrifying, I began to remember the resilient youth I had met, the young people who were putting aside their feelings about the United States government to play an active role in building a better life for themselves, free from the ruthless oppression they had suffered under Saddam Hussein.

I was lucky to have escaped the war in Iraq unscathed. Rather than falling into the hands of insurgents, I now found myself again in northeastern Syria, sipping tea and eating kebab as my Kurdish friends smiled at me affectionately.

EPILOGUE

THE YOUTH PARTY

After my misadventures in Mosul, I returned to Lebanon. Then, after a series of unreturned phone calls and ominous text messages, I realized that I'd now fallen out of favor with my Hezbollah contacts. My travels were finally beginning to take their toll on me. I was physically and emotionally spent. After trips to Iraq, Iran, Syria, Lebanon, Afghanistan, and all over Africa, I also owed it to my parents to spend some time with them in Connecticut and New York. It was time to go home.

I was thrilled to reconnect with family and friends after two years abroad, but just as I'd done after arriving home from Iran, I started planning for my next trip not long after my return. I wanted to return to Lebanon: I hoped to thaw my relationship with Hezbollah and see if I could go deeper into the organization and perhaps even reach some of the leadership. I also knew how much fun Lebanon would be in the summer; I was excited for another round of parties.

One friend described the weeks of late June 2006 as the "most amazing summer in the history of Beirut." He told me, "Everybody is talking about it, you must come." As I listened to friends tell me about the newest bars and beach parties, all I heard over and over again was "You have no idea what you are missing."

Optimism in the summer of 2006 was even greater than it had been the previous July. There hadn't been a bombing since December 2005, when Gebran Tueini, the outspoken anti-Syrian editor-in-chief of *An Nahar*, was killed in a car bombing. Also contributing to the sense of hopefulness was the fact that there were negotiations taking place between Shi'as, Christians, and Sunnis within the government. Beginning in January 2006, these negotiations were even addressing the issue of how to disarm Hezbollah. While no conclusions had been reached, many Lebanese were encouraged that the country's rival powers were at least talking about how to better the country. Finally, tourism was at an all-time high. Reservations in hotels were fully booked for the whole summer, new buildings were springing up, new recreational sites were opening, and tourism revenue was four times higher than in the previous summer. Families who had been part of the diaspora were coming back to Lebanon to visit and thinking about moving back permanently.

Even when a conflict between Hamas and Israel erupted at the end of June, most Lebanese hardly blinked. They had grown accustomed to violence next door in Gaza and the West Bank, and this new skirmish was not a threat to their borders. An average Lebanese might catch a glimpse of what was going on by watching the news in the morning, but by day they would be at the beach and by night they would be at the bars and clubs.

Suddenly, out of nowhere, Hezbollah entered the conflict. Since 2000, the organization had claimed that it was not interested in destroying Israel, but was instead focused on protecting Lebanon's sovereignty and winning back Shaba Farms near the Golan Heights. But in July 2006, Hezbollah militants entered Israel, killing three Israeli Defense Forces (IDF) soldiers and kidnapping an additional two. The attack by Hezbollah was a sudden and unexpected departure from what many believed the organization had become. There was no doubt that historically, Hezbollah has been responsible for some of the worst terrorist attacks against the United States and Israel; there was also no way of being certain that its self-imposed halt to high-profile terrorist attacks would be anything but temporary. Still, Hezbollah had been out of the kidnapping business and had seemingly moderated its behavior substantially since it had claimed victory in ousting Israel from Lebanon in 2000.

On July 12, Israel reentered Lebanon for the first time since it had left in 2000. The beginnings of a ground operation led to the capture of two more IDF soldiers by Hezbollah. The following day, the IDF bombed the airport in Beirut, killing forty-four Lebanese civilians and leading to widespread fear among Lebanese that they were once again trapped in a war zone. Hezbollah responded by launching Katyusha rockets into northern Israel, killing two Israelis and wounding more than thirty-five. The attacks continued over the next week as Israel continued the ground and air strikes and Hezbollah launched thousands of rockets aimlessly into Israel.

As the international community struggled to find a solution to the rapidly escalating conflict, Hezbollah continued to launch hundreds of rockets each day into the Israeli city of Haifa, while the IDF followed its air strikes with a ground invasion by more than ten thousand troops. In response, Hezbollah leader Hassan Nasrallah vowed to turn south Lebanon into a graveyard of Israeli troops. By mid-August, the fighting between Hezbollah and Israel had completely destroyed much of the country. As bombs dropped and rockets flew, the "war children" of Lebanon had once again fled to the mountains to watch their beautiful country being reduced to the rubble they remembered from their childhood. Only, this time it was different: They'd had a taste of the good life and knew what was being taken away from them. In the words of one of my Lebanese friends, "Lebanon is a country that almost was, but will never be, because it has bad neighbors."

As I received phone calls from Beirut, I could hear the planes and the bombs in the background. I could hear the fear in the voices of my friends. "Jared, they are destroying our country," they told me. My friends were not referring specifically to Israel or Hezbollah; they referred to actors that didn't represent them. Some said they hated Israel, while others blamed Hezbollah. I heard some blame America and I listened to others blame everybody. "We have no way out," I was told after the airport was bombed and the road to Damascus was destroyed. For almost two weeks straight, I sat on the couch of my apartment in New York, one eye on the news on television and the other on my laptop, where I was using MSN Messenger and Skype to communicate with dozens of my Lebanese friends. The Lebanon I saw on television was not the Lebanon I knew; it was the Lebanon of the past, the war-torn country that my friends had shown me photos of, had described for me in detail, and had hoped would never resurface. When I was in Lebanon, my friends would always remind me that nothing was as peaceful as it seemed. They said violence could come again, but I didn't believe them; I thought they were captives to the paranoid scapegoating of their childhood. Besides, with all the partying we did, it was hard to imagine the country could return to war.

As I watched Lebanon fall apart, I was reminded of one of the first things I'd been told when I arrived in Beirut a year earlier. Upon finding out that I was American, someone said to me that "on 9/11 we prayed for you and our hearts were with the people of America." I remember being touched by the warm embrace of a people who demonstrated such compassion for what they knew had been a difficult time for the United States.

The post-9/11 years have not been easy for Middle Eastern youth. To most of the rest of the world, the Middle East seems caught in a perpetual cycle of violence, sectarian conflict, and fanaticism. On TV, we watch both Shi'a and Sunni insurgencies mounting in Iraq; mujahideen fighters trying to revive Taliban-style rule in Afghanistan; and Hezbollah and the IDF fighting a war in Lebanon. In the newspapers, we read about the publication of cartoons depicting the Prophet Muhammad in an offensive light, sparking massive riots in Europe; the president of Iran calling for the destruction of Israel; and terrorists in Britain conspiring to blow up ten commercial airplanes with liquid explosives. The images and rhetoric we see on the news lead us to believe that the world is on an inevitable path to catastrophe, even apocalypse.

And that's wrong.

My journeys have taken me from wild underground parties in the Islamic Republic of Iran to the military headquarters of some of the most dangerous Palestinian camps in all of Lebanon to the emotionally shattered villages of Syria and finally to the war-torn streets of Iraq. As an American Jew traveling in the Middle East during this age of terror, I should have been unwelcome, I should have felt unsafe, and it should have been impossible for me to engage on any level with people who I'd been told hated my country and my religion. But I found that the easy, monolithic characterization of "us versus them" fails to take into account the humanity and the individuality of all of the people who make up "us" and "them." And the "them" I met—the young men and women of the Middle East—should make all of us very hopeful for the future.

The war in Lebanon, the violence in Iraq and Afghanistan, and the growing threat of terrorist attacks are by no means insignificant. But these events have not—and will not—change the fundamental nature of youth culture in the Middle East. And that's why I believe that despite the almost daily setbacks we see on television and read about in newspapers, there is a better future ahead of us; I've seen it with my own eyes.

I am optimistic about the future because of the people I met: Sharif, Fouad, and Asharaf, the three members of Hezbollah who told me they hated the Israeli and American governments but had no problem with Jewish or American people. These young Hezbollah boys showed me that even they—young people linked to a known terrorist organization—seem to know the differences between religions, governments, and people; the unnamed young taxi driver who didn't charge me because I was American; the Iranian university students who told me they had wept for me on September 11; the young couple enjoying each other's company in the bushes, always one step ahead of the morals police; Gita and Leila, who wore elaborately pink and blue hejabs while denouncing the Iranian regime behind their menus; Omid, who had prevented me from taking photos of anti-American propaganda in Esfahan out of fear that I might show it to people in America and give them the wrong idea about Iran; Cirrus and his friends, who took me to underground parties in Iran where alcohol was made in bathtubs and Western music was blasting; Nezam, my trusted hotel receptionist in Iran who simply wanted a way out of his country; Mariam and Nassim, who showed me how boys and girls pass their phone numbers to random love interests on Fereshteh Street in Iran; the feisty girl in Shiraz who, once shown the cost of the nuclear program, realized that she would prefer the ouster of the clerics to all the nuclear weapons in the world; the girls from southern Iran with their meticulously applied makeup, telling the Basij forces to get out of their faces; the hard-liners in Esfahan, who described the skyscrapers in New York as so amazing that "they must be with the hand of Allah"; the Iranian hipster who pointed me in the direction of the synagogue; the Jews who worshipped freely on the Sabbath in one of Iran's eleven synagogues; Lebanese Christians like Ziad, Walid, and Naylah, who reminded me that, despite sectarian divides, the Beirut evening temporarily unites Christians, Muslims, and Druze as Lebanese who love to party; Lebanese Sunni like Hibah, who told me that during the Cedar Revolution she stood before Muslims and Christians and realized for the first time that she was Lebanese; the

Hezbollah youth I would interview in the afternoon and run into at the club at night; Ayman, who wanted to take me into Ayn al-Hilwah so that I could see for myself that there was more to the Palestinian youth than meets the eye; the Palestinian militants, who told me they wanted pens, not guns; Haifa and Maya, who took me on a tour of the conservative town of Homs, comfortably wearing Western clothing and flaunting their own interpretation of modesty in the face of glaring Sunni fundamentalists; Mazen, who spent hours driving me around on his moped in an effort to make sure I would not feel lost or unsafe in the predominantly Sunni region of Syria; the soccer-playing boys of Hama, who gave me a candid political assessment of Syria; the shopkeeper in Palmyra who knew I would not change my religious beliefs, but still enjoyed the chance to teach me about the Quran; the Bedouin nomads, who had their satellite television in the Palmyra Desert with 963 channels; the Sunni youth who sneered at my taxi driver's decal of Osama bin Laden; and the Iraqi Kurdish youth who lived in a region that seems to be an oasis of stability amid the chaos of war in other parts of their country.

None of this is what I expected to find. With each debunked myth, with each overturned stereotype, I began to see that widely broadcast images of violent, angry, and fanatical Muslims are hardly representative of the majority of the Middle East. In fact, youth, the majority demographic in the region, share more similarities with their American peers than most of the world realizes.

Middle Eastern youth are far more sophisticated than earlier generations in their ability to distinguish between governments, people, and religions. Hardly fans of their own governments and the ruling circles, they themselves bristle at being associated with regimes they don't support. Most know the difference between Americans and the American government and they know the difference between Jews and Israel; they want Americans to know the difference between, say, the supreme leader of the Islamic Republic and Iranians. And though they might not support the American government and other practitioners of democracy, Middle Eastern youth appreciate the concept of democracy, practice it on a daily basis through technology even if they don't make the association, and desire many of its benefits.

As I saw from the dual lives of young people with their evening and daytime identities, the majority of youth are relatively progressive when it comes to their social and recreational activities. This isn't simply a reflection on the innate rebelliousness of youth: Because of increased access to diverse perspectives and an enhanced ability to interact through digital, audio, and visual media, the current generation of young people enjoy an independence that their parents and grandparents could not have imagined. Such autonomy has never before existed in these police-state societies or tension-ridden environments, but it has become impossible for the watchful eye of the government or the vigilance of their own parents to be everywhere without the complete banning of technology that has already become intertwined into Middle Eastern society.

While young and old alike use and enjoy satellite television, radio, Internet, and mobile phones, the generations are using them in completely different ways. For young people, technology is first and foremost a means to express themselves, interact, generate their own media, and shape a digital identity that may or may not be in sync with real life. They rely on this technology for their autonomy and as a result, it is through this digital means that the youth have been emancipated from the rest of the population. They are incredibly proficient at learning the innovative uses of technology, in part because of what technology brings them and in part because they actually read the instruction manual.

The youth are not only using technology to communicate with one another; they are using it to communicate with the rest of the world. And that's the most significant difference between the young people and the older generations: Unless they have deliberately shielded themselves from technology, nearly every single youth in the Middle East is accessible.

Middle Eastern youth are just an e-mail or text message away. However, their thoughts, opinions, and feelings are very much in contention. When I left the Middle East, it wasn't clear who was winning this fierce battle of ideas. It seemed then, as it does now, that extremists and ideologues have already made tremendous inroads into shaping the opinions of these young people. I can say from my own experience, living and traveling in this volatile part of the world, that reaching this under-thirty generation is our best hope for greater communication—but only if we engage with them on their own terms. Amid the despair of war, poverty, and oppression, they are the ones who respond to creativity. Could it be that they will also find creative solutions for peace someday? In a world of unremitting grimness brought on by lack of opportunity, they are the ones who delight in entertainment and the allure of adventure. Could it be that they will be able to rise above their despotic regimes to live interesting and successful lives? And, finally, they are the ones who can be reached by breaking down the traditional means of communication and speaking a language that appeals to them. Could it be that we will truly find a common language so that this generation everywhere can communicate their hopes and ideals? Or, is it possible that we will fail and the extremists and ideologues will hijack the hearts and minds of this entire generation?

What I have discovered is that the language they speak is not exclusively the language of politics. Instead, it is more about a common set of norms and values that are characteristic of young people around the world regardless of their religion, nationality, or ethnicity. Like us, young people in the Middle East all desire better education; they all have a fascination with innovative uses of technology; they all get bored and crave adventure and entertainment; they all seek interaction and global connectivity; and more than anything, they all want to feel as though they belong, have a purpose in this world, and can have a better life. Those were the things that mattered to the young people I met, and this is the common ground on which we can appeal to them.

Young people in the Middle East *are* reachable—and they could be waiting to hear from us.

ACKNOWLEDGMENTS

This book would not have been possible without the support, guidance, hospitality, and generosity of family, colleagues, mentors, friends, and informants.

I am first and foremost grateful to the young people from the Middle East who made this book possible. These brave souls took tremendous risks in speaking with me, arranging for meetings, and guiding me in the right direction. As most of my interactions with young people took place above the grids of the various police-state apparatuses that comprise the Middle East, I choose to not thank anyone from the Middle East by name. To all of you who talked to me, protected me, sheltered me, fed me, transported me, and aided me in my research, I give you my thanks. You know who you are.

I would next like to thank my family, in particular my parents. Despite your concerns about my safety, you remained supportive and let me follow my passion. My sister, Emily, has always been a major support and source of encouragement. To my granparents, Max, Paul, and Annette, I am so glad that you have been a part of these experiences. I owe a particular thanks to my great-uncle Alan Mirken, whose pearls of wisdom about what it takes to write a good book kept me focused and motivated.

I was fortunate to have worked with a number of mentors from Stanford who have had a tremendous impact on me in writing this book. These include Larry Diamond, Stephen Krasner, James Lowell

Gibbs, Michael McFaul, David Kennedy, Norman Naimark, Stephen Stedman, Lynn Eden, Abbas Milani.

The travel for this book would not have been possible without the generosity of the Rhodes Trust, whose stipend enabled me to trek about the Middle East to do this research.

Working with Gotham Books proved to be a remarkable experience and there are a number of people that made this book possible: my publisher, Bill Shinker, who believed in the manuscript from the very beginning and gave me a chance to share the story with the world; my editor, Brett Valley, for really working through the manuscript and imparting his creative wisdom upon me. I also owe my thanks to Brendan Cahill, Patrick Mulligan, Lisa Johnson, and Amanda Walker. And, at Trident Media, thanks also to Claire Roberts and Randall Klein.

I never realized how complex the publishing world can be and as a result, I owe a particular debt of gratitude to my agent, Mel Parker, at Mel Parker Books. You believed in the book from the very beginning and pushed me to write the best manuscript possible. Thank you for the countless hours you have put into this project. I would also like to thank David Parker, who worked very closely with me to find my voice, shape the manuscript, and produce an early draft. I am grateful for having benefited from his guidance and expertise.

My housemates at Oxford—Alex Pollen, Dov Fox, Decker Walker, Trevor Thompson, and Jeff McLean—thank you for giving me your feedback and for your support as I traveled from Oxford to the Middle East. You all kept me sane during the writing process and helped keep me motivated. I would also like to thank some of my dear friends who read parts of the manuscript and gave me feedback: Parag Khanna, Zahra Almufti, Souha Charbel, Haifa al-Bedrawi, Erik Kramon, Pete Blaustein, Tarek Hamman, and Tamara al-Gabbani.

Finally, to my colleagues in and out of government: You have all been an amazing support network and source of inspiration. Thank you for all that you have taught me.

AUTHOR'S NOTE

The individuals I met throughout the Middle East took a tremendous risk in speaking to me and making this research possible. This story is as much theirs as it is mine. My two obligations were to give these young people a voice and to protect their identity. Without changing the content of my experiences, I adjusted names and minor personal details in some cases in order to ensure that none of the stories can be traced back to any particular individuals.